D0202584

VISUAL LITERACY CONNECTIONS TO THINKING, READING AND WRITING

VISUAL LITERACY CONNECTIONS TO THINKING, READING AND WRITING

By

RICHARD SINATRA, Ph.D.

Professor and Chairman
Human Services and Counseling
St. John's University
Jamaica, New York

CHARLES C THOMAS • PUBLISHER
Springfield • Illinois • U.S.A.

Published and Distributed Throughout the World by
CHARLES C THOMAS • PUBLISHER
2600 South First Street
Springfield, Illinois 62717

© *1986 by* CHARLES C THOMAS • PUBLISHER
ISBN 0-398-05192-5
Library of Congress Catalog Card Number: 85-22202

With THOMAS BOOKS *careful attention is given to all details of manufacturing
and design. It is the Publisher's desire to present books that are satisfactory as to their
physical qualities and artistic possibilities and appropriate for their particular use.*
THOMAS BOOKS *will be true to those laws of quality that assure a good name
and good will.*

Printed in the United States of America
Q-R-3

Library of Congress Cataloging in Publication Data
Sinatra, Richard.
  Visual literacy connections to thinking, reading,
and writing.

  Bibliography: p.
  Includes index.
  1. Visual literacy. 2. Learning. 3. Cognition in
children. 4. Language acquisition. 5. Literacy.
6. Computer literacy. I. Title.
LB1068.5.S56   1986   371.3′35   85-22202
ISBN 0-398-05192-5

FOREWORD

I AM CONVINCED that the approach taken in this book is of the utmost importance in helping learners become independent thinkers. There seems to be little question that visual literacy plays a vital role in the learning process. I see visual literacy as an organizing force in promoting understanding, retention, and recall of so many academic concepts with which students must contend.

As I have worked with young people in our schools and with graduate students in universities, it is evident to me that, as they organize for the tasks of composing and comprehending, their greatest strengths come from whole-brained thinking. When they brain-storm either on their own or with the guidance of a teacher, organization of major points comes alive through diagraming and recognizing relationships in broad visual structures. In this book Sinatra presents important rationale for the interaction of the various literacies and explains how right-left brain processing is able to take place. He then goes on to present specific reading and writing strategies that capitalize on inter-literacy strengths.

Visual Literacy Connections to Thinking, Reading and Writing makes an important contribution to our knowledge and procedures in relationship to composing and comprehending. It should be welcomed by theorists and practitioners alike.

H. Alan Robinson
Coordinator of Doctoral
Reading Programs
Hofstra University

FOREWORD

THIS IS A BOOK for everyone who cares about the nurture of children to adulthood, and who is concerned about literacies and their consequences. Through this book, a thoughtful reader may arm himself with new means for understanding children and improving teaching. More importantly, perhaps, the reader can equip himself with new, powerful perceptions of literacies, of the breadth of the role and value of literacies, and with superior ways for achieving higher levels of culture and intellect through both traditional and the new literacies.

To me, this is an exciting book. Richard Sinatra has provided answers to two long-felt needs: he has introduced and explained many aspects of Visual Literacy, and he has offered a plethora of classroom practices that can be used to help children reach new high levels of both verbal and visual literacies.

The Visual Literacy movement sprang up because observant educators and scholars were puzzled by changes they saw in young children after television had arrived in the average United States home. The I.Q. scores of school-entering children were rising sharply; but the numbers of students having difficulty learning to read and write were increasing. Contradictory seeming facts such as these and the classroom observations led to the First National Conference on Visual Literacy. Those concerns remain, and are reflected in Richard Sinatra's pages, where theory and technique for enabling children to achieve do promise assets from these contradictions.

We tend to think of the child of today as being a child in the way he was yesterday, or at least as he was when we were children. It is a crippling mistake. Our families, our schools, and our society are plagued by forces within our children that we struggle to comprehend. Our streets are filled with illiterates, our jails with the out-of-step and under the impact of those forces, the gap between the "literate" who succeed and the illiterate who are increasingly disfranchised steadily grows wider. We conjecture uneasily about the causes, perceiving the potentially enormous threats, but, despite perceptive research, showing the irresistable impact of TV on our young, we continue to act as if it is not there.

John, Viscount Morley, in his **Life of Richard Cobden**, observed that "Great economic and social forces flow with tidal sweep over communities that are only half conscious of that which is befalling them. Wise . . . are those who forsee what time is thus bringing, and endeavor to shape institutions and to mold men's thought and purpose in accordance with the change that is **silently** (my emphasis: the visual image!) surrounding them." By his insistence throughout this book that we systematically attend to the alterations in our young being wrought "silently" by TV, Richard Sinatra has placed himself in Viscount Morley's fold.

John L. Debes
Macedon, N.Y.

INTRODUCTION

THIS IS FIRST and foremost a book about the influence of visual literacy upon the thinking, reading, and writing proficiencies of learners. Its thesis will be that there are two facets or stages of visual literacy. The first stage may be considered a given, a human necessity, for all seeing-proficient peoples. Through interaction with the environment, the first stage establishes some deep underlying thoughts about the construction of reality. The second stage flourishes as a result of the unique way individuals strive to capture and express reality through nonverbal representational systems. The failure to separate these two facets of visual literacy has resulted in a confused sense of the impact of nonverbal learning in literacy development.

Secondly, this book shows how different types of literacy interact with one another. An essential aim is to show that visual literacy is primary in human learning and, as such, lays the foundation for the more "literary" literacies that follow. An over-indulgence in correct forms of written literacy production has permeated even early childhood education, much to the detriment of children's thinking and conceptual development. This book will show, however, that there are at least five faces of literacy available to any participant in a modern culture; one uses that literacy mode necessary for social, professional, informational, emotional, or aesthetic fulfillment at particular times and places. These five faces of literacy that will be developed in interactive stages are:

1. Visual Literacy as primary
2. Oral Literacy
3. Written Literacy
4. Visual Literacy as representational
5. Computer and Technological Literacies

We will discover that while each literacy has a rich communicative style of its own, each interacts with the others during the thinking processes of composing, comprehension, and creativity. Furthermore, verbal and nonverbal modes of expression which make up the different literacies have distinctive features that are processed differently by the two hemispheres of the brain.

The view of visual literacy espoused in this book is that visual literacy precedes and lays the foundation for thinking, composing and comprehending which, in turn, manifests themselves in such activities as writing, reading, computer programming and the visual and creative arts. The first one-third of the book will develop this thesis. To think that writing and reading are synonymous with composing and comprehending is erroneous. Composing and comprehending are mind processes that demand facile interaction between the two hemispheres of the brain as well as the lower brain stem structures controlling emotions and levels of alertness. These mind processes help us to understand ideas as we read and to put our thoughts down in some logical, communicative way as we write. How the brain and individual styles of learning operate during verbal and nonverbal learning will be explored in the second-third of the book.

Aptly expressed by Moffett and Wagner is the notion that "the best way for the receiver to learn to comprehend is to compose" (1983, p. 10). Composing, according to the book's philosophy, has its genesis in nonverbal thought while receiving encouragement from the other facets of literacy. Moreover, current beliefs for increased holistic input in reading and writing instruction cannot be fully implemented without nonverbal, visual literacy modes of thought. This book will provide both rationale and technique for practitioners in using our first literacy — visual literacy — to enhance composing and comprehending processes. Practitioners will see in the final third of the book, a number of strategies that capitalize on the power of the visual literacy modes of experience, analogy, imagery, metaphor, and synthesis to increase written literacy development. The continuous direction of the later chapters will be to explore "visionary" ways to compose in order to build the mental framework for comprehension and composition.

ACKNOWLEDGMENTS

THE AUTHOR wishes to thank many people who assisted in the production of this book.

First, there is my friend and colleague, Josephine Stahl-Gemake. She not only constructed most of the figures and illustrations that reinforced important visual literacy concepts but also acted as a constant springboard for my ideas.

Jack Debes and H. Alan Robinson, both noted authors in their own right, provided two valuable reviews which appear in the Foreword section of this book. While both are strong believers in visual, nonverbal modes of learning, they criticized and commented on visual literacy ideas that needed clarification. Jack Debes, acknowledged as the Father of Visual Literacy, reinforced and challenged many of the integrative verbal/nonverbal strategies while H. Alan Robinson lent a strong focus on the holistic emphasis of the book.

I wish to thank my friends and colleagues of International Visual Literacy Association, particularly Roberts Braden, Priscilla Hardin, Jim Sucy, and Richard Ball. They dialogued with me on a number of occasions and gave me additional ways that nonverbal strategies interfaced with the verbal.

Then, of course, there were teacher acquaintances, Barbara Schrift Geven and Manny Rodriquez, who promoted nonverbal thinking in their classrooms and graduate Reading students at both the Jamaica and Staten Island campuses of St. John's University who implemented many of my visual literacy ideas. Their excellent implementations and connections to verbal/nonverbal thinking can be found in the latter third of the book.

Finally, the author wishes to thank his office staff and graduate assistants. Secretaries Anne Bottari, Claire Caramore, and Ann De Paulis painstakingly worked through the many drafts while remaining in constant good humor and graduate assistants William Waked, Kerry Thornhill, and Laurie Delle Donne, Linda Fortuna, and Jeanette Magnuson provided much technical and mechanical assistance in the way of reference searches, proofreading, and indexing. Also, special thanks go to Patricia and Daniel Cleary for completing the subject and author index and for completing the final page proofs.

Richard Sinatra
St. John's University

CONTENTS

VISUAL LITERACY CONNECTIONS
TO THINKING, READING
AND WRITING

CHAPTER ONE

THE PRIMACY OF VISUAL LITERACY
ON THOUGHT

THIS CHAPTER will examine how components of visual literacy are basic to human thought. How these components interact with four other stages of verbal, nonverbal, and computer literacies that follow will be the subject of the next chapter. These five stages of literacy will be viewed from a developmental perspective, meaning they will be presented in a way that most youngsters experience them regardless of culture or circumstances. However, it is fully realized that the five-stage sequence is an oversimplification for some learners at some times. For instance, some artistically gifted youngsters may progress from being visually literate to a stage four level of artistic, nonverbal creation without achieving the full benefits of the abilities to read and write.

It must be noted as well that some cultures, especially those not yet homogenized with others due to technology and mass media, may excel or accent one literacy mode more than another. Because visual literacy is basic to human thought, the more primitive the peoples of a culture, the more likely that visual literacy and its representational forms will be the dominant literacy. For instance, in Kleinfeld's excellent paper regarding the intellectual strengths in culturally different groups, he showed that in the processing of visual information in the Eskimo arctic hunting culture, the Eskimo surpasses the Caucasian (1973). Furthermore, he added, due to the spatial demands of arctic hunting, the grammatical character of the Eskimo language has come to be a powerful intellectual tool for the processing of visual information. The Eskimo, for instance, can tell his listener through prefixes and suffixes added to words in one sentence, the shape of an object, the shape of the surface in which the object is to be placed, and also the directional position of the object on a surface. The English language, on the other hand, would require more verbal information to code the same amount of figural information. This illustration serves well to show the primacy of visual literacy in the development of an ensuing literacy, one that we call "speech."

The notion of literacy itself needs to be explored before the five stages are accentuated one by one. Webster's **New World Dictionary** defines literacy as "the state or quality of being literate; ability to read and write." Notice that the second part of the definition explains what is meant by being literate and that there is a functional quality ascribed to literacy. That is, one must show that he or she is literate by demonstrating the ability through reading and writing. Doughty, Pearce, and Thorton also supporting a functional view of verbal literacy note that verbal literacy means "the ability to draw upon a wide experience of the language system in order to meet the linguistic needs of a particular occasion for using language" (1972, p. 112). Thus, a verbally literate person must be able to know how to use the language system appropriately to communicate personal and social needs on any particular occasion. Are there other ways, however, that people can be literate, using other symbols or coding systems to communicate thought? For instance, is a painter, a sculptor, or a musical composer creating in his or her medium without the use of verbal language literate? By the same token, is a young child in rudimentary stages of oral language development in actuality literate if the child is able to use concrete objects to represent natural life? Are other children who master turtle graphics or the computer language of LOGO before book reading involved in a new, modern dimension of literacy?

THE BASIC COMPONENTS OF VISUAL LITERACY

Because visual literacy emanates from a nonverbal core, it becomes the basic literacy in the thought processes of comprehending and composing which underlie reading and writing. While many conceptual models of the language arts show nonverbal experience as the foundation of the listening, speaking, reading, and writing experiences, educators do not acknowledge the real importance of the meaning of that core. The nonverbal components of visual literacy are the real "basics" in literacy learning and not the three "R's" as is often proclaimed in the educational establishment. Because this concept is basic to the thesis of this book and the later stages of literacy development, the definition of visual literacy will be offered here and periodically reexamined in subsequent chapters to test its applicability.

Visual literacy is the active reconstruction of past visual experience with incoming visual messages to obtain meaning. The reader will see how this definition differs from others offered in the field and how it brings a functional, process perspective to the meaning of visual literacy. Three essential aspects of the definition need to be examined but the most important notion is the aspect of "acting on" or interpreting visual information. The active reconstructive nature of the thought process means that as visual information is presented to the brain, it is modified and interpreted in light of what information already exists there. The stored information, generally known as imagery, or schemes to a follower of Piaget, is coded in a way that is immediately accessible to the brain. This accessibility allows the brain to match new visual information, presented rapidly and holistically, with that which is stored to see if additional processing in the form of assimilation or accommodation must take place. Finally, meaning must result; that is, the intake and reconstruction of visual information results in some kind of meaningful recognition for the literate processor. Many times, a perceiver will not act on information immediately presented to the eye but will store it for later use when it is needed to modify and amend other information.

This active aspect of visual literacy develops immediately in life and may precede or develop concomitantly with stages of oral literacy. But not vice versa. Words do not precede the visual/motor experience. Piaget (1963) maintains that the sources of thought are not to be found in language, but in the nonverbal, visual-motor reconstruction performed by the very young child during the first two years of life. The eye and the hand coordinate to build a sensorimotor base for thought that is eventually expressed in words.

Physiologically, we now know that the auditory nerve is ready to receive verbal information seven months after conception. Robeck (1975) notes that the peak period of myelination, the growth of fatty tissues around the axons essential to the transmission of impulses, occurs in the seventh month of foetal growth. As early as the first day after birth, the infant has been shown to move in patterns that are coordinated with adult speech (Condon and Sander, 1974). After analyzing films of neonate movements, these two investigators found a correspondence of 90% agreement between neonate body movements and the structures of adult speech. In contrast, there was only about 50% agreement between movements and sound when continuous vowels were spoken or when tapping noises were employed.

Visual Seeking as Primary

While the neural pathways are being laid for the understanding of the oral language, the young child is also active as a viewer and visual explorer of the environment. Harris (1975) cites research which indicates that the visual cortex of the right hemisphere matures faster than that of the left hemisphere and that newborn infants tend to lie in a position which allows most of the incoming sensory information to be processed by the right hemisphere. This evidence, and that consistently showing facial recognition to be a right hemisphere related task, led Harris and others to believe that the cognitive development of the right hemisphere precedes that of the left. Restak (1982a) highlights research showing that from the moment of birth, newborns are enormously responsive and visually interact with their parents. In fact, in one children's hospital, mothers of premature babies are taught to gaze at their newborns. This gazing is felt to strengthen the communicative bond between both, leading to a stronger emotional well-being for the developing youngster.

Because many neuroscientists now believe that the right hemisphere of humans is the more predominant one in the early years of life and because visual literacy is the literacy generally processed by the right hemisphere, it follows that visual literacy must be fundamental to human thought. A remarkable case study exists on record which shows how the right hemisphere develops normally even with meager visual stimulation while the left hemisphere will not develop as genetically programmed without language interaction. Genie was a 13 year-old "wild" girl discovered in California in 1970. Genie, isolated and literally confined to a small room and not spoken to by her parents since infancy, was not able to speak nor stand erect when her blind mother brought Genie's plight forward to Los Angeles authorities (Fromkin et al., 1974; Pines, 1981). It was found that right-handed Genie had normal right hemisphere lateralization for nonverbal functions, but abnormal left hemisphere development for language. In fact, language processing appeared to be lateralized to the right hemisphere as well.

Fromkin et al. (1974), hypothesized how both verbal and nonverbal processing modes lateralized to Genie's right hemisphere. At the time of her experiential and social deprivation, Genie was a normal right-handed child with potential left hemisphere dominance. The inadequate language stimulation during her early years inhibited or interfered with language aspects of left hemisphere development. This would amount to a kind of functional atrophy of the usual language centers, precipitated by disuse or suppression. What meager visual stimulation Genie did receive from the single room was apparently sufficient for normal right hemisphere specialization. The authors also feel that Genie's normal right hemisphere development is consistent with the theory that the right hemisphere develops first because it is more involved with perception of the environment. Furthermore, Pines (1981) indicates that Genie's earliest vocabulary showed an extraordinary attention to the visual world — to such qualities as color, shape, and size.

The discussion of right hemisphere processing and its relationship to visual literacy will be resumed in a following chapter. For now, we can say that the first stage of literacy development is that of visual literacy. Figure 1 shows that this first stage rests not only on the aspects of viewing but also on the feedback provided by active exploration of the environment and by the genesis of nonverbal, representational thought.

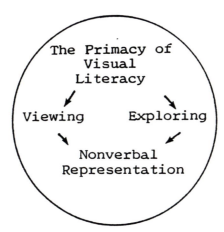

Figure 1. Stage one of literacy development: Visual literacy and its active components.

The Necessity of Exploration

How does the tiny tot learn according to the eminent Swiss psychologist, Jean Piaget? Children learn by doing, by interacting with their environment and by constructing mental schema of how the natural world operates. They discover their own rules regarding how the environment is put together through active participation of their own intelligence.

Piaget (1967) maintains that the young child must operate upon the environment to bring about change. In fact, the very essence of young children's learning styles require that they actively experience the environment through sensory-motor manipulation and actively perceive what is happening through that manipulation. These coordinated visual, sensori-motor actions are coded in neurological patterns that are embedded in the brain throughout life. The eye, the essential receptor of visual literacy, needs the hand to continue to build nonverbal logic.

This active view of visual literacy exploration is much akin to Gibson's view of the active nature of perception (1966). Gibson views perception as a process of exploring, seeking out, and responding in continual interaction between viewer and environment. This is far more than the simple interpretation of sensory message. Murch (1973) adds that the kind of information extracted by an active perceiver and the resulting analysis and redirection of search schema develop as a function of the observer's previous experiences with the environment. Incoming sensory messages play an integral but subordinate part in the view of perception as a dynamic process. Of greater importance are the programmed experiences of the observer in the form of motor actions and hypotheses of how the natural world operates. In short, neurobiologists now believe that the visual cortex is more concerned with the interpretation of visual stimuli rather than just with matters of "sight" (Restak, 1982b).

Children construct what they know about the world through their actions (Duckworth, 1973a). These actions provide feedback to the eye and help children construct their logic, found in such thinking processes as classifying, ordering, and conserving. Children learn, for instance, that some things can be grouped, some cannot, and that some things can move when they're pushed while others cannot. A bit later they will learn to see that changes of physical appearance, such as when a quantity of milk is poured from a bottle to glass, does not mean that a loss of volume has occurred. Or they learn that changes of physical structure, as when a rolled-out piece of clay is divided into a smaller number of segments, has not resulted in a loss of material. As noted by Duckworth (1973a), all of these insights are independent of language. Children's thinking, therefore, is qualitatively different from that of adults in terms of its basic structure. This basic structure emanates from a nonverbal core and forms the basis of symbolic thinking, classification, and reversibility of thought which develop through a sequence of stages found across childhood of all cultures.

For young children to actively learn the environment must provide a field of experimentation. They must manipulate materials and get visual/motor feedback regarding the outcome of their behavior. In so doing, they learn how to adapt and accommodate themselves to changes caused in the environment, some of which may have been self induced, and they learn how to adjust to these changes. In effect, they construct mental schemata of past experiences. According to Piaget, a schema is a mental image or a pattern of action, and becomes a way of representing and organizing all of the child's previous sensory-motor experiences.

For the tiny infant at the preverbal level, schemata or schemes are what the infant knows how to do. Schema will not develop unless the infant can construct and reconstruct experience. For instance, initially an infant may be handed a rattle and because of fortuitous shaking of the hand, the rattle may sound. By repeated activity, the child will learn that visual exploration of the rattle is not enough for it to sound and, secondly, that the sound is something desirable — it is fun. Now, because a schema of the rattle has developed, the infant is establishing an important nonverbal concept, one of object permeance. That is, something which was previously seen or experienced exists even when its' out of sight. However, when the rattle is brought back into view as the infant looks up from his/her crib position, the infant's face lights up with smiles. This can occur because the youngster is actively reconstructing the schema of the rattle movement with the pleasurable sound. Piaget's view of schema development is not far removed from Arnheim's view of the nature of how perception actively builds visual concepts (1954). Visual concepts are the organization of forms and relations that represent experience.

We see young children rapidly enlarging their mental schema during the early years of life. At first, all four-footed animals may be called either a dog, a cat, or a cow. Then, as the youngster comes into more and more visual or physical contact with each type, the schema for each begins to take on a clearer focus. The child has accommodated his or her previous perceptions and adjusted to the new view of each animal. Schemata, then, are mass representations of all of life's experiences and become the basis of the child's conceptual filing system.

It is through such activities as cooking, cleaning and sorting dishes, modeling with clay, finger painting, block construction, playing house, and the hundreds of other visual/motor activities that children do, that they form schema and learn the cognitive skills of comparing, contrasting, categorizing, sequencing and so on. In actuality, a conceptual base for verbal understanding and expression found in the oral and written literacies is developed before children come to the experiences of reading and writing. The more meaningful and different the encounters the young child has had with the real world, the stronger will be the "thinking foundation" on which learning to read is based (Furth, 1970).

So, teachers must truly ask themselves, do they really teach children such skills as sequencing and classifying through paper and pencil activities as they claim to do later during reading and writing instruction? Or is it that children bring these conceptualization skills to the task on the printed page and teachers merely provide another mode to practice those particular skills?

The Double Knowledge of Representational Thought

A critical outgrowth of active experimentation and viewing noted in Figure 1 is the formation of nonverbal, representational thought. This thought process is also the driving force of Stage Four of literacy development, in which nonverbal creativity gives rise to artistic masterpieces. Nonverbal, representational thought is thinking by analogy, metaphor, and symbols. For the young child and for that matter, adults acting as children, representational thought will be expressed through such forms as gesture and body language, play, modeling or imitation, and art.

The developing, sensorimotor child has already developed a number of schemata or mental blueprints where the child does not directly have to see an object as the family dog in order to know that is exists. But now in representational, symbolic thought, one schema can represent another. One concrete object or thing can become another, one that has another experiential context. For instance, a rough block can represent a train, a lid from a glass jar can be a dish, and small beads or colored stones can represent all the child's favorite foods on that dish. This is thinking of pretense, but highly important for cognitive growth. As expressed by Furth (1969), it is the preoperational child's double knowledge, in that this child from about age two to six, knowing what the block is and knowing what a train is, can use one schema of knowing to represent another purpose.

This creation of representational form also involves a distinctive mental orientation by the child (Franklin 1973). An object or pattern of movement is not a representation in and of itself. It achieves its identity as a symbol through the child's mental reconstruction of one form for another. For instance, the child can use a fluff of cotton to represent a bunny during play time because the child "sees" the connectedness as he/she conceptualizes a specific intent or purpose. The whiteness, softness, and fuzziness of cotton provide the basis for the nonverbal representation of rabbits. Thus, Franklin notes that the relationship between the representational form and that which it represents rests on the basis of similarity or resemblance, a correspondence between the two which is established in the process of symbol formation.

Through play and social interaction, children share representational thought. However, the connectedness between the real object (cotton fluff) and the representational form (the rabbit) must be in each child's experience, embedded in nonverbal schema. For instance, if one child says, "This brillo can be the porcupine," during animal-form play, and the second youngster has never seen or experienced a porcupine, the representational connectedness may not occur.

Now, notice what happened in the above illustration. Language was used, and in the usage of a verbal name, one child did not comprehend the other. "What's a porcupine?" he or she might ask? This illustration serves well for the classroom as well, where teachers often use verbal expression beyond the experiential framework of the child. It suggests, even more, that with the institutions of preschools for inner-city children reared in poverty backgrounds, the practice of emphasizing names of things, of emphasizing the names of the attributes of things, and of extracting the correct verbal answers to an abstract type of teacher question may not be as productive in helping the child's intellect to advance as actual experience with the phenomenon (Schwebel and Raph, 1973).

Language, then, becomes the natural extension of symbolic thought, and symbolic thoughts help form the mental schemata of a visually literate person. To Piaget (1963), the development of symbolic thought provides the basis for language development; furthermore, language, besides imitation, play, art, and graphics, is just one way to symbolize thinking. The reader must fully realize the importance of this notion — that the foundation of mental activity in young children is grounded in their potential capability as explorers or "doers" and not on passively receiving the words of wisdom from others.

CHAPTER TWO

DEVELOPMENT AND INTERFACE OF
ENSUING LITERACIES

L ANGUAGE DEVELOPMENT is highly important in the human
road to fulfillment. The human brain, in fact, is uniquely wired for
language reception and production, and nature has favored this importance by insuring that the auditory nerve is maturated quite early to receive auditory input from the environment — a full two months before
the normal birth of most children (Robeck, 1975). Language frees children from the immediate. It makes it possible for children to objectify
and conceptualize their world while giving them the responsibility for
shaping their environments (Smith, Goodman, and Meredith, 1970).

ORAL LANGUAGE: OUR SECOND LITERACY

The relationship of the components of visual literacy to oral language
development can be seen in Figure 2.

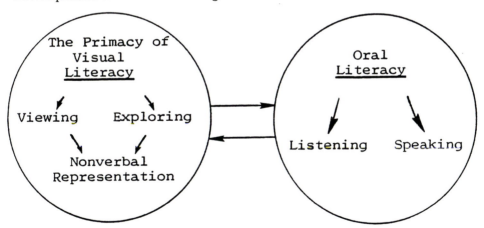

Figure 2. Stage two of literacy development: Visual literacy and its interaction with the oral
language.

Young children initially hear language used in actual, immediate contexts which Frank Smith calls "situation — dependent speech" (1982). Initially the object and later the schema of the object become referents for the verbal name. Thus, a mother is likely to ask, "Do you want milk?" as the bottle or milk container is visually displayed before the child. Once again the child must see the connectedness between the object and the words used; this connectedness has to be neurally woven; it has to be fabricated by the individual thinker. As noted by Duckworth (1973b), connections have to be made by youngsters themselves even if adults take great pains to point out the connections they themselves have already made. The language connectedness emanates from a nonverbal core and from what psychologists call "deep structure" thought.

Duckworth (1973b) suggests that words develop from the natural inclination of children to imitate in the sense that imitation means the nonverbal representation of something else. At first, the child's own body is the first object available to use for reproductive thought. Later words, which have been used in specific situational settings, become available to youngsters as a way to imitate the situation. They become a useful short-cut to acting out the physical aspect required to get the communication meaning across. For instance, in the milk example above, if the child says "wan milk," he/she is shortcutting the nonverbal necessity of going to the icebox, struggling to open it, and finding the milk container to bring to his/her mother. Language, then is both cued by the concrete, visual world and is a cue of what information that world holds. When the writing system develops as we shall see in Chapter 8, nonverbal gesture, a bodily cuing system, is one of the earliest developmental signs of the composition process.

Connectedness and Inner Development

This connectedness of words for referents in the immediate environment develops from the inside, out. In other words, children learn the meaning for words by attaching them to nonverbal schema prior to their verbal expression. Children develop a "deep structure" meaning which becomes reflected in their personal but meaningful holophrastic and telographic utterances, such as, "baby, doggie bad, daddy good." Because meaning is learned in wholes, the search for meaning proceeds outward from the child's inner self to become gradually modified according to the language conventions established by the speaking community. By using language more and more to achieve more and more satisfaction from the

world, the child provides his/her own continuing motivation and reinforcement; in a sense children are their own paymasters (Berry, 1969).

In the early stages of language production, children produce rather
grammatical utterances that reflect deep unlying thoughts. Smith,
Goodman, and Meredith (1970) regard this as the unitary stage of language development in which the child has underlying meaning and
structures but not the transformations to put words together at the surface level of language. Knowledge of how to manipulate and transform
language utterances to achieve surface structure conventions advances
with two important language stages — that of expansion and structural
awareness. In the stage of expansions, language utterances become
more complete and precise but still reflect one basic idea. For instance,
in the previous holophratic utterance, "baby," what did the youngster
mean? Was he/she pointing to another or to himself/herself? In what
context was the word used? In the expansion stage, the youngster might
next say "me baby" and later "I am the baby?" Notice the deep structure
meaning was the same in the sense that the youngster was referring to
himself-herself. However, with expanded constructions the youngster
has moved closer and closer to the correct surface-structure, language
conventions of adult speech.

The process of cultivating expansions can occur rather naturally by
youngsters. Rather than teach children early in life the names of the
parts of sentences (subject, predicate, direct object, etc.), they can be
stimulated to produce more expressive and creative sentences. This can
be done through the sentence-expansion strategy which requires a scaf-
folding of questions by the parent or teacher. Watch how naturally this
can occur as demonstrated in the following example with four-year-old
Anthony.

Anthony was asked by his teacher if he wanted to play a language
game. He became very excited and showed a willingness to play. He was
told he would have to remember and repeat the short sentence, "The
boys play," each time a question was asked. "The boys play" represented
a kernel idea which could be expanded by questioning used in a skillful
way. The teacher in this case wrote down Anthony's responses after each
question. However, in the classroom setting, the teacher can ask youngsters to write their novel sentences on a couple of blank lines inserted between each question. The reader has the opportunity to watch how a
young child can be encouraged to learn language naturally in the following dialogue between Anthony and his teacher:

Kernel Sentence	— The boys play.
Question (Teacher)	— What do the boys play?
Answer (Anthony)	— The boys play school.
Question	— When do the boys play school?
Answer	— The boys play school on Saturday morning.
Question	— Where do the boys play school?
Answer	— The boys play school on Saturday mornings in the livingroom with a chalkboard.
Question	— Why do the boys play school?
Answer	— The boys play school on Saturday mornings in the livingroom with a chalkboard and a piece of chalk to write their mommies' names on the chalkboard.

When you try the sentence expansion strategy in your classroom setting, please be tolerant of children's spelling errors. Remember they are attempting the creative use of words in new syntactic structures. Thought process is on originality and not necessarily on words whose spellings are unknown.

Reconstruction and Cognitive Growth

In the second stage of structural awareness, children begin to generalize about the patterns and rules of language. These conventions aren't taught, they are learned in the sense they are reconstructed by youngsters as they experiment with language. The connectedness is established between things in the environment and language just as connectedness was established during the nonverbal representation of brillo for porcupine. Smith (1982) considers that infants invent grammar by hypothesizing rules for the formation of utterances and by testing the adequacy of these hypothesis by putting them together to represent a meaning. For instance in the earlier example of "wan milk," if the child expands his/her meaning to become more exact, he/she will say "I want milk" or "I want even more milk." But if the child generalizes about language, he/she invents an utterance not previously emitted. For instance, the young child might be apt to say, "I want beer." No one ever said to the youngster, "Say, I want beer. . . .I want beer." The utterance was reflected on, generalized, and induced consistent with the grammar and meaning of English. The child reconstructed the meaning for himself/herself and tested that meaning to determine its effectiveness. Now feedback must occur to determine the appropriateness of that utterance, regarding both its content and surface structure correctness. But notice that the schema for beer was in the same frame of reference as milk. The word was used as a means of getting a drink. The youngster was willing to take a gamble for appropriateness since he may have seen his mom or dad enjoy that particular liquid with the dinner meal. The ability to actively reconstruct meaning through lanuage is an important cognitive landmark for youngsters.

Anastasiow cites research to show that the ability to reconstruct meaning through verbal expression reflects a higher degree of cognitive maturity than the tendency to omit words (1973). Researchers using a repeated sentence technique have found that children will omit elements of a sentence that are beyond their stage of cognitive development. Omissions of words or a syntactic element are in indication of lower stages of language development. For instance, while the three-year-old will eliminate the passive, the five-year-old will not. Anastasiow has shown that inner-city, five and six-year-old children will reconstruct about 70% of the words they hear in sentences to conform to their own sense of meaning expressed in nonstandard dialect. Nonstandard dialect speakers who reconstruct sentences to conform to their own language are exhibiting an active thinking process concludes Anastasiow.

During oral language learning the accent is on meaningful, functional interaction. Later, for that matter, should be the case for written language learning. Smith (1982) is quite emphatic on this point, indicating that youngsters do not learn language conventions first which they can then use for various contexts. The learning of language comes with the use of language and with the increasing understanding of how language structures can be transformed in different ways, on different occasions, and for different people. "Children do not learn language as an abstraction, as an end in itself, but in the process of achieving other ends, like getting another drink of juice, learning to distinguish cats from dogs, or striving to enjoy a story from a book" (Smith, 1982, p. 96). Hence, the strength of the dual direction noted in the arrows extending between the visual and oral literacies of Figure 2. In the presence of significant others providing both visual and oral cues, the child binds oral language competencies to visual features and to mental, representational images of those features.

The Affective Side to Language Development

Language learning also has an affective, emotional component. Smith, Goodman, and Meredith summarized the relationship between language and affect (1970, p. 13):

> Language is always experienced by the child in the context of the situation. . . The child's reaction to the situation is also part of the language-learning process. His emotions and his developing ability to think, to process his perceptions, and to begin forming concepts, actually become part of the situation as the child experiences it.

The child's earliest private language is akin to lived experience and becomes even more meaningful if the experience is colored by interest and emotion (Sinatra and Taber-Kinsler, 1976). When interest and emotion are linked to an experience, memory for that experience becomes stronger. The memory of an experience touched by emotional impact becomes strongly established through a coded pattern of neuronal activity and language learning that is meaningful has more logically associated bonds with previous experiences (Schnitker, 1972). Thus, motivation, attention, and memory operate in an interlocking ring, each interacting with the other to enhance learning (Berry, 1969).

The early-reading child is often reared in a language enriched, emotionally supporting environment as well. Elkind (1975) found that early-reading children come from homes in which immersion in the oral and written language was rich, in which parents frequently read to their children, and in which social motivation to please adults who model and reward reading behavior was important. Because feelings like language are linked to brain activity, the brain systems responsive to emotionality and attitude will be reviewed in a bit more depth in a later chapter.

THE THIRD LITERACY: WRITTEN LANGUAGE ACQUISITION

The active, reconstructive nature of literacy learning resurfaces once again during written literacy attainment. Figure 3 shows the interactive effects of the three literacies which begin to impinge upon young learners' lives between the ages of 5 to 7 in most Western cultures.

The two-way traffic between the literacies shows how one can influence the other. In other words, visual literacy can sharpen the language used in the oral and written literacies while the verbal literacies can interface directly with how we perceive visual experience. However, many popular models of the language arts as well as Piagetian wisdom are based on the developmental progression from nonverbal experience,

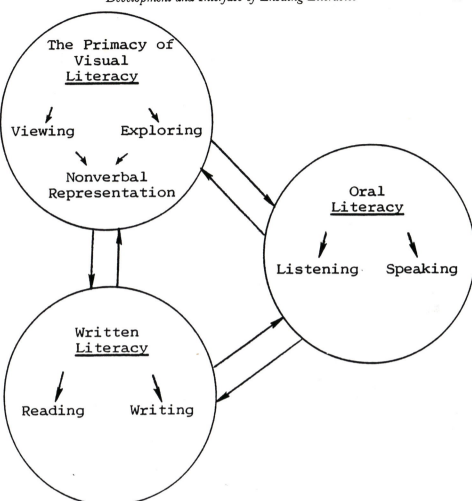

Figure 3. Stage three of literacy development: Visual literacy and its interactive relationship with the oral and written languages.

to oral language development, to written language usage. For instance, in Ralph Kellogg's model of the development of the relationship of the elements in the language arts shown in Figure 4, experience is the foundation of language development with reading and writing hierarchically removed from earlier receptive and expressive verbal development (1972). While Kellogg uses the generic word experience to represent the foundation of literacy learning, we saw that viewing, exploring, and nonverbal representation are the essential components of that experience.

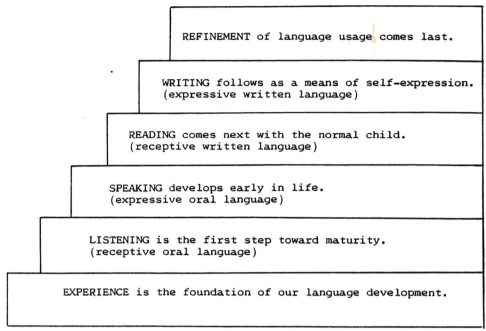

Figure 4. How experience provides the building blocks for the oral and written literacies. From Ralph E. Kellogg: Listening. In Pose Lamb (Ed.), *Guiding Children's Language Learning*, 2nd. ed., Dubuque, Iowa: William C. Brown, 1972. Courtesy of William C. Brown Pub. Co. and Pose Lamb, editor. (Feb. 15, 1983).

The Naturalness of Comprehension

The content of messages whether identified by the oral or written languages can be traced to nonverbal schemata that were experienced earlier in life. However, once competency in written literacy is achieved, a comprehender or composer of written discourse does not need to evoke the oral language to achieve meaning. As a reader processes text and converts chunks of print to imagery, the reader can see in his/her "mind's eye" the author's meaning. Likewise a writer can visualize past experience or generate sensory images to create a flavorful text.

Unfortuantely, many parents and educators have been lead away from the importance of the nonverbal, representational core and rich oral language development as healthy prerequisites to successful written literacy development. They have been lead to believe that a method or a particular reader brings knowledge of the written symbol system to children. This is a totally erroneous assumption. Children bring their internalized meanings to the printed page and as with experimentation with the oral language, they search for meaning and connectedness in print. Unfortunately, when teachers focus children's attention on letters and sounds that may unlock the names to printed words, they remove children from the search for connectedness and bring about a false concern in the learning to read. They take children away from learning what print means to analyzing what print looks like.

The Goodmans have conducted a good amount of research in such lands as America, Mexico, Australia, Uruguay, Canada, Switzerland, and New Zealand and have found that youngsters who are brought up in a literate environment know a substantial amount about the nature of print before school entry (Goodman and Goodman, 1981). Furthermore, when they investigated the reading ability of four groups of children speaking English as a second language, they found that children could understand and read much more than they could talk about (Goodman and Goodman, 1978). This finding contradicted the belief that non-native speakers who did not have enough control of the rules of English would read at the surface structure level only by decoding words without understanding what they meant at the deep structure level. Even children with limited English proficiency construct meaning when they read. The Goodmans found over and over again that children's ability to understand English, as reflected in reading comprehension, was far better than their expressive language ability, as reflected in their oral fluency and accuracy. Children who were native speakers of Spanish in Texas, of Navajo in Arizona, of Samoan in Hawaii, and of Arabic in Michigan strived to construct meaning in English as they read even in a language with which they were not fully competent. These studies show that meaning or deep structure understanding precedes accurate production or knowledge of decoding.

Since children, all children regardless of cultural or socioeconomic levels, have had similar life-related experiences and have evolved some familiarity with the oral language, shouldn't the beginning stages of written literacy be based on what they know? What they know is embedded in schemata related to their own inner-directed energy to construct and reconstruct the environment. Their vocabulary ranges from about 8,000 to 20,000 words (Smith, Goodman, & Meredith, 1970) and their oral language facility includes mastery of the basic sentence arrangements used in standard English (Dawkins, 1975). Surely this is the frame of reference for the language-experience and Sylvia Ashton-Warner's organic method (1963) approaches to beginning reading. I listened to one charming reading professor recall the days when she taught reading to native American children on Indian reservations. She claimed that she always had three natural things in her class as a basis for her reading programs — a place to cook, musical instruments, and animals. What essentially occurred was an experience-language approach to written literacy attainment in which children read and wrote about experiences that were lived in the classroom. They cared for their animals, prepared food for lunch every day, and sang songs in accompaniment to music. These real experiences provided a functional necessity to learn to read and to write, as for instance in preparing and reading recipes.

Both Goodman (1979) and Smith (1982) maintain that written literacy development naturally develops from immersion in language use. Goodman feels that written literacy must be regarded as an extension of natural development and learned in the same way that the oral language is learned. Literacy must always involve whole, real, natural, and relevant tasks. Translated to the classroom this means that teachers must engage children in real functional uses of written language — to label, to chart, to inform, to stimulate imagination, and to develop story sense. Smith suggests that the majority of children are as much immersed in written language as they are in the oral language because of the vastness of print accessible to visual bombardment. He writes (1982, p. 96):

> I am not referring to school, nor to those overrated books that are supposed to surround and somehow inspire some privileged children to literacy. I refer instead to the wealth of situation-dependent print to be found on every product in the bathroom, on every jar and package in the kitchen, in the television guide (and in television commercials), in comics, catalogs, advertising fliers, telephone directories, on street signs, store fronts, gas stations, billboards, at fast-food outlets, supermarkets, and department stores. All of this print is meaningful; it makes a difference. We no more predict cereal in a package labeled **detergent** than we expect candy in a store advertising **cleaning** or a concert in a television program announced as **football**.

Reading as Concrete Reasoning

Elkind presents an added dimension to the successful early reader — often overlooked in the discussion of reading readiness development — that of the logic to perform concrete operations (1975). Generally this Piagetian stage is usually reached by children who are 6 or 7 years of age and continues to age 11. However, in two studies of early readers, Elkind found that early reading children were superior to non-early reading children on Piagetian measures of conservation — a reasoning ability of the child at the concrete operations stage. The mental reasoning of the conserving child involves the ability to focus on more than one attribute of an object at a time so that changes or transformations in the object can be observed, to discriminate between relevant and irrevelant qualities, and to reverse the direction of thought. This type of thinking involves mental operations using imagery. This occurs for instance, when a child visualizes the mental change of a piece of clay rolled from a ball into a doughnut and then back to the ball. The understanding that the same amount of clay has remained in both transformations cannot be arrived at through the clay's visual appearance; imagery and mental reasoning was necessary. The core of this reasoning ability rests on the formation of representational thought which, as was noted earlier, is highly nonverbal and creative in nature and which, as we will see shortly, emanates from the brain's right hemisphere.

Schema — Pictures in the Head

Psychologists, psycholinguists, and reading theorists have long maintained that the background information a reader has on any particular topic has a powerful influence on how well the reader will comprehend that topic (James, 1890; Smith, 1971 and 1982). Picking up on cues from Piaget (1963) and Bartlett (1932), reading theorists have more recently evolved a theory of reading comprehension called schema theory (Anderson, 1977). Schema theory attempts to deal with the essence of comprehension by proposing that what is comprehended during reading or listening integrates in some conceptual way with what exists in the mind of the learner beforehand. A fundamental belief of schema theory is that oral or written messages do not in themselves carry meaning. Conversely, the spoken or written text provides cues and directives for listeners and readers as to how they should construct intended meaning using their own, previously acquired knowledge (Adams and Collins, 1979). This previously acquired knowledge is stored in memory in the form of abstract cognitive structures called schema (Hacker, 1980), and a schema becomes a knowledge "structure" because it indicates the typical relations among its components (Anderson, 1977). For Rumelhart (1981), schemata (plural of schema) are more. They are, as the building blocks of cognition, the fundamental elements upon which all information processing depends. Schemata allow us to interpret sensory data (both linguistic and nonverbal), to retrieve information from memory, to organize actions, to determine goals and subgoals, and to allocate resources in guiding the flow of information processing.

Monteith (1979) expands the building block metaphor by likening a schema to a description of a particular class of concepts, composed of a hierarchy of schemata embedded within other schemata. The embedded schematas fit into slots or placeholders of the conceptual hierarchy. Furthermore, the schema topic at the top of hierarchy must be general enough to capture the essential aspects of all attributes of the concept of class. Rumelhart and Ortony (1977) have suggested that during comprehending, the purpose of a schema is to serve as a cognitive template against which incoming data can be matched and in terms of how it can be comprehended. Pearson and Spiro (1982) liken schema to the little pictures or associations conjured up in the brain as words and sentences are heard or read.

Notice in the above discussion defining what a schema is and how schemata operate during comprehending that visuospatial and nonverbal descriptors are used by theorists as they attempt to describe how the mind works to assimilate new information. Piaget, himself, saw a schema as a mental image or pattern of action which represents just one of a child's many stored sensory-motor experiences. As youngsters interact with the environment whether it be through language or sensori-motor means and construct mental schemata of how the natural world operates, they file these sensory-motor images into a massive network of schemata which again become modified as new learnings are integrated with the old. Thus, schema theory integrates the verbal with the three essentail components of visual literacy: viewing, sensorimotor exploration, and nonverbal representation. Two more important concerns need to be mentioned regarding schema development, concerns which will be developed in later chapters. First we shall see how the brain's right hemisphere is an important contributor to the connections made amongst schema and second, we shall see how semantic networks extend schema theory to a practical reality in the classroom.

Resolving Conflicts in Written Literacy Instruction

During the 1970s those concerned with written literacy development expressed a growing concern with discovering how readers read and how writers write — essentially the processes involved in each act. This represented a shift in the product-perspective view of how reading and writing are learned held by the "back-to-basics" enthusiasts. Language experts became aware that to encourage process and more creative aspects of language development, they had to forego criticism of students' results produced during the early stages of reading and writing instruction. Furthermore, Piaget's belief that children's errors hold valuable clues to their thinking (Duckworth, 1973b) became reflected in this process, functional view of written language learning.

Roger Shuy (1981a) noted that the major difference in educational perspective brought about by the language research of the 1970s was the reexamination of the natural directions of language learning; essentially that it occurs holistically in social contexts. Successful language learners begin with a need to use written language and gradually learn to acquire the forms that best reveal how language functions. Gone was the idea that written perfection should occur in a first or second draft. This was surplanted with the idea that writing continuously evolves more writing and one learns through actively manipulating linguistic elements in reconstructing text. In essence, Shuy maintained that students using natural language need to be more concerned with getting things done through the medium of language than with the surface correctness of it. They should experiment and learn to use language holistically, not by applying isolated skills.

Shuy provides us with the nonverbal metaphor of the iceberg to show how the visible features of written language are those that the "back-to-basics" advocates essentially test and teach (1981b).

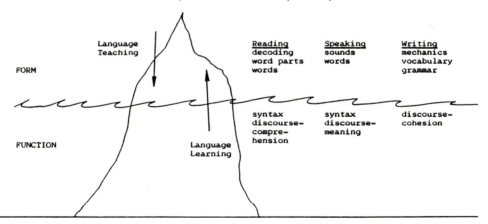

Figure 5. Tip-of-the-iceberg literacy forms contrasted with expansive, holistic functions of language. From Roger Shuy: The rediscovery of language in education. *Educational Leadership*, March 1981, p. 435. Courtesy of Association for Supervision and Curriculum Development, Alexandria, Va. (2/9/83).

The tip of the iceberg represents those features of written literacy which one can see and count. In reading, the visible aspects are related primarily to decoding concerns while in writing, they are related to matters of mechanics. Shuy points out that most standardized tests measure just the surface aspects of literacy. Much more difficult to measure and harder to see, count, and teach are the beneath-the-surface concerns of language and literacy: Those aspects which deal with meaning relationships, language use, and text structure. While the "back-to-basics" enthusiasts stress form before function, natural language learning highlights function before form. This represents the same progression noted earlier with young speakers who move from deep structure internal concerns to correct usage of language forms.

The latter third of this book will emphasize functional, holistic ways to help student get beyond the basics in reading and writing. We will see that representational modes of visual literacy such as art, graphic patterns, and photography can assist students process verbal statements. Furthermore, visions that develop from both Stage One and Stage Four levels of Visual Literacy underlie what readers and writers "see" during reading, writing, and computer activities.

SYNTHESIS: THINKING OF CONNECTEDNESS AND CREATION

Henry (1974) clarifies why the part-to-whole theory best represented in the skills management and grammer-based approaches to written literacy are quite deleterious to the thinking and imaginative capability of our students at whatever grade or learning levels. Henry notes that two modes of thinking — analysis and synthesis — are always present, for example, in the act of reading. Analysis requires that separation occurs as when a passage is broken into parts or when a word is broken into its structural parts. This analytical process, Henry feels, has become the main way of teaching reading for appreciation and comprehension. The justification for analysis is that, in time, pupils will learn to do the dissection of parts on their own, and, above all, analysis may reveal how a literacy work as an entity holds together.

Synthesis necessitates a joining or relating of things that seem to exist separately. Synthesis then becomes a discovery of the nature of the relation between two or more disparate things. The key to synthesis is, of course, the search for connectedness. Grouping, composing, and generalizing are forms of joining that require synthesis.

Henry's point is that throughout the academic establishment, kindergarten to graduate school, we teach how to analyze and not how to synthesize. There is an underlying assumption that by constant, continual analysis, students will somehow learn to read and write for synthesis. But this does not appear to be the case. Very little comprehensive synthesis is taught to youngsters, because teachers have not had much experience with it in their own reading and writing.

Henry also suggests that the reason why many teachers shy away from using synthesis and encouraging intuition and imagination in the language arts is because many times it initially leads to failure. However, the groping for discovery, the bungling along the way is part of the creative process. Since synthesis in reading requires search for connectedness, students may awkwardly connect textual information that is inappropriate at first due to inventiveness and experimentation of intuition. Shuy (1981a) reiterates, however, that there is no way to learn a language without being wrong in it and without being allowed to be incorrect in it as one learns the right forms.

Essentially, synthesis is to composing that analysis is to dissection. When students write an original sentence, they are involved in synthesis. When they locate and label the parts of speech, they analyze. When students read or work through a collection of subskills in a skills management program, they engage in analysis. When they read a few books or excerpts from which they must induce a pattern or a generalization, they embrace synthesis.

Synthesis is powerful because in each discovery of relation or in each creation of structure such as in the writing of a sentence, poem, or story, the individual gives something of his/her self. The idea is not there until it is intuitively perceived or insightfully discovered. Teachers can point out features of characterization and plot in a story, but the relationship of one to the other in creating a compelling tale is not there until it is synthesized by each student. The discovery of relation and connectedness that occurs in synthesis is one of the processing strengths of the brain's right hemisphere.

I will point out in far more detail in an ensuing chapter how the right brain operates in holistic learning, but the reader can sense at this point, why a coding-emphasis view of written literacy limits not only individual student potential but also the learning style strengths of entire populations of youngsters. With continuous manipulation of only surface-level parts of the verbal coding system, students do not engage in discovery, in creation, in acts of synthesis and thereby do not learn to see relationships amongst the messages transmitted by the code; a process we label "comprehension." A major focus of the nonverbal strategies presented later in this book will be to show educators how to activate exercises whereby students synthesize large amounts of information and construct mental relationships that embed parts within the whole. As Henry deftly suggests, synthesis supercedes and embodies analysis when a design or overall structure has to be invented to incorporate all the parts or separate relations of a work. But next, let's look at the second level of visual literacy to see how it enriches our thinking capabilities in other ways.

VISUAL LITERACY AS REPRESENTATIONAL COMMUNICATION

Stage four of literacy development is based on humankind's desire to represent meaning in nonverbal, creative, and symbolic ways. Figure 6 shows the interactive relationships that exist amongst the four literacies as well as the interactive components within the representational systems of the second stage of Visual Literacy. This second stage of Visual Literacy encompasses the world of the visual and graphic arts, the media, and the aesthetic. The words imagining and producing represent the receptive and expressive processes of this literacy stage. The second stage of visual literacy, having direct linkage to the basic stage, is composed of the receptive processes of imagining or composing, the expressive processes of producing or creating, and the interactive effects of aesthetic engagement and appreciation. The advance of filming and videotaping of the 20th century has made the technology of media literacy a powerful means to influence thinking. While many visual literacy advocates focus on the media aspect of visual literacy only, they need to be aware that the dual processes of nonverbal composing and producing underlie that technology.

Note that all four literacies are not bound in some kind of rigid hierarchy. For instance, the representational systems of the artist or filmmaker can interact directly with the basic components of visual literacy, with those of oral literacy, or those of written literacy. Written literacy can be processed directly through interaction with nonverbal, representative thought and so on. We can say, however, that the comprehension gained from each literacy provides a richness, a fullness to the others experienced and mastered in a lifetime.

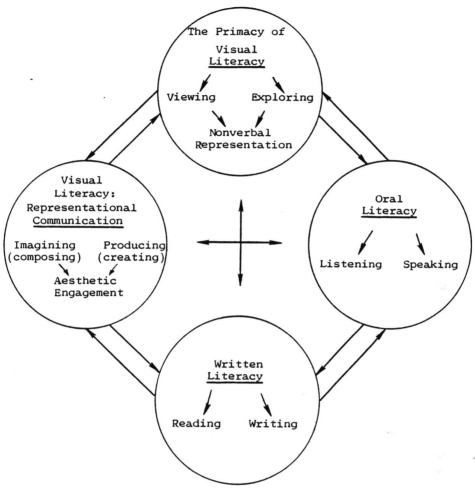

Figure 6. Stage four of literacy development: Visual literacy and its interactive relationship with the verbal and nonverbal literacies.

Similarities Amongst Nonverbal Literacies

In actuality, only degrees of cultural value and appreciation separate the young child's symbolic representations synthesized during stage one of literacy development from those of the aspiring or proclaimed artist. The end product (and price tag) may be viewed differently by the admiring and possibly buying aesthetic, but the process is the same. The young child expressing himself/herself through pictures, clay, or dramatic play is reconstructing nonverbal experience without the immediate necessity for language. Furthermore, when your children begin their first writing experiences, their drawings often become the driving force, the rehearsal for the printed message (Graves, 1979). So, while the young child can "create" a picture, symbolic design, or nonverbal composition without full fluency in either the oral or written literacies, the visual composer or producer often purposefully bypasses verbal language to get at the essence of the nonverbal creation. In fact, speaking or writing about the experience may initially get in the way. This does not mean that the artist will neglect the oral and written language systems to help explain the meaning of the nonverbal message. It does mean, however, that the incubation or conceptualization of idea that became through the process of discovery and creation the artistic end product, was conceived holistically, nonverbally, without the use of language. Synthesis of idea occurred that didn't need the appendages of language for conceptualization and clarification. During the time of the creative process, however, other images can crowd into the mind of the artist to suggest other views or approaches (Shahn, 1960). These images can be accepted, embellished, or discarded as they suit the original fullfillment of nonverbal conceptualization.

Later, language can be used to explain the insight; to break the insight down into logical component parts so that the whole can be discussed and evaluated. Such was the thought process of Einstein as creator when he conceived his "theory of relativity." It was first conceived holistically in an image — a mental picture — and later translated and refined by Einstein into the analytical and sequential symbols of mathematics and words (Clark, 1971). Modern art teachers such as Betty Edwards (1979) are showing their students how to mentally shift from a verbal, logical way to create art to a global, imagistic, intuitive mode which, as we well see a bit later, activates the processing mode of the brain's right hemisphere.

However, while the verbal literacies may get in the way during the critical moment of holistic conception, they may be critical for the visual composer, artist, and aesthetic during the apprenticeship period. The artist listens and reads about the creation and discoveries of others. This knowledge bank expands his/her landscape, allowing the artist to know and understand not only precedents in history but also the technology of his/her craft. The years of schooling in which the verbal literacies are stressed, on the other hand, will not guarantee the future artist his/her skill or craft. The oral and written literacies are means of learning and outlets for expression and criticism. But for the artist, the creative moment rests on the direct exchange between the representational idea conceived from the visual literacy base and the implementation of craft.

Another essentail quality separates the emergent artist as creator from that of the young child as representational designer. That quality is centered on purpose and need. The artist knowingly strives to reconstruct experience so that it can be perceived anew. The artist examines the earthly, the mundane to discover even the tiniest elements of beauty. The visual composer or creative producer work through their respective crafts to establish new and fresh connections. Madeline Grumet (1983) suggests that the essential distinction between art and craft rests on the process of estrangement. The objects of craft, which could be film equipment, zoom lenses, brushes and easals, are bound within daily life and are intended to enhance the common order. The artist reconstructs experience through the tools of his/her craft to transcend the ordinary or to make the ordinary appear fresh. For the viewer or aesthetic involved in estrangement, "the work of art simultaneously draws the viewer to it, engaging expectations, memories, recognition, and then interrupts the viewer's customary response, contradicting expectations with new possibilities, violating memories, displacing recognition with estrangement" (Grumet, 1983).

The Need for Cultivating Aesthetic Literacy in Young People

Many art educators and neuroscientists see a failure in Western school systems in their presentation of the arts. They don't train young thinkers in the powerful process of estrangement, the process of aesthetic literacy, but focus whatever art training they do, on glimpses of finished products. The thesis of Sykes's paper (1982) is that students should be trained to become critics as a way to achieve aesthetic literacy. Rather than be presented the arts as 'givens,' students should become involved in the creative process. Too often, Sykes notes, the arts are taught as finished products — completed symphonies, paintings, films, or poems — in art and music appreciation courses. Students need to be brought closer to the conditions in which art is created by being engaged in the arts. This means that while most students will not become artists, "they can be taught to respond to the aesthetic levels of meaning in literature, music, painting, film, sculpture, architecture, and other manifestations of art" (Sykes, 1982).

Many in the educational field feel that schools have systematically

ated those experiences which develop youngsters perceptual, ... native, and visualizing abilities. Having a dual perspective of the school curriculum as a professor of education and art, Elliot Eisner (1981) adds that sensory deprivation is a glaring cause of illiteracy in our nation's schools because schools fail to provide programs that allow youngsters to express meaning through sensory forms of representation. Eisner feels that literacy can be employed, developed, and refined within any of the forms of representation the sensory systems make possible. Sensory forms of representation found in such activities as poetry, the visual arts, music, and dance can provide the conceptual basis for meaning that will be represented later in the oral and written language codes. He maintains that children who have not learned how to see and mentally explore the forms of nature and the forms of art and science that constitute our culture will not be able to write, not because they can't spell, but because they have nothing to say — nothing to reconstruct from sensory exploration of the environment. Nature provides the raw material for basic experience as was noted in Stage One of literacy development. Cultural forms of representation, on the other hand, are purposeful, traditional, have specific syntaxes through which meanings are conceptualized and shared, and require the perception of subtle qualities according to Eisner.

Lewis (1980) disparages the isolation of the arts as a separate school subject. The isolation limits the extension of thinking that often occurs when a young child initiates an art project. The teaching of separate disciplines, reading, writing, and the arts, prevents children from letting different forms of expression emerge from and into one another. In other words the creation of a toy puppet or painting can be the impetus for an oral or written composition. The interfacing of the arts with written literacy expression allows children to put tone and feeling into written works.

THE LITERACY OF AN ELECTRONIC AGE: COMPUTER COMPETENCE

Within the past two decades, interest in another form of literacy has overshadowed, even eclipsed, preoccupation with the traditional stages of literacy. This interest is in, of course, computer literacy and the way that information can be transmitted through electronic media. We must realize that a type of linguistic, cultural, and social revolution is presently in effect equal to the impact of the printing press some 500 years ago. In fact, Watt (1983), who helped develop the computer language of LOGO, believes that computer literacy is truly a lifelong process of acquiring a culture. Bork (1981) notes that students of today have both their present and their forthcoming future dominated by electronic wizardry. He adds that unless students have the understanding of and the ability to use the new technology, they will be as illiterate as people of today who can not read and write. Furthermore, if the aim of the computer industry is to have the personal computer installed in every household, instruction can be managed in the home thereby altering the traditional concept of school. The futurists see even beyond the technological present and advocate preparing students to be able to communicate information at any time and any place with any other peoples who have a two-way communication systems capability.

However, the reader of this book will need to consider what is really meant by computer literacy and secondly what type of mental processing does this literacy demand. We need to make a distinction between programming the learner and programming the computer. The former encourages the type of mental processing feared by many and which becomes the fruit of fantasy for science fiction and alarmist writers. In this mode, peoples are dominated by an electronic mind which monitors all of life's daily movements and thoughts. Programs and packaged-learning modules transmitted by a benevolent "Big Brother" are a major source of the control. In today's technological world, we do see a good amount of such pre-arranged packaging, labeled software or courseware, in which the learner's mind is programmed to deal with information in a didactic, controlled sort-of-way.

While many computer advocates consider the packaged use of the computer as "literacy," the reader of this book will sense that this usage lacks the thinking requirements inherent in the other facets of literacy. Recall, we noted that literacy meant competency in the use of a symbol system and that a mental requirement was the acting on or the interpretation of meaning consistent with what was already stored in the head. Finally, we noted that literacy had a functional component, the ability to "do" in that symbol system.

When the learner programs the computer, on the other hand, we can note that a literacy in that mode does exist. As programmer, the learner is involved in very similar receptive and expressive processes that were found in the other forms of literacy. While the technology is modern and its mode of delivery extremely rapid, the information processed and manipulated by the computer is still bound by the same distinctive features that make up the verbal and nonverbal coding systems. These coding systems will be covered in depth in Chapter 5, but for the moment we can note that the computer programmer does use sequential, digital and simultaneous, imagistic modes during thought process.

Let's examine the scope of computer literacy as viewed in its largest context. In one recent **Curriculum Update**, Gawronski and West (1982) looked at a number of definitions and arrived at the following consensus of what should be covered in the topic of computer literacy:

- How computers are used
- What a computer can and cannot do
- What a program can and cannot do
- How computers work
- How to use a computer
- The impact of computers on society
- How computers can develop the skills of decision making and coping with change
- An introduction to or an awareness of programming (p. 3)

Note that these authors place the interactive aspect of computer usage last and maintain "as important as that last item is, educators should remember that there is no need to create a world full of programmers" (p. 3). These author like many others in the field miss the crucial aspect of the mental processing involved in programming and fail to see how this usage essentially fulfills the requirements of literacy.

Following the consensus of topics listed above, seven applications of computer technology exist in the educational field at the present time:

1. There exists an administrative use of the computer at the superintendent's office or school principal level. Administrators can manage the affairs of the "shop" and keep such records as attendance, coursework, and grade point averages at their fingertips. In this context, the author could sense the orderly, disciplined mind of the administrator at work when three of them were overheard during a break at a computer conference. Their interest was to know the **exact** skill in each subject domain that each student was mastering on a weekly or even daily basis. This is a fine notion if one holds a narrow, skills approach to curriculum. However, consider the point that for the administrator to access that information instantly with the press of a key, someone (probably the forlorn teacher—) had to enter all that data on a continual basis.

2. There exists the concept of computer-managed or computer-assisted instruction. In this vein, the computer assumes the role of teacher and provides instruction on either a one-to-one, tutorial level or on a network-of-students level. This is where the software or courseware is all important. While children or youths sit in front of the computer, they interact with the program that has been preset for them. If the network approach such as that of Radio Shack's Network II is being used, one teacher can monitor the responses of eight or sixteen students who are keyed into the program. In this tutorial usage, concepts and skills may be taught through some computer interaction. The computer leads and the student responds. The notion of branching is also important here in that the computer program branches the information to the student's skill level and branches the student through a series of retaining steps when errors are made. According to one spokesman, Emmett (1983), "the computer-assisted instruction or CAI programs may be used to present material in a tutorial format, the better ones guiding the student through the material, setting the pace to suit the student, prompting, cuing, asking questions and presenting relationships — much of the time in a strict alternative or multiple-choice mode."

3. The drill and practice usage generally indicates that the skills or concepts have been taught beforehand and now the student is getting practice or reinforcement with that skill. This would be similar in usage to traditional roles of flash cards or pages of arithmetic computation problems. The CAI programs often have some of the electronic flash card drills built in after teaching segments.

4. The computer can be used to stimulate experiences that are too far fetched, too difficult, too dangerous, or too expensive to bring into the classroom. In this usage, an experiment or a social, political, or economic problem can be established that the learner has to work through to a logical, manageable solution. One important point that Balajthy (1984) makes is that simulations can provide a fund of experiential information not normally faced in real life by the average child.

During the simulation, the learner's thinking processes are stimulated and skills are taught often unbeknown to the software user. For instance, during challenging sequences such as figuring out what is wrong with a car's motor based on facts provided through various auto diagnostic tests or during an adventurous search for the secrets of Science Island (Grolier), the learner is involved in very active, inquisitive reading processing. While engaged in the Treasure Hunter software program (Grolier), the student uses reference skills to manage his/her history and geography facts. Some programs make good use of the icon to fill in children's imaginations and to provide relevant experiential background. For instance, in Dinosaur Dig (CBS Software), one screen says, "Press → to compare a four-legged apatosaurus with a two-legged struthiomimus as they walk." By pressing →, the child first sees a four-legged dinosaur lumber across the screen followed by the two-legged animal, with a very different bodily configuration, prancing across the same screen.

5. Then, of course, the computer games remain popular even for classroom use. They serve to motivate low achieving students and to help them learn computer operations. Those games that have learning sequences built in are often used for disabled and reluctant students as a means of reinforcing reading or math skills often without student awareness that they are working on such skills.

6. Use of the computer as a word processor is one of the stronger ways in which interaction between the learner and the tool is achieved. In word processing, the learner must initially use the keyboard as a typewriter to enter or type in a paper, report or composition. For many students, a first or second draft may have been completed already by the more traditional paper and pencil mode. When the paper is typed in, however, the word processing component allows the writer to modify, replace, and transfer text. Words, paragraphs and sentences can be moved from place to place within the composition. Because editing and revision-writing are practices highly unfavored by student writers, and word processing component is a high motivator for increased competence in composition writing. Students sense they can edit and revise rapidly rather than undergo a series of laborious rewrites in order to reach a finished written product. In fact, word processing undoubtedly encourages revision. This feature of the computer is highly favored at high school and at college levels.

7. A final, but most important use of the computer as a means to literacy, is that of programming. To program, the user must learn a langauge that allows the computer to work and to solve problems. The computer than translates the keyed-in language through the use of tiny pulses of electricity into its own binary code. Young children can learn the language of LOGO as their first computer language while older youngsters and adults can learn the language of BASIC, which stands for Beginner's All-Purpose Symbolic Instruction Code. Knowledge of one or more of these high level computer languages allows the learner to write programs which are a sequence of rules or steps in the solution of a

problem. When one writes and executes computer programs through the use of a computer language, one has achieved another stage in literacy development that is distinct from competency in either the visual, oral, or written literacies.

The New York City Board of Education has recently published two rather inexpensive curriculum guides that will help youngsters become proficient in the languages of LOGO and BASIC. These guides, listed under the curriculum offerings in Appendix A, highlight how verbal, nonverbal, numeric, and symbolic interactions occur to achieve uniqueness in computer programming.

Let's see how this unique literacy is achieved. To communicate in either the oral or written literacies, the communicator uses the language of his/her culture and receives and expresses messages among participants who share the same language. While misunderstandings may sometimes occur, there is little need for direct translation. The programmer, on the other hand, must arrange his or her thoughts and convert them to a language that can be electronically converted by the computer. These thoughts can be prearranged in the form of an algorithm which is a written set of instructions in computer language such as BASIC or can appear as a flow chart which is a nonverbal/verbal flow of steps in the program. The algorithm statements or flow chart diagram express the logic of the literate user.

When the computer operates the program or "discusses" stages of the operation with the programmer, it must present the information back to the programmer to read in a language that the programmer can understand. While words in any spoken language can have multiple meanings, only one meaning is assigned to a word or phrase in computer language. For instance, the BASIC word RUN means only one thing to the computer — to operate the program that was just programmed. This one word or one symbol meaning allows for exact interpretation to occur. Thus, use of a computer language allows the user to convert thoughts into a system that can be translated by the computer and reinterpreted by user when the computer has processed the program.

There is another highly important distinction that separates the learning of the verbal literacies from that of computer literacy. This distinction is missed by many computer enthusiasts who favor the more passive coursework and CAI features of computer usage rather than the active role required during programming and during the composing and revision stages of word processing. During these stages, the expressive aspect of literacy development precedes the receptive. Developmentally, the other literacies generally work in reverse. Listening is achieved before speaking, and, for most of the population, reading is achieved before writing. Because the LOGO or BASIC programmer is using a language to operate a tool, the expressive component directs the operation while the receptive output is read as completion of a satisfactory operation. The mind has searched for the appropriate connections and has used the logic of programming to make the tool work.

This expressive feature is what is making John Henry Martin's computer-based reading and writing program so successful for kindergarten and first-grade children. Recently acknowledged in the March 1983, ASCD **Update** and in New York Times Magazine of February 26, 1984, Martin's Writing to Read program teaches youngsters to interact by typing-in words into the computer before they can read. The program uses a simplified phonetic alphabet, and children learn to associate letters with sounds as they begin to write their first words. Interacting with the computer, which also talks to the five and six-year-olds, the youngsters discover they can write anything they can say. Eventually, the simplified phonetic alphabet is discontinued and the children learn to spell words as they appear in books. According to Asbell (1984), never before have children of five had a chance to write as well as they can think and talk. They regard the computer interaction as "talking with their fingers." While . Martin has begun the youngsters on written language parts, soon they are typing whole stories.

Figure 7 shows how computer literacy interfaces with the written language and the stages of visual literacy. This would be the triad relationship experienced by most verbally and visually literate users of the computer since they have had prior experience with various language systems. For most adult users of the computer, written literacy would subsume fluency with the oral language and visual literacy as representational communication would subsume visual literacy as primary thought. However, for the five-and-six-year-olds in the Writing to Read Program, the triad relationship experienced would be that of Oral Literacy, Computer Literacty, and the basic components of Visual Literacy.

Programming and word processing, especially where a paper is keyed-in directly from thought, may be regarded as expressive activities. Receptive functioning occurs during the reading of print, designs, and computer symbols or computer statements. The reading of print would be similar to the reading of graphemes of language that appear in

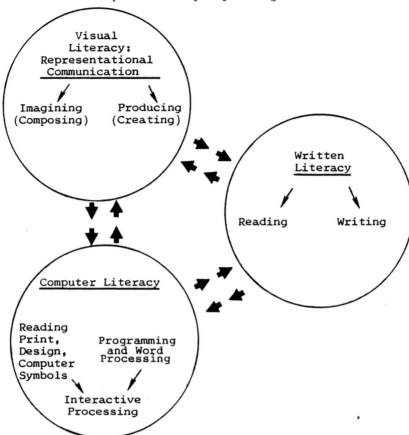

Figure 7. Interactive relationships among computer literacy, written literacy, and visual literacy as representational communication.

a printed text while the reading of computer symbols or statements would involve the reading of those characters which are special to computer operation alone. For instance, in BASIC, the * sign is used to designate multiplication and the ↑ is used for raising the number before the arrow by the number written after the arrow. The statement GO SUB while having some near resemblance to English is a singular computer command which branches the program to a subroutine written in the program. Interactive processing is mediated by the expressive input and the receptive feedback provided by the computer screen during program operation.

There is a strong visualizing aspect to computer literacy that is often achieved through the rapid communicative mode of the electronic media. This aspect may be more appealing and motivating for some to capture if their thinking style is more right-brain preferent. These users may also prefer the use of flow chart conceptualization rather than the listing of algorithm statements. However, White's thesis (1983) is that electronic learning evokes more sensory interactions than print because electronic technology can produce images, sound, simulations, and fresh dynamic graphics. For the graphics to appear, the computer user has to visualize the effects he or she wants before they are programmed and then has to work through the creative steps to produce the graphic display.

College students are receiving preparation in these ideas in the area of "micrographics" (Bloom and Braden, 1984). In this usage of computer, students are required to create microcomputer graphics which integrate a wide range of word, picture, and design, and design combinations. The goal of the programmer is to achieve a harmony of visual/verbal symbiosis in displaying messages and to consider, as well, the mood value of words and images when they are displayed on the screen for reading. Bloom and Braden maintain that interactive images with text are far more possible through the microcomputer than they are to document on paper. Students are able to program displays that develop gradually on the screen and to move and modify images through simulation and association. A critical visualizing feature for student programmers is also the ability to mentally anticipate likely human responses to the verbal/nonverbal program displays.

THE IMPORTANCE OF COMPLETING
THE LITERACY CYCLE

Throughout this chapter, the receptive and expressive components that are inherent in each of the five literacies have been developed. We have also seen how the literacies impact upon each other and how the components of visual literacy provide the sensory data for the other literacies to flourish. My efforts have been, in part, to show that Western educational horizons have been narrowly conceived during the past decades. Those entrusted with the cognitive and affective growth of youngsters have overlooked how they themselves learned, through active sensory exploration of the environment in an atmosphere of cultural enlightment.

In efforts to cut back so-called curriculum "frills" and intensify time-on-task for written literacy acquisition, educators may have been cutting the real basics from the curriculum. David Rockefeller (1977) as spokesman for the Rockefeller Report, **Coming to Our Senses**, maintains that the arts are the real basics in our school curriculum and that the concept of literacy should be expanded beyond word learning skills. Also limiting is the notion that a curriculum which does not give students the opportunity to become literate in the forms of representation available in a culture handicaps their ability to use other forms of representation (Eisner, 1981). Finally, literature, music, and art contain the best evidence we have of the unity and continuity of the human condition reflected from past to present times (Postman, 1980).

Besides narrowing the focus of the total curriculum, educational leaders have imposed an adult-oriented, analytical schema in the content disciplines that remain, particularly in regards to the learning of the three R's. This analytical approach can be seen in the pre-occupation with decoding skills and formal grammar mastery before written language has gone through processes of experimentation and discovery.

Even Western notions about science and mathematics instruction are based on narrow thinking. In a recent edition of the Association for Supervision and Curriculum Development's **Update** (1984) was a revelation of what occurs in the Japanese curriculum as compared to what school boards and legislatures are doing in the American curriculum. The title of the piece was "Arts and Humanities Education Undergirds Japanese Success." The aritcle reported that educators and school administrations are mandating more years of study in science and mathematics in the belief that better academic preparation in these subjects will narrow the gap between U.S. and Japanese success in technology and industry. Because of the insertion of more science and math, the arts and humanities have been completely eliminated in some schedules because students don't have time for much coursework. "By contrast, Japanese students not only receive a superior technical and scientific education, but also a superior arts and humanities education." The mental stimulation provided by the arts and humanities education is just as important to the Japanese students' success as mathematics and science, the article adds. While the American educational system focuses narrowly on verbal and numerical thinking, the Japanese learn many symbol systems. This allows them to compose and create patterns and to imagine organizational structures, systems designs, and computer software through many symbolic and representational modes.

However, with shifts to process-oriented, holistic approaches to written literacy instruction stored sensory experiences and nonverbal representations can be integrated with language. One reading methodology does attempt to fuse the arts directly with reading instruction. **Reading Through the Arts** presents a number of manifestations of the arts — painting, music, dance, drama, graphics, filming and recording — to youngsters of all grade levels to involve the youngsters in the vital component of visual literacy before or in conjunction with their reading and writing. The strength of such an approach is based on the organizational marriage of the sensory and the visual with a need to express meaning through the written language.

The thesis of this book will be to show educators how to couple other nonverbal representational strategies with reading and writing processing. When this occurs both brain hemispheres will necessarily contribute to the learning process. The point of the discussing selected brain research studies in later chapters will be to show that interhemispheric exchange of information does occur during print acquisition and that nonverbal representation is a thinking strategy that can be activated during the acts of reading and writing. There does exist a wide range of individual differences for both the verbal and nonverbal modes of thinking within the human species. However, even in today's jargon, individualization generally focuses on presenting written literacy in a variety of subskill guises to youngsters without cultivation of sensory, artistic forms of representation. In our highly literate culture, we continue to look at just verbal growth and deficiencies and do not particularly esteem nor reward the nonverbal mode. We may praise and reward the artists, inventors, and technological geniuses when they achieve their feats but we do not reward them during their schooling years if their nonverbal strengths interfere with written literacy attainment. For those youngsters who don't attain written literacy early or rapidly enough, we may label these youngsters disabled and subject them to analytical, parts-specific verbal remediation. By so doing, we curtail the power of holistic, analogic thinking for those youngsters and minimize the opportunity to cultivate the nonverbal, creative mode in which they may excel. We shall see, however, a bit later, that a major quest of the learning style practitioner is to match the preferred thinking styles of youngsters with educational opportunity.

This discussion of the five stages of literacy development can be ended with Roger Sperry's opening remarks delivered at a conference on thinking processes in which he noted (1973):

> . . . our educational system, as well as science in general, tends to neglect the nonverbal form of intellect. What it comes down to is that modern society discriminates against the right hemisphere.

Educational practices must be widened to include a more enlighten-ing process perspective embracing the arts and a readmittance of the ba-sic nonverbal curriculum that was an early, essentail part of youngster's lives. By so doing we will restore the components of visual literacy to an influential role in shaping creative thought.

CHAPTER THREE

PERSPECTIVES OF VISUAL LITERACY

VISUAL LITERACY remains a concept unfamiliar to many educators in America. The term visual literacy, generally credited to John Debes, a pioneer in the use of visuals in the classroom (Fransecky and Debes, 1972), became fashionable in the late 1960's and early 1970's when the impact of television viewing on modern youth began to be a national concern. However, while visual literacy conferences have been held through the years and publications have appeared in various professional journals, visual literacy concepts and approaches are downplayed in most curriculum offerings throughout our country.

PROBLEMS WITH VISUAL LITERACY'S ACCEPTANCE

There are at least five reasons why Visual Literacy has not made a substantial impact on Western education. First of all, as indicated earlier, the meaning of visual literacy has not been clearly defined in functional, realistic terms. This is undoubtedly due to the expansiveness of the concept, the meaning of visual itself, the academic leanings of the educators applying the term, and preoccupation with the forms and techniques of media communication. Debes (1969) indicated that the field of semantics, linguistics, philosophy, psychology, pscholinguistics, art, screen education, and the industrial, vocational, and graphic arts have contributed ideas to the meaning of visual literacy. At an educational media leadership conference held in 1976, delegates were asked to define the term "visual literacy." Analysis of the 62 definitions indicated that 52 different phrases were used to define the adjective "visual" and that three major meanings evolved for the word "literacy," as a group of competencies, as a process or method of teaching, or as a movement (Cochran, 1976). All the delegates agreed, however, that visual literacy is used to refer to three major diverse categories: human abilities, teaching strategies, and the promotion of ideas.

A major problem for visual literacy enthusiasts is that they have been using a catch-all term to mean anything that is delivered through visual sensory input. They have focused more on the Stage Four aspects of visual literacy particularly on the technology of media communication than on the fundamental Stage One level of visual literacy as a thought process. Horton (1982) notes that while the concept has been with us since 1969, no substantive theory of visual literacy has been developed. The two-stage model advanced in this book does represent, however, a viable way to advance the theory of visual literacy.

A Language Contradiction

Secondly, use of the term visual literacy suggests a contradiction. How can a literacy be visual? Does a visual language exist subject to the analogous rules of syntax and word arrangement as for the verbal language? From the school's perspective, how can time, resources, and teacher energy be devoted to an ill-defined literacy when so many of the nation's youngsters are already underachieving in reading and writing development? The issue becomes one of conflict concerning the ultimate goal of schooling.

Chall and Mirsky (1978) point out another danger in stressing a curriculum approach that may favor the learning style of some youngsters, particularly children of the poor, but may, in actuality, widen the gap between written literacy proficiency of the affluent and the poor. They indicate that national surveys show that children of the less affluent tend to be low achievers while other research indicates that many of them prefer to learn through right-brained activities such as through visual and artistic literacies. If schools concentrated on right-brain activities to match a preference in learning style, it is conceivable that even lower achievement in reading and writing could result among the less affluent. We will follow these issues a bit more in Chapters Six and Seven.

Effectiveness of a Media Curriculum

A great deal of controversy exists regarding the place of media in the school curriculum. For instance, many instructional technologists advocate the use of film and television within separate curriculum offerings. Foster (1979) in his book **The New Literacy: The Language of Film and Television** feels that one of the main skills in acquiring visual literacy is acquiring an understanding of the structural devices basic to all films and how they are used. Structural devices such as composition, lighting, color, movement, editing, and sound are used by filmmakers to create powerful emotional responses in audiences. When the viewer learns how these devices are used to elicit feelings, he/she will be helped to resist media influence and manipulation and will develop a more sophisticated perception of film or television. Kundu (1976) has suggested further that television and videotapes can be used to capture nonverbal interaction between teachers and learners so that this interpersonal communication can be properly observed and analyzed during playbacks.

While these ideas may have merit for the modern classroom, are they truly realistic? Can the schools of today experiencing tightening budgets afford the hardware and film rentals necessary to implement a motion picture and television curriculum? Furthermore, aren't modern-day youngsters viewing more than enough television so that while they're in school for literacy instruction, they are not engaged in more of the same media conditioning and manipulation? Postman (1979, 1981) is probably the electronic media's severest critic in the way that it influences and conditions children's lives. Labeling television the "first curriculum" in modern technological cultures, he points out that between the ages of 6 and 18, the average child spends roughly 15,000 to 16,000 hours viewing television while school, the second curriculum, consumes about 13,000 hours for that same life interval. Thus, we come back to the issue of what literacy the schools should teach and if a media literacy, based on electronic technology, is really necessary to teach in the first place?

While filmmaking is not generally a major part of the academic program, the receptive, information-giving quality of film has long been valued by educators. Teachers often use the film as a prelude, as a motivater for the verbal experience to follow, or as a substitute for those students who lack the verbal abilities to understand specific contents if they were to listen or read about them. Content area and grade school teachers know the value of using film to help students comprehend and conceptualize events too remote or too abstract for them. Film takes youngsters to places and eras of history that may not exist in the imagination and thus fills in the schema related to time and distance. Such recording of images has given viewers the opportunity to examine the events recorded in those images, to relive an event symbolically, and to develop more novel, complex ideas (Cromer and Thompson, 1980).

Secondly, skillful use of a particular film can help student writers see parallel constructions between written and visual themes. Green (1978) has pointed out five such ways that film and written compositions overlap: the importance of context and focus, organizational principles, effective emphasis given to a particular idea or quality, juxtaposition for contrast and comment, and the effectiveness of concreteness compared to generalities.

Since film and television are obviously here to stay, schools should accept the responsibility of training literate and perceptive viewers as they have accepted the responsibility of training literacy in reading and writing (Foster, 1979). Morrow (1980) warns, however, that although English teachers of the 80's will undoubtedly favor the term media literacy over the less translatable term visual literacy, they will still have difficulty translating the concept of media literacy into unambiguous, teachable competencies in which print can stand along with media. Because a major goal of this text is to show educators the parallel connections between verbal and nonverbal modes, subsequent chapters will develop positive ways to use media, pictorial messages and visuospatial configurations to help students understand text and create compositions.

Teacher Training

Another reason why many educators are unfamiliar with the ideas and components of visual literacy is because they weren't covered in college coursework. Of course, this may be due to the lack of unity among the differing camps of visual literacy and the general diffusion in establishing a conceptual and theoretical framework of the meaning of visual literacy. Secondly, while Stage One awareness of visual literacy is often covered in early childhood education courses through discussion of Piaget's stages of cognitive growth, the connection is not made for prospective teachers as the carry-over of these thinking processes of the ensuing stages of literacy developed in Chapter Two. Little of the ideas of visual literacy as representational communication are presented to teachers during literacy course work as ways to help youngsters compose and comprehend as they learn the rudiments of reading and writing. Artistic, aesthetic and media training also appear to be covered as separate curriculums in order to prepare prospective neophytes for entry into specific art or media-dominated fields.

By briefly examining types of visual communication curricula offered at various colleges, we can note once again the various perspectives and diversity of the visual literacy concept. Media ecology is defined at New York University as the study of the effects of communication technology on a culture and on the people of the culture to include their life styles and personal values. Dake (1977) describes a visual literacy methodology program at Iowa State University for future art teachers. Student teachers plan and prepare visual lesson plans designed to promote right hemisphere processing. Ragan and Huckabay (1978) describe a course in visual communications at the University of Oklahoma for a general undergraduate population. The course, designed to stimulate visual awareness and visual thinking processes, deals with graphic and media techniques, visual/verbal message design and delivery, and purely visual message design. At the American University, all School of Communication majors were required to take a new course entitled **Visual Literacy: Learning to See** (Sutton, 1982). It was felt that this would be a key course for students later moving to upper level work in any of the four programs offered by the school. To assist students to "see" in a discerning manner and to deepen their understanding of the contents of Art History, Photography, Film, and Video, the awareness of the image was highlighted.

In reviewing various elementary and secondary school programs that have reported success in visual literacy approaches, teacher training, particularly in media usage, appears to have occurred at the in-service level when a program was initiated in a specific district, school, or classroom. For the concept to have national educational impact, visual literacy notions would have to be implemented at many more higher schools of education than is the practice at the current time. Teachers collectively will need more background and training in both Stage One and Stage Four Levels of literacy as is done in methods courses which focus on verbal literacy procedures and methods for all levels of the school population. With more teacher involvement, more familiarity with the concept will occur, and more visual literacy methodology will be attempted. For instance, imagery exists as a powerful influence on composing and comprehending. However, in teacher education course work, how often are techniques of visualization taught as a processing mode to aid youngster's reading comprehension?

Research Problems

Problems in researching visual literacy methodologies is the fifth rea-

why the concept is still in its infancy of development. Sigel (1978) feels that a dearth of experimental and empirical data exists, particularly in the area of pictorial comprehension. He strongly suggests that a major research question should be devoted to finding out if picture comprehension is related to other cognitive competencies. A problem in visual literacy research noted by Debes (1981), on the other hand, is that it deals with single images, or single pictures. The single picture paradigm in visual research is very misleading according to Debes for the real test of visual language research should be concerned with sequence and continuous movement. "If we ever are to understand visual languaging and visual literacy, we will do so after we begin to aim our experiments and our research questions at visual statements consisting of sequences of visual signs" (Debes, 1981, p. 2). Hennis (1981) notes that most research conducted by psychologists and media researchers has been aimed at discovering the effects of visual presentations on viewers. Little research has dealt with the processes a composer uses when creating a visual message or in determining the processes by which meanings are made from specific images. Fork and Jonassen (1976) add that even with the diversity of fields represented, the results of visual literacy research efforts have shown to be largely ineffectual in providing teachers and other practitioners with any established guidelines to apply.

The relative differences amongst literacy research is revealed in a computer search of the ERIC data base conducted in February 1985. The descriptions used in the search were research and either reading, writing, or visual literacy. The research score for the various literacies was as follows:

Reading Research	— 7,511 studies
Writing Research	— 1,916 studies
Visual Literacy Research	— 6 studies

The large discrepancy amongst the literacy studies may reveal not only the relative importance afforded to one literacy over the other, but also to the ease in which research can be conducted in each mode.

One of the major reasons for the lack of studies in the nonverbal area may be due to the way that the components of visual, media, and artistic literacies are transmitted and codified. Kundu (1976) feels that for media literacy the answer lies in recent developments and applications of technology. When the spoken language was analyzed and codified into a written form, it was transfixed in a mode where its patterns, structures, and meanings could be studied by linguists and others. However, until recent times with the major inventions of the motion picture and television, there had been no way of capturing the rapid flow of nonverbal communication and momentarily halting it for analysis and study. Now with the added dimension of videotape, nonverbal indicators between respondents could be fixed and replayed for analysis by scientists and researchers. For instance, Restak (1982a) describes how infant researches through slow motion, frame-by-frame analysis of videotape can show how an eight-day old newborn responds visually and emotionally with his father. Kundu indicates that since 65 percent of all communication between people is nonverbal, teachers and counselors would profit from studying gestures, expressions, and postures, used in the process of communication.

EXAMINING THE DIVERSE VIEWS
OF VISUAL LITERACY

Let's examine how others have viewed visual literacy from their various educational perspectives as a prelude to reexamining the functional view of visual literacy raised in Chapter One.

Debes and Williams (1970), editing the Proceedings of the First National Conference on Visual Literacy, identified four major concepts within the visual literacy movement:

1. a visual language exists,
2. people can and do think visually,
3. people can and do learn visually,
4. people can and should express themselves visually.

Hewes (1978) suggests that from an anthropological perspective these aspects of visual literacy may be viewed as the general human condition. Since almost all of the world's people have normal vision subject to the same physiological constraints and since they are exposed to rather similar visible phenomena, the notion of visual literacy can be viewed as simply superfluous. However, Hewes adds, because different cultures offer different visual arts and man-made visual experiences to their members, visual literacy can be conceived of being on a continuum from very restricted competence, even where vision is normal, to high competence. Just from simple interaction with the environment, range of visual information reaches the brain.

The essential characteristic of visual information, whether it be the result of a natural occurrence in the environment such as a hunter visually tracking an animal or a representational occurrence such as a picture or film of the same event, is that it is nonverbal.

Categories of Nonverbal Language

Nonverbal forms of communication have been studied in depth by Ruesch and Kees (1956). They established three distinct categories of nonverbal language — sign, action, and object language. The commonality among these three nonverbal categories is that they transmit information through analogic representation.

Sign language occurs when gestures and manual signs are used to communicate meaning. Their meanings may involve complete systems such as the sign language of the deaf or the Indian sign language. Individual gestures or body movements may indicate singular messages, such as when the thumb is extended for the hitchhiker pose or when the horizontally extended index finger is pointed menacingly at someone. The advantage of sign language is that people who can not speak the language of a culture can communicate with one another through facial expressions, gestures, and manual signs. If cultural meanings are similar for the visual signs, peoples of differing verbal language backgrounds can also communicate in an open, direct way.

This level of visual communication is also unconsciously learned by students in our classrooms. They learn to "read" the teacher's face and specific body movements to determine how they will act or not act in a given situation. Young children can be taught to modify their behavior based on the information conveyed by adults during sign and gesture language. If a visual literacy curriculum were to be implemented on a school-wide basis, young children should be consciously taught to use and interpret sign and gesture language in social situations. By using signs and meaningful gestures themselves, young children will associate physical activity with meaning just as they had during natural development.

An important concept needs to be noted regarding the rapidity of meaning communicated through nonverbal forms. One gesture or sign can communicate a complete and instantaneous meaning that may take many words to explicate. Moreover, meaning communicated through signs and gestures can be transferred to verbal referents. For instance, signs and gestures can begin a communication cycle and as young children ask "What did that expression mean?" their oral language can be developed and refined. Their oral statements, in turn, can be transcribed to written stories. When children read the stories, they will have clear, concrete referents, both verbal and nonverbal, to aid the process of comprehension.

While human communicative behavior is more verbal than nonverbal, behavioral scientists are placing more emphasis on the meaning of nonverbal signals communicated during day-to-day human activity. MacLean (1978) adds that many forms of nonverbal behavior displayed by humans show a striking parallel to the behavior patterns of animals.

Action language is the second category of nonverbal communication discussed by Ruesch and Kees. It involves body movements and actions not specifically related to direct signs and signals. The key to action language is that it is transistory, ongoing, and can exert a kinesthetic effect upon the viewer. For example, hearing and perceiving movements of someone or something else can set in motion other actions on the part of the perceiver. Movements involved in eating, swinging a golf club or viewing television may serve the personal needs of the actor, but they can be interpreted as statements by those that perceive these acts. Observing the actions of others can then influence how a perceiver might act.

Another aspect of action language is that it can express emotion. When in the course of a verbal argument, a person slams his/her fist on the table, the action is understood although possibly not appreciated by the perceiver. Thus, coupled with specific gestures, action language can convey powerful visual statements through such activities as dance, pantomime, mimicry, and acting found in Stage Four levels of literacy. The performers are engaged in conveying meaning through movement while the audience is emotionally aroused to feel a particular way about the performer's actions. Possibly, it is this aspect of action language that allows us to feel catharsis while viewing drama but rarely through participation in verbal communication.

Furthermore, the "show and tell" activities of kindergarten and first graders take on an important dimension when viewed as an aspect of action and gesture language. Notice the sequence is not "tell and show." Young children should "show" the material or demonstrate their actions first before the rest of the group. As they "show," they become involved in movement and bodily action so that words are coordinated with the internalized meaning of the activity. The showing aspect provides a clear referent for the verbal accompaniment. When a child talks about something he made, for example, and the object is held in his/her hands, the words used about the object are complemented and reinforced by the object's presence. The group, in turn, will provide visual, emotional, and verbal feedback about the success of both dimensions of the "show and tell" activity. Lewis (1980) adds that, by nature, young children's actions evolve in an integrated meaningful manner: dancing evolves into a story, a story into a painting, a painting into a poem.

Object language, the way that material objects can be displayed or represented, is the final category of nonverbal communication categorized by Ruesch and Kees. All material things such as implements, machines, art objects, architectural structures, still and movie photography are included in object language. Because of its time-enduring quality, object language has played an enormous role in archeology, anthropology, and history. Also, since letters themselves as they occur in various written forms or displays have a material substance, they can be considered a form of object language as well. Until fairly recent times, engraving, drawing, painting, and sculpture were the principle ways that people recorded their visual impressions. However, with the development of photography and motion pictures, candid, unstaged and naturalistic events of human and animal life could be captured and recorded for all time. In fact, the photographic document has become a codification system and portrays an external visual model of the world. Kundu (1976) has suggested, the visual recording of historical events allow us to examine the nonverbal cues that influence both trivial and worldshaking decisions.

In considering the potential impact of nonverbal communication on the school language program, we will be most interested in the category of object language and the compelling way that its messages are transmitted. For now, we can say that still and movie photography are modern examples of object language which can convey to the viewer themes and details that the verbal language is often incapable of expressing. Furthermore, computer technology has emphasized the importance of visuospatial design, directionality and arrangement found in such techniques as flow charts, diagrams, graphs, and other nonverbal configurations. When educators capture the power of such visual meaning and visual structure to help students articulate verbal expression, they create learning situations in which students are using their full learning potentials.

Range of Visual Literacy Definitions

The three nonverbal forms of communication categorized by Ruesch and Kees emerge in the standard definition of visual literacy which grew out of the early conferences of the visual literacy movement (Debes, 1969; Fransecky and Debes, 1972):

> Visual literacy refers to a group of vision competencies a human being can develop by seeing and at the same time having and integrating other sensory experiences. The development of these competencies is fundamental to normal human learning. When developed, they enable a visually literate person to discriminate and interpret the visible actions, objects, and symbols natural or man-made, that he encounters in his environment. Through the creative use of these competencies, he is able to communicate with others. Through the appreciative use of these competencies, he is able to comprehend and enjoy the masterworks of visual communications.

This early definition does suggest that viewing integrates with other sensory modalities and that creative and appreciative aspects of visual literacy are possible once earlier visual competencies are developed. However, this definition is too expansive and unsatisfying from a pragmatic perspective. As argued in this book, all seeing people are potentially visually literate and this condition, as reflected earlier in Chapter One, starts immediately after birth. Secondly, visual literacy as representational communication can resurface and provide creative insights at the fourth stage of literacy development for many thinkers at many times. This second stage allows for a distinction amongst individuals as to how much more they will develop nonverbal modes of representation and creative expression beyond the basic level of visual literacy.

We will discover in the book's second section, how the visual perceptual system influences thinking and the stages of verbal and nonverbal literacies. The contribution of vision to learning allows for the second stage of visual literacy to flourish. This notion is closer to Randhawa's belief that because the mind is influenced more by inputs through the visual channel than the combined effects of inputs delivered through the other four sensory senses, vision is our most powerful sense (1976). Randhawa states that "visual literacy is concerned with the mode of our most powerful sense, vision — a channel which provides at least 60 percent of the raw material for our minds to process, integrate, and direct action."

Debes and Williams (1974) then included the notion of visual imagery in their definition, and suggested that visual literacy is aided by technology for creating visual images and using them to communicate. They felt that a visual literate person could perceive and expertly interpret patterns and sequences of visual images and use them for effective and even eloquent expression. The process of visualizing was also a major component of Greenlow's (1976) visually literate person. During viewing, a person responds to the surface patterns, but during "visualizing" the person brings meaning to the image and reacts to the image in a critical manner. The visually literate are those who have acquired the ability to make viable judgments about the image they perceive.

Finally in 1978, Debes and Williams argued that the concept of visual languaging represented a basic component of visual literacy. Visual languaging is the invention and use of visual signs and symbols and the systematic utilization of these in communication. Furthermore, the authors suggest that there are at least nine ways in which the intentional use of visual sequential arrangements resemble verbal sequential arrangements.

Recent definitions of visual literacy focus almost exclusively on the imagistic aspect of thinking. Horton (1982), urging the instructional technologist to take a leadership role in defining the scope of visual literacy, writes that "visual literacy is the ability to understand and use images and to think and learn in terms of images, i.e., to think visually." Braden and Horton (1982) expressed the same view in their formulations of visual literacy proposed during the 13th Annual International Visual Literacy Conference held in Lexington, Kentucky. Their problem has been in reconciling input via picture and media viewing with that of active reconstruction that occurs during imagery.

Others such as Ross (1972), Lamberski (1976), and Ausburn and Ausburn (1978) focus on nonverbal, communicative techniques and skills in their views of visual literacy. Ross referred to visual literacy as the numerous techniques used by people to communicate with each other in nonverbal ways, such as through body language, art forms, pantomime, graphic expression, and picture stories. Ausburn and Ausburn add that such skills are intentionally communicated during visual literacy communication. Lamberski sees visual literacy as related to the creation and use by students, teachers, and designers of visual communicative activities, devices, and systems essential to the teaching-learning process. Finally, Whitsitt (1976) suggests that visual literacy refers to anything that isn't in print.

VISUAL LITERACY AS A RECONSTRUCTIVE THINKING PROCESS

At this point we can review the definition of visual literacy offered in Chapter One to see how it encompasses the range of definitions expressed in many of the earlier views. It was noted that visual literacy was fundamental to human thinking and evolved through the interaction of three basic components — viewing, exploration, and nonverbal representation. Visual literacy itself is defined as the active reconstruction of past visual experience with incoming visual information to obtain meaning.

Within this framework, we need not have separate concern about the skills level of the visually literate person, the various nonverbal communication techniques and modes, and the distinction between the sensory input and the resultant images. The focus in my definition is on a process, thinking perspective fundamental to all seeing persons. Furthermore, the definition works for those involved in any levels of artistic, media, and electronic literacies which, in turn, are bound in thinking process to the very nature of visual literacy.

Let's examine how the definition works at both Stage One and Stage Four levels of literacy. An object, event, or nonverbal representation exists in the natural world and the viewer brings his/her mind set to bear upon the natural circumstance. The mind set however is already conditioned by previous sensori-motor experiences regarding the nature of the particular circumstance, and we saw that these mind sets are housed in the brain in a network of schema relationships. Furthermore, the way that the natural circumstance is being perceived at the moment in a certain light, at a certain angle, from a particular spatial perspective impinges new information upon the visual cortex of the brain. This level is what Ihde (1977) calls the straight-forward visual experience; in which the viewer attends to the visual event in the present.

Brain researchers, Restak notes (1982b), have modified their most cherished notions about how we perceive reality. Restak indicates that the view of vision is no longer the belief that the eyes operate like the shutter of a slide projector transmitting impressions "ready made" to a silent screen somewhere in the brain. Rather, as we shall trace in the following chapter, reality involves a two-way process. We impose "meaning" through our reconstrucion of reality even as the immediate world "holds up the cue cards" (Restak, 1982b, p. 112).

Thus, incoming visual information is understood or modified in light of which is previously stored in schemata in the brain. The notion of active reconstruction indicates that a perceiver can reflect upon the information contained in a visual experience as the experience is being viewed. For instance, at a basketball game you have previously viewed the opponent's team guard steal the ball from one of your team's forwards. Now, as the selfsame forward dribbles the ball down court, you can sense the movement of the opponent guard as he maneuvers himself for another steal. In a sense, you are reconstructing the guard's moves and you have apprehension for your team. The closer the guard gets to his original stance, the more able you are to visualize the liklihood of a second steal. The more that the forward stays away from that guard and does other ball handling that is different from the original event, the more likely you would be to repress the impact of the steal. However, the act still exists as an internal visual event retrievable at any time during the game, or for that matter, throughout your lifetime.

Even more important for the educator to realize is the discovery that the recognition stages physiologically existent within the brain's visual cortex need outside stimulation in order to develop normally (Restak, 1982b). That is why a child with strabismus (crossed eyes) or cataracts is now operated on quite early in life. With these conditions, a dominant eye usually develops causing a suppression or disuse of the neural cells in the other eye. Thus, Restak notes, the importance of environmental stimulation on brain function persists throughout life and gives brain researchers vital clues as to how to prevent such mental disorders as senility.

The importance of the two-way direction arrows noted in Figure 6 needs to be emphasized as well. The arrows indicate that an interactive relationship among all four stages of literacy exists within one individual. We shall see in an ensuing chapter, however, that differing individuals have a propensity or bias to learn through one literacy mode more than another, conditioning them to adopt a mindset or learning style to complement that continually evolving bias. The arrows indicate, for instance, that media and artistic literacies have a direct interactive relationship with a visual literacy base. This base is composed of the processes of viewing, sensorimotor exploration, and nonverbal representation which are housed in schemata or mental images. Now, when literate individuals at the Stage Four level compose or comprehend through their respective crafts, they imagine, create, and engage themselves in their creations, tempering past experience with present enlightenment.

The processing at the Stage Four level incorporates some of the very same mental activity found at the basic level of literacy learning. For instance, for a media specialist to compose through filming, he or she must have an imaginative sense of how the visual composition will unfold. Likewise, when a youngster "creates" a rhinocerous from molded clay complete with horn and tail, he or she had visualized that animal taking shape through the clay. In Chapter Five, we will examine the distinctive features of this imagistic, holistic mode to see how the filmmaker and the young child are akin in their thinking processes.

A NEW PERSPECTIVE FOR VISUAL LITERACY

Since the mid 1970s, a new exciting perspective has been added to the concept of visual literacy from experiments and studies conducted in brain research. This research clearly indicates that because of their very nature and mode of transmission, Stage One components of visual literacy and Stage Four modes generated through artistic and media literacies are primarily processed by the brain's right hemisphere. The finding does pose an additional potential conflict for the school curriculum. While the traditional school activities in the language arts, such as phonemic discrimination, word attack, spelling, and writing are generally processed by the left brain, visual messages are processed and comprehended by the right brain. Furthermore, the right brain appears to excel in holistic, spatial, and kinesthetic learning in which visual perception and integration are just a part. Therefore, visual, artistic and media literacies are means of engaging global, holistic mind sets in learning tasks. Since many language activities as presented to youngsters in beginning stages involve an opposite-type processing, generally analytic and sequential, the thinking generated in early schooling is unfortunately conditioned along one dimension.

In this chapter, the perspectives of visual literacy have been reviewed so that the reader can sense difficulties theorists have had in establishing a singular perspective. Ideas developed in this chapter have also helped us to see that one comprehensive definition of visual literacy was needed so that its essence can be differentiated from that of verbal literacy. Shortly, we will examine the uniqueness of the visual mode of transmission and why many educators and parents are justifiably alarmed about the unchecked use of television and other electronic media on their children's lives.

CHAPTER FOUR

THE VISUAL SYSTEM
AND BRAIN PROCESSING

THIS CHAPTER will explore recent brain research findings especially as they effect the visual processing system and some of the underlying neurological structures involved in learning the various literacies. In Chapter Five we will take note of the distinctive features that exist between verbal and nonverbal communication modes. Because learners have differing degrees of brain organization to assimilate these modes, there exists the possibility of a wide range of individual differences in humankind with regard to literacy competencies. This focus will allow us to consider in Chapter Six how people come to differ in their thinking and learning style habits and to investigate what can be done to assist those learners who develop "mind sets" not congruous to how the mainstream learns their written literacy skills.

Since visual literacy is the literacy concerned with nonverbal communicative forms whose messages reach the brain through one sensory route, albeit one that eclipses the combined effect of the other four sensory pathways in the human species (Randhawa, 1976), it is fitting that we focus on the two-way traffic between eye and brain. However, we must remember the interactive effects of the other sensory systems upon the act of viewing. We saw in Chapter One, how the integration of motor and kinesthetic activity with viewing enlarged schema development.

The human brain is a complicated piece of evolutionary engineering. As noted by Wittrock (1978), since the brain also specializes within each hemisphere as it does across hemispheres, no functional dichotomy can do justice to the sophistication and complexity of the human brain. Yet, popular notions today may tend to oversimplify the processing modes of the two brain hemispheres — the left and right cerebral cortex. We see in some recent writings discussing Visual Literacy the erroneous assumption that visual presentations are processed by the right brain and language presentations are processed by the left brain. The truth is a bit more complicated than that and this chapter and those that follow will attempt to separate fact from speculation in the brain lateralization area. Furthermore, we can't just look at the well-documented findings from hemispheric asymmetry research regarding the specializations of the two brain hemispheres, but need to consider, as well, the potential impact of Epstein's findings (1978) showing that there are distinct stages of brain growth akin to Piaget's stages of developing mental operations, and of MacLean's (1978) discoveries that the brain processes information through three distinct, vertically arranged systems: the reptilian complex, the limbic system, and the neocortex.

Brain research is attempting to show us what the brain does during specific learning tasks under differing conditions for different types of learners. The modern era of research was fueled by Roger Sperry's experiments with split-brain patients during that mid 1960s and continues with six other major procedures used to determine which hemisphere does what during specific sensory and information-processing tasks. These procedures encompass the following:

1. Examining damaged or diseased brains, either a complete hemisphere, sections or lobes of a particular hemisphere, or tissue below the neocortex to determine the effect of damage or removal on subsequent behavior;

2. studying brain wave activity particularly alpha rhythm from surface electrodes placed on the left and right sides of the scalp during the Electroencephalogram (EEG) or the Event Related Potential (ERP) procedures;

3. studying the sex hormones — the male endrogens and female estrogens and progesterones produced by the sex glands — to determine physical differences in male and female brains;

4. measuring the changes and intensity of blood flow to various areas of the cortex activated by subjects' performances on specific sensory, motor, and mental tasks;

5. using the Wada Test to determine which hemisphere is dominant for speech for right and left handers;

6. and activating the sensory/motor systems or half visual field opposite to the brain hemisphere being studied through such techniques

as dichotic listening, visual half-field tachistoscopic testing, eye movement, and tactual stimulation to letters or numbers.

The brain research perspective presents a host of implications as well as inconsistencies for educators. Some implications appear to be quite outlandish such as those which postulate that creative, artistic people are right brained and logical, rational people are left-brained and these two extremes if sexually joined would make for a good marriage! Inconsistencies have arisen in the use of nonsurgical techniques such as in the dichotic listening and split-visual field procedures. These studies, have revealed, as well, poor validity and reliability (Satz, 1977; Zaidel, 1979). Hellige (1980) adds the dimension of proper piloting with normal subjects whose behavior is predictable and confirmed with such a technique as the visual half-field tachistoscopic procedure before the procedure is used to note individual differences with another atypical population. Finally, Galin (1979) tells us that another major reason the tachistoscopic tests correlate poorly with the dichotic listening tests is because the one involves the testing dimension of reading and the other involves listening. Not only are the tasks not the same, but different brain systems are involved.

However, regardless of the procedure used, brain researchers are making educators aware of the nature of brain processing during all learning. Knowledge of how the brain works may have important bearings on specific learning strategies presented in the classroom during different stages of learners' lives. This awareness level is important not only for reading and writing instruction, but also for those educators involved in visual, media, artistic, and computer forms of literacy. We shall see that because we are aware of the highly complex cooperation between the two hemispheres and amongst the vertically arranged brain system, we have the opportunity to deliver curriculum content through more than one literacy mode to insure likelihood of success.

Let's now look at the intricate workings of the human brain, expecially those recently revealed by the split-brain researchers and other neuroscientists tracing the remarkable activity from brain to mind.

SPLIT-BRAIN FINDINGS

The modern era of brain investigation began shortly after the mid 1960's when Dr. Roger Sperry and his associates published their findings regarding patients who were operated on to control life-threatening epileptic seizures (see Gazzaniga, 1967 and Gazzaniga & Le Doux, 1978 for historical reviews, and Wilson, Reeves, Gazzaniga, 1977 and 1982 for more recent reviews). Scientists had known well over one hundred years before that time that two specific regions in the left hemisphere mainly Broca's and Wernicke's areas were primarily responsible for the expression and comprehension of language (Geshwind 1972 and 1979). However, behavior analysis after surgery of the epileptic patients altered the view of brain functioning especially in regard to the functioning capability of the right hemisphere, long believed to be the "dormant" one in the human species.

Sperry, teaming with a neurosurgeon, Dr. Joseph Bogen, had known that epileptic seizures began in one brain hemisphere of each of the patients and traveled across the corpus callosum to the other hemisphere resulting in uncontrolled generalized convulsions. The corpus callosum is the largest of the neural tracts that connect the left and right hemispheres of the brain, allowing the hemispheres to communicate with one another and insuring that the perceptions arising from the differing processing modes of each hemisphere integrate into a unified whole. When Bogen severed the corpus callosum of these epileptic patients confining the epileptic seizures to one hemisphere, Sperry and his research associates were able to test the individual processing capability of each hemisphere.

Results from a group of studies on nine commissurotomy (split-brain) patients showed that the surgically separated left hemisphere had its own mode of thinking that was distinctly different from the thinking mode of the right hemisphere (Sperry, 1973 & 1982). In fact, elsewhere Sperry (1968) described the split-brain syndrome as dealing with two separate spheres of conscious awareness, each with its own sensations, perceptions, cognitive processes, and learning experiences. It became clear in the post-operative testing of the nine right-handed subjects, that the disconnected left hemisphere processed information from the right hand and the right-half visual field and was the hemisphere that essentially did all the talking, reading, writing, and mathematical calculation (Gazzaniga, Bogen, and Sperry 1967). Conversely, the disconnected right hemisphere remained essentially speechless, was unable to write, and was unable to carry out mathematical calculation beyond simple addition problems with sums under twenty. However, the right brain was found to be the superior and dominant one for perceptual recognition of whole figures and patterns, for dealing with visuospatial relationships, for nonverbal thinking, and for making direct perceptual transformations when verbal language did not have to be used to tell what happened during the perceptual task.

For a number of years, the commissurotomy was performed as a one-stage operation. The surgical procedure involved severing the corpus callosum and many of the other cerebral commissures. Wilson, Reeves and Gazzaniga (1982) noted that the one-stage operation frequently caused major, irreparable damage to surrounding areas of the brain. Many patients suffered from "acute disconnection syndrome" which included states of apathy, confusion, and infantile behavior.

A present technique used by a team of surgeons at the Dartmouth-Hitchcock Medical Center, Hanover, New Hampshire is to perform the operation in two stages (Wilson et al., 1982) and to use the "central" commissurotomy procedure. During the partical commissurotomy, or first stage, 75 percent of the corpus callosum is divided. Furthermore, the "central" commissurotomy procedure uses a microsurgical technique in which only the corpus callosum and hippocampal commissure is divided. After a minimum interval of two months the remaining 25 percent of the corpus callosum is severed while the anterior commissure is left intact. Documenting a number of such commissurotomies at the Dartmouth-Hitchcock Medical Center, Wilson et al., (1982) felt that the two-stage, "central" procedure helped make convalescence smoother and diminished the acute discrimination syndrome.

A PERUSAL OF THE VISUAL SYSTEM

At this point let's examine the anatomical structure of the visual system in humans to see how the split-brain researchers accomplished their finding about the human brain using the visual half-field technique. Look at Figure 8 which shows how information presented to each eye is registered in each hemisphere (Lindsay and Norman, 1977).

Information in the visual field falls upon the cornea, the outside protective covering of the eye. The cornea has the slight bulging shape on the outer edge of each eye in the diagram. Then the information, in the form of light waves, passes through the pupil and the lens, which focuses the light reflected from an object or a scene onto the light-sensitive receptors at the rear of each eye. In the figure, the oval shape through which the lines cross coming from the outer boundaries of the visual

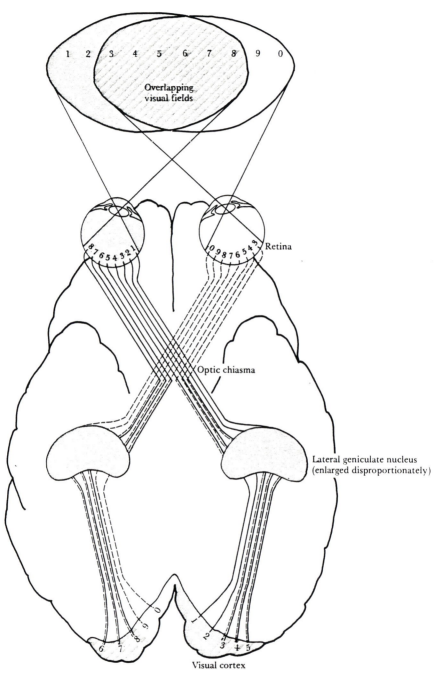

Figure 8. The visual processing system and brain input. From P.H. Lindsay and D.A. Norman; *Human Information Processing: An Introduction to Psychology.* NY, NY, Academic Press, 1977, p. 74. Courtesy of Academic Press, Inc. and Peter H. Lindsay (2/22/83).

field is the lens. The light-sensitive receptors found at the back of each eye are commonly known as the retina.

Each retina is composed of approximately 125 million light-sensitive neural receptors called rods and cones which, in turn, respond to the light energy falling upon them. Beginning with the neural processing of the rods and cones, the physical energy of light is now converted to electrical energy necessary in neural transmission. Generally the cones have the greatest density in the fovea or center of retinal field and they decrease in the peripheral region. The fovea is thus optimally located to receive the central part of the image around which the forward part of the eye is fixating.

At the retina, neural cells pass the light information from the rods and cones to the brain. One cell, known as the ganglion cell, contains the axon which makes up one fiber of the optic nerve that leaves the back of the retina to pass to the next relay station before it reaches the brain center known as the visual cortex. The reader needs to be reminded at this point about the basic components of the nerve cell or neuron. The neuron is composed of the cell body, an axon or nerve fiber that carries information from one neuron to another, and a host of threadlike projections called dendrites which occur on the cell body itself or at the end of the axons. Once myelination occurs, nerve fibers and dendrites can be considered insulated conductors necessary to transmit the electrical signal of the neurons. The gap between neurons and dendrites where chemical transmission of information passes from one neuron to the next is called the synapse.

According to Lindsay and Norman (1977), approximately 800,000 relatively long fibers of the ganglion cells form the optic nerve which is as big around as the thickness of a pencil. In Figure 10 the solid and dotted lines leaving the backs of the left and right eyes respectively represent these long fibers of the optic nerve. These fibers cross at the spot called the optic chiasma which lies anatomically just below the corpus callosum. All of the fibers from the right half of each retina (roughly those bound by numbers 1-4 in the left eye and those bound by numbers 3-5 in the right eye) then go to the right visual cortex found in the occipital lobe in the right hemisphere of the brain, while the fibers from the left half of each retina group together and go to the left visual cortex. Because these nerve fibers are actually axons of the ganglion cells, no new synapse occurs at the optic chiasma.

The nerve fibers regroup again at the lateral geniculate nucleus which serves as the next important relay station after the retina in sending visual information to the brain. At the lateral geniculate nucleus, synapse occurs between the axonal extension of the retinal ganglion cells and new cells to carry a sensory message to the visual cortex, the primary visual receiving area of the brain.

It has been found, as well, that inputs to the lateral geniculate nucleus do not arise extensively from the retina cells. A particular midbrain area of interest to us called the reticular formation also sends signals to the lateral geniculate nucleus. Because the reticular formation is an activation and alert mechanism, there exists the possibility that neural activity in this nonsensory structure may help to determine whether the signals that arrive at the alteral geniculate nucleus are transmitted to the higher cortical levels of the visual processing systems (Lindsay and Norman, 1977).

Upon leaving the lateral geniculate nucleus, there are no more synaptic connections to modify the path of visual information before that information arrives at the visual cortex. In the visual cortex, signals are processed in neural circuits arranged in layers which operate similarly to those found at the retinal level. Fibers leaving the visual cortex generally go to adjacent visual association areas of the visual cortex and from there the information passes to the temporal lobes found at the left and right sides of the cortex. Throughout cortical processing, features are extracted from the original sensory input so that perception occurs. For instance, some cortical cells are sensitive to visual patterns of edge, others to contour, others to movement, and some to color and the spacing of light and dark areas of the visual image. From their analysis of the perceptual processes involved in pattern recognition, Lindsay and Norman feel that the system requires top-down, conceptually driven processing, as well as the inputs from signals presented to the visual field (1977).

As indicated by Figure 8 information taken in from the left half of a visual scene is transmitted to the right side of the brain, and everything to the right of the fixation point (generally found in the center of the visual field) is registered in the left half of the brain. Notice the overlapping of the two visual fields on the cortex bounded by numbers three through eight. The primary emphasis in the processing of visual information becomes concentrated in the central part of the visual field, the fovea or region of maximum acuity. In the visual cortex, to show the neural importance given to foveal processing, more than 50 percent of the neurons have to deal with analysis of the central 10 percent of the visual field.

A bit later we will see some major implications for tasks such as reading due to the organizational scheme of the visual processing system. We will see that configurational features presented at the periphery do make a contribution to how fluently we read even though meaning is processed through foveal fixations.

RIGHT HEMISPHERE COMPREHENSION

In the split-brain studies, patients were tested when sensory input was restricted to a single hemisphere. With the corpus callosum severed but not the underlying optic chiasma, the hemispheres could not readily communicate with one another. During visual testing with appropriate visual fields masked or occluded, when an object such as a cup of coffee was presented to the opposite field, very discernable results occurred (see Figures 9 & 10).

When the cup was presented to the right hand or the right visual field, the response would be "it's a cup." In this case, the sensory input crossed appropriately at the optic chiasma, reached the left visual cortex, and was recognized for naming by the left hemisphere, the normal language center for most humans. When the coffee cup was presented to the left hand or to the left visual field, no verbal recognition occurred.

However, in many instances, the left hand could recognize what was seen although it couldn't say what it was. Experimenters ingeniously had a patient tactually feel an object and then select it from amongst a larger group of objects, placed into a closed bag. They found that while the right half of the brain is seriously limited in language production, it does have capability in language recognition and comprehension. We will see later how this capability aids the general population in terms of reading and writing processing. Another interesting finding resulting from left-visual field recognition of objects was that these patients often responded with analogy, metaphor, or a functional quality of the object seen. Thus, if recognition occurred for the outer rim of the coffee cup, the patient might be apt to respond "doughnut" because of the metaphorical quality of roundness. Another patient might be shown a key in the left visual field and respond by trying to insert it into a car dashboard because the key reminded him of a basic function.

An important observation noted in the post-operative behaviors of

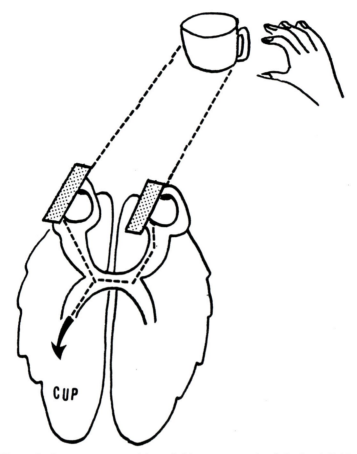

Figure 9. Language recognition of object presented to left visual field.

the split-brain subjects was that their left hemispheres continued to dominate. Sperry felt that this phenomena was due to the highly developed cognitive and expressive capabilities of the left hemisphere and its tendency to take control of the motor system (1973). The left hemisphere, in other words, because it could verbally express itself, gave reasons for right hemisphere behaviors, even though these reasons were not based on complete truth. For instance, when the word "pencil" was tachistoscopically flashed to the left visual field (right brain) of one split-brain subject, he was able to select the pencil from a group of other objects with his left hand. When asked why the pencil was selected, the subject could not answer correctly because the brain responsible for speech was cut off in the act of perception. He said something like "I must have done it unconsciously" (Sperry, 1968).

In a later experiment with a different callosal-sectioned 15-year-old

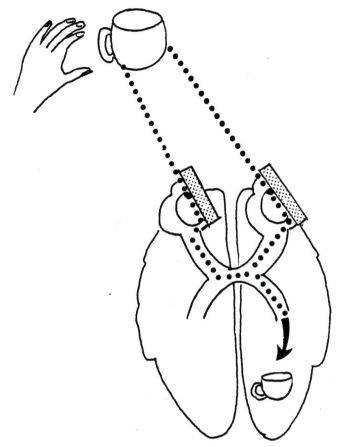

Figure 10. Nonverbal recognition of object presented to left visual field with no verbal output.

patient, Gazzaniga, Le Doux, and Wilson (1977) felt that it was the boy's verbal system which attributed cause to the behavior produced by right hemisphere motor activity. They noted that in exercises requiring the right hemisphere to initiate motor acts, the left brain was forced into a role of observing responses of unknown origin. Yet, in trial after trial, the left hemisphere was quite adept at providing a reasonable explanation for the response. For instance, when the word "rub" was flashed via tachistoscope to the right brain, the boy rubbed the back of his head with his left hand. When asked what the command was, he said "itch." In this case the response of moving the hand back and forth was observed by the left hemisphere and the boy immediately characterized it with what he thought was the best word to described that behavior — "itch."

The important implication noted by these authors is that the existence of two major, yet independent language systems allows for a rationale of how normal people go about constructing a personal sense of conscious reality. The verbal system may not always be aware of the origins of our everyday actions, yet it attributes cause to our behavior as if it knew for sure. In fact, it may be a very common phenomenon for the left brain to rationalize and take credit for right-brain perceptions of the world.

Right-hemisphere functioning is also quite important for the apprehension of full meaning from oral or written communication especially regarding emotional and interpretive levels of content (Levy, 1983). This evidence is gleaned from patients with right-hemisphere damage who are asked to provide an account of the stories read to them. They usually omit emotional and humorous content. Expressive language production is almost always under the control of the left hemisphere, however, the right hemisphere can generate some spoken words if prompted to do so by the stimulation of strong emotion.

For the normal population full and rich language comprehension requires right hemisphere contributions. Hellige (1980) and Levy (1983) point out that as mental tasks become more complex, the more likelihood that hemispheric cooperation is the rule rather than unilateral hemispheric processing as might be the case in simple one-task experiments. Levy adds that normal brains are made to be challenged and "they only operate at optimal levels when cognitive processing requirements are of sufficient complexity to activate both sides of the brain and provide a mutual facilitation between hemispheres as they integrate their simultaneous activation" (1983, p. 70). Moreover, Levy suggests that because the right hemisphere plays a large role in general activation, arousal functions, and emotion, when the student has a motivation, desire, or an interest to want to learn a particular content or skill, both brain hemispheres will be activated.

Ross (1982), discussing research conducted with some of his own patients and that of brain researchers in Copenhagen, goes one step further on the importance of the right hemisphere in the emotional aspects of language and behavior. The Copenhagen researchers, Lassen, Ingvar, and Skinhj (1987), measured the cerebral blood flow in normal brains of 80 patients and over 400 patients who had diseased brains. Some of their findings were remarkable. They showed that while the patterns of blood flow increased to designated language centers in the left brain during speech, a concomitment pattern of blood flow occurred in the right side of the brain during speech. They also found that reading aloud activated even discrete cortical regions on the surface of each hemisphere, while silent reading involved the activation of four areas in both hemispheres. Finally, they noted that blood flow is always substantially higher in the frontal part of the cortex (the brain area of planning and will) than in the central and rear parts.

Ross became convinced "that both halves of the brain have responsibilities during speech and that, since the blood-flow patterns mirror each other in the two hemispheres during speech, the areas controlling language in each hemisphere are probably organized similarly" (1982, p. 10). Thus, Ross concludes that for every type of aphasia, there must be a corresponding syndrome existent in the right hemisphere which involves the emotional components of language. Summarizing the division of language functions between the two hemispheres, Ross states it this way, "The left is responsible for what we say, and the right for how we say it." Can the same maxim be transferred to the reading experience? Is the left strongly responsible for processing what we read while the right for how we think and feel about what we read?

WHAT DICTATES THE HEMISPHERIC PROCESSING MODE?

Other emerging conclusions also became clear in the years of brain research conducted since 1967 on split-brain and normal subjects. It was clearly not whether the stimulus was verbal or nonverbal that determined whether the left or the right hemisphere would respectively process the information, but rather the processing demands of the task. This meant that the left hemisphere would tend to dominate if the processing demands were time-oriented or sequential in nature and the right hemisphere would dominate if the information was to be processed holistically and simultaneously. Secondly, the intent or predisposition of the learner could influence how information was to be processed. This second consideration will be covered in depth in Chapter Six.

To illustrate how the nature of the task can dictate which hemisphere would process pictorial or verbal material, Tomlinson-Keasey and Kelly (1979) flashed words, pictures, and picture-word pairs to the visual hemi-fields of junior high and undergraduate college students and they found, as predicted, that both groups matched pictures more efficiently in the right hemisphere. However, when they had to translate words into pictures or pictures into words, the task was performed better by the left hemisphere. The latter occurred because meaningful matching involved analysis and sequence; tasks better suited to left hemisphere processing.

Bogen himself (1977) indicated that hemispheric differences are more usually considered in terms of process specificity rather than material specificity. He considers the mode of cognition of the right hemisphere to be more appositional in nature in contrast with the left hemisphere's dominance for propositional tasks such as occurs during speaking, writing, and calculation. All of the latter generally demand serial ordering. A key to the understanding of what appositionality means is reflected in the meaning of a more common term — configuration. Configurational processing is useful for describing the conglomerate of behaviors in which the right hemisphere excels such as recognizing the whole, recognizing and retrieving shapes and patterns that cannot be easily named, and recognizing faces.

Bogen feels that the key distinction between the hemispheric modes is the extent to which a linear concept of time participates in the ordering of thought. Thus, according to Bogen, the distinction in processing lies between the right hemisphere's specialization for processing time-independent stimulus configurations and the left hemisphere for time-ordered stimulus sequences.

To test out the spatial-holistic superiority of the right hemisphere, Nebes (1974) carried out three experiments with seven of Bogen's split-brain patients. Previous studies on these same patients had shown that higher-level cognitive functions in each hemisphere went on fairly independently of activity in the other hemisphere (Sperry, Gazzaniga, and Bogen, 1969). Nebes found that the right hemisphere excelled in generating from partial or fragmented information a percept of the whole stimulus. What distinguished the mental operation between the two hemispheres in these tactile and visual hemi-field experiments was the mental manipulation required to see the whole in the part, a factor to be closely related to synthetic reasoning.

In efforts to understand the reason for the verbal deficit in the right hemisphere, Levy (1974) presented a number of tasks requiring varying amounts of visual manipulative skills to brain-divided patients. She found that their left and right brains used different strategies. The left hemisphere did best on items which lent themselves to analysis and verbal description, and the right hemisphere did best on those items which lent themselves to perceptual, spatial differentiation.

The right hemisphere dominated when immediate recognition and memory of visual shape was the only requirement and the left hemisphere dominated when some form of verbal and/or conceptual, symbolic transformation was required. In fact, the right hemisphere was correct in visual matching 87 percent of the time regardless of the stimuli. However, in a matching task, when pictures which rhymed were substituted for identical pictures, a complete switch was produced from right to left hemisphere functioning. Why the switch? While the right hemisphere had a clear advantage over the left in visuo-visual mapping, visuo-phonic mapping was totally beyond the capability of the right hemisphere. Internal language was, for the most part, absent in the right hemisphere. Levy felt that the left hemisphere is disabled in visualization and constructional skills while the right hemisphere has an expressive aphasia due to a lack of internal language.

Levy (1974) suggests that the abilities and deficiencies of a given hemisphere may, of necessity, stand in reciprocal relation to one another. In other words, whatever provides the possibility for one function excludes the possibility of another. Given that humans are the only animal with language, cerebral asymmetry of function may have been nature's design for a brain which fully utilizes both linguistic and Gestalt perceptual functions. She points out that research dating back to 1924 has repeatedly shown that differentiation of hemispheric functions has to do with distinctions between part and whole perception; the left excels at perception of parts while the right hemisphere shows the reverse — good understanding of Gestalt but lacking in detail. The biological usefulness of an analytic deficiency in the right hemisphere thus becomes easy to understand if an analytic part-to-whole mode of information processing specifically interferes with Gestalt perceptions.

Levy concludes that the left hemisphere can be described as an abstract, temporal analyzer which placed stimulus input into sematic and phonemic categories while the right hemisphere is a concrete, spatial synthesizer which maps information into a visuo-structural realm. These two functions, then, would seem to be logically incompatible, but provide an animal with language greater specializations for survival.

HOW THE INTACT BRAIN FUNCTIONS

Now we can turn our discussion to the intact brain and why nonverbal and visual literacy experiences are quite important in the early lives of children. We saw earlier that the hemispheres are connected by several bundles of neural connections, the largest being the corpus callosum. These neural connections allow the hemispheres to communicate with one another and integrate the perceptions arising from the differing processing modes of each hemisphere into a unified whole.

Consider the natural learning style of the young child through the primary route of visual literacy and how schema representations form in the brain through interaction with the environment. Just prior to the beginning of formal schooling, the young child has been reacting to the world more like a generalist with both verbal and nonverbal modes of consciousness operating successfully in each hemisphere. It is also believed, as discussed in Chapter One, that the right hemisphere is the more predominant one in the early years of life as the young child visually and spatially explores the environment. Fadley and Hosler (1979) feel that early experience arising from right hemispheric thought and organization is our most natural state of consciousness and provides our fundamental structure in all life. Recall how Genie had normal right hemisphere development from even simple exploration of her environment but due to extremely limited social and verbal interaction did not develop the specialization for language in the left hemisphere.

One key to how the left and right hemispheres eventually achieve a coordinated balance of verbal and nonverbal communication may be in the maturation of the fiber systems that connect the differing brain systems. One such fiber system, the corpus callosum, connects the hemispheres laterally while other fiber systems pass from the hemispheres to the lower brain stem structures particularly the reticular formation. Both of these major systems mature slowly through early life and the smoothness of neural maturation and account for maturation of the child's cognitive powers.

The process of nerve fiber maturation is called myelination. Gazzaniga (1975) and Galin (1976 & 1979) feel that because the connecting nerve systems, especially the corpus callosum, are the last to myelinate during childhood, the young child may be considered to have a functional split brain with each thinking system developing independently.

Myelination is the development of a fatty sheath around the nerve fibers particularly the nerve axons. The axons conduct impulses from the cell body to the thread-like projections called dendrites which transmit the coded message to adjoining cell bodies. The myelin sheath acts to fa-

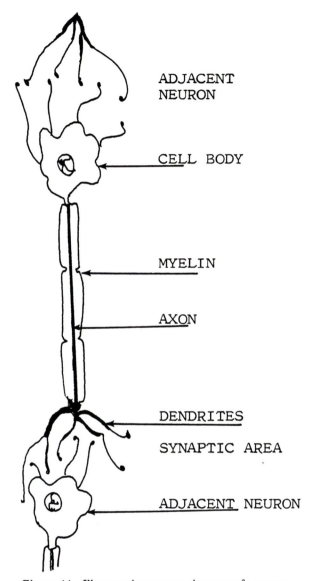

ADJACENT
NEURON

CELL BODY

MYELIN

AXON

DENDRITES

SYNAPTIC AREA

ADJACENT NEURON

Figure 11. Illustrated neuron and means of synapse.

cilitate electrical transmission through the neuron since its axonal fiber
is insulated just as an electrical cord is insulated for the transmission of
electricity (see Figure 11).

Yokovlev and Lecours (1967) have indicated that myelination of the
horizontal and vertically arranged fiber systems are hardly noticeable
until about two years of age. Then, the corpus callosum and other commissures between the two hemispheres myelinate rapidly from two until

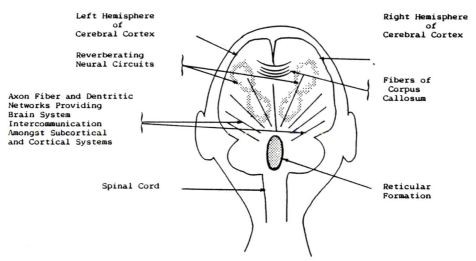

Figure 12. Illustrated brain showing fiber connections amongst subcortical and cortical brain systems.

seven years of age while the fibers from the reticular formation to the hemispheres myelinate rather rapidly from two until twelve and continue maturating until old age.

Both Galin (1976) and Kraft et al. (1980), have reasoned that these physiological myelin stages correspond with Piaget's landmarks in cognitive development. Kraft et al., noted that certain Piagetian conservation tasks having to do with the transformation of physical matter can be regarded as behavioral indicators of interhemispheric integration. Even more so, and extremely critical to proponents of visual, nonverbal literacies, may be the belief that visuospatial, manipulative activities stimulate myelin and dendritic growth, forcing nonverbal/verbal integration between the hemispheres (Sinatra, 1983c).

The more that language assumes command of the child's thoughts and actions, the more that the left and right hemispheres begin to take on distinct processing and memory roles and the more that full lateralization occurs. However, as we saw in the first two chapters, the left brain learns words and proper language usage best when it is guided by right hemisphere exploration of natural experience. This means that when the child sees and explores wholes of natural experience, he or she attaches the language that goes with components of that experience. The image of the whole appearance remains stored in the right hemisphere as well. Therefore, language learning is anchored to something concrete, something that lives in the child's mind. When language learning is covered in school as abstract bits and pieces of sounds and letters, we can see how sensory experience and imagery provide little assistance in the learning. This is one reason why many young children fail in beginning reading and writing attempts and why use of the naturalness of visual literacy and its representational form's can insure that both brain hemispheres contribute to full literacy success.

The central issue, then, is not that there is a dichotomy of consciousness between hemispheres but that there is one awareness or one consciousness which can rapidly switch between right and left informational banks. With the intact corpus callosum of normal learners, a flow of information can occur almost instantaneously between the two hemispheres. The corpus callosum is composed of some 200 million fibers of which at least 60 percent are myelinated (Wilson, Reeves, Gazzaniga, 1982). These fibers are really axonal extensions of cells that begin in one hemisphere and terminate in the other. Shortly, a powerful model of brain and mind based on the work of Luria (1973) will be examined. The model helps account for how consciousness directed by the frontal lobes can mediate between the left and right modes of thinking.

GROWTH BY SPURTS

Myelination is just one major physiological process that is important for increased brain efficiency. Neurologists had known that the basic unit of brain functioning — the neuron — developed in stages. Most felt that there were three distinct stages of neural development; the first during pregnancy, the second during the first year of life, and the third from the end of the first year to about the 16th year of life. Herman Epstein (1974, 1978) reported that his experiments showed a five-stage series of rapid, intensive brain cell growth followed by periods of little growth. He equated brain cell growth with increase in brain weight. The first of his five-stage periods did occur during the first year of life and the other four occurred between the ages of two and roughly 16.

The first pound of the adult, three-pound brain forms by birth. This means that during pregnancy, particularly beginning about the third month there is a rapid development of neurons or brain cells so that at birth the neurons that regulate vital life functions like breathing and blood circulation are functioning. These neurons are generally complete in cell body but they lack connective bridges with other neurons. What immense roles these bridges called axons and dendrites have in human development will become clear shortly.

The second pound of brain weight develops from birth until about the child's first birthday. So, in roughly one year of life another pound of brain weight has been added. Why has nature evolved this process during a time period when the baby seems like an empty vessel incapable of any controlled functioning? Essentially, we now know this is the time that the youngster is laying the neurological foundation for consciousness and language. While parents can't control such genetically determined circumstances as the number of neurons with which their child will be endowed, they can influence brain development during the second and third periods of brain-weight growth.

The third period extends roughly between the ages of two to sixteen. Herman Epstein has found that the growth during this third period does not occur in smooth, continuous fashion as was long assumed, but more in the form of discrete brain growth spurts. Between 2-4, 6-8, 10-12, and 14-16 years of age (the latter two stages occurring somewhat earlier for girls), occur rapid, intensive brain growth spurts which add some 35 percent of weight to the brain. The increased weight results due to a greater network of branched axons and dendrites which form amongst the neural cells, an increased level of energy and material in the form of blood to fuel the developing cells, and the formation of the insulating sheath — the myelin — around the axon fibers. Transferring this information to Figure 13, we can see how Epstein's brain growth periods correlate with the outset of the main stages of intellectual development defined by Piaget.

Let's examine some of these important processes that help add two pounds of additional weight to human brains by the end of the 16th year of age. At birth, scientists know that neurons are generally located in genetically determined areas in the brain that are responsible for such important life processes as hearing and seeing. Furthermore, all human beings seem to be born with about the same number of neurons — about 10 billion or so — in the brain area. While these neurons are in place, ready to receive stimuli from the environment, they lack connections with other nearby neurons. Without a connective link, information could not be transmitted amongst neurons. These connective links occur when a projection called the axon develops from the cell body of the neuron and when threadlike fingers called dendrites develop at the end of the axon and on the cell body itself. Both the axonal and dendritic growth allow the neurons to connect with the dendritic growth of other neurons in such extensive ways that by maturity one neuron may be relaying and receiving information from over hundreds of other neurons in the axonal/dendritic network.

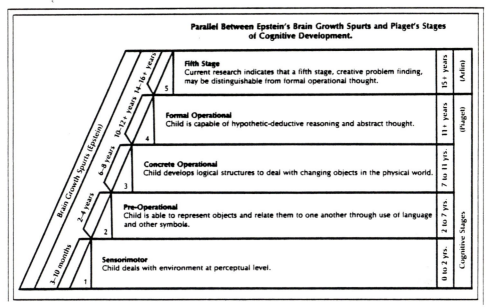

Parallel Between Epstein's Brain Growth Spurts and Piaget's Stages of Cognitive Development.

Fifth Stage
Current research indicates that a fifth stage, creative problem finding, may be distinguishable from formal operational thought.

Formal Operational
Child is capable of hypothetic-deductive reasoning and abstract thought.

Concrete Operational
Child develops logical structures to deal with changing objects in the physical world.

Pre-Operational
Child is able to represent objects and relate them to one another through use of language and other symbols.

Sensorimotor
Child deals with environment at perceptual level.

Figure 13. Parallel between Epstein's brain growth spurts and Piaget's stages of cognitive development. From M. Brooks, E. Fusco, J. Grennon: Cognitive levels matching. *Educating Leadership, 40*: 4-8, 1983. Courtesy of Association for Supervision and Curriculum Development (Feb. 14, 1984).

Dr. Richard Restack points out in Chapters Seven and Eight of his book, **The Brain: The Last Frontier,** how the immature brain is dependent upon sensory stimulation for normal growth, development, and function. In fact, he compares sensory stimulation to a "nutrient." He explores the tantalizing concern that possibly learning, memory, and perhaps other brain functions depend to a large part upon the quality of environmental stimulation. Is establishment of the dendritic network important? To quote from Dr. Restak, "In many ways the number of dendritic connections is considered even more important than the total number of neurons in the brain, since the density and complexity of dendritic connections probably has greater psychobiological consequences for brain development and human intelligence" (1979, p. 101). We can see now how the primary components of visual literacy — viewing, exploration, and nonverbal representation, exert a powerful influence upon the quality and quantity of nerve network interconnections especially during the first year of life when a pound of brain weight is added.

Information reaches the developing brain through the natural sense — through vision, hearing, touching, tasting, smelling, and bodily feel. The youngster must be stimulated **to hear** language as the other senses, especially viewing, are brought to bear upon an experience. Then, the infant develops and begins to reach out and clutch things in the environment that catch the eye. Once again, parental language should reinforce the experience and discuss not only the object grasped in the youngster's hand but the dangers inherent in such possibilities as dropping it, tasting it, or rubbing it. In this way the neural development of the meaning inherent in language forms before the child voluntarily uses language in his or her own talk. Neural networking responds to learning and once new learning has become automatic, newer neural pathways can be established for yet more novel learnings.

IMPACT OF SUBCORTICAL BRAIN SYSTEMS ON LEARNING

Besides the horizontal view of brain organization discussed thus far, another neuro-scientist has contributed a vertical view of brain organization during his work of the 1970s. Paul MacLean (1978) found that the brain processes information through three distinct but interconnected areas which he called from bottom to top, the reptilian complex, the limbic system, and the cerebrum or neocortex. The three areas or brain complexes actually lie on top of one another and according to MacLean represent a separate evolutionary step in the development of the human brain.

This three-layer arrangement of the human brain, in fact, reflects millions of years of evolution. The cerebrum, rather new in evolutionary development, accounts for about five-sixths of the total brain or about 85 percent of its size. This newer, larger brain actually envelops vestiges of the past and allows thinking or consciousness to occur unrestrained by such concerns as breathing, heartbeat, or pupil dilation. Furrows or convolutions appear on the outer surface of the third brain layer to increase its capability to deal with conscious verbal and nonverbal thought. Only a five-millimeter layer of nerve cells arranged in a vertical fashion of six neural circuits (see Figure 14), the cerebrum interprets sensory data and acts on it based on the basis of previously stored schemata and problem-solving techniques that it has found successful in the past. The cerebrum is horizontally composed of the left and right hemispheres whose processes and specialities were discussed earlier in this chapter. Each hemisphere, in turn, is composed of four lobes arranged

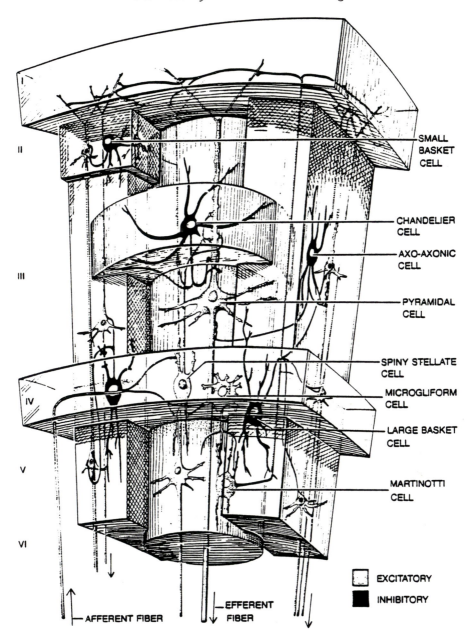

I

II   SMALL
       BASKET
       CELL

       CHANDELIER
       CELL

       AXO-AXONIC
       CELL

III

       PYRAMIDAL
       CELL

       SPINY STELLATE
       CELL

       MICROGLIFORM
       CELL

IV

       LARGE BASKET
       CELL

V   MARTINOTTI
       CELL

VI

☐ EXCITATORY

■ INHIBITORY

AFFERENT FIBER   EFFERENT FIBER

CELLULAR ARCHITECTURE of the cerebral cortex is organized into columnar modules made up of vertically arranged circuits of nerve cells. A typical column, some 250 micrometers (10^{-3} millimeter) in diameter, is shown in this highly simplified diagram based on one by János Szentágothai of the Semmelweis University Medical School in Budapest. Hundreds of incoming nerve fibers carrying sensory information converge on the spiny stellate cells in Layer IV of the cortex. The vertical circuits of interneurons, arranged in a highly specific spatial configuration, transform these raw data into the subtleties of conscious experience and behavior.

Figure 14. Vertical arrangement of nerve cells in five millimeter layer that comprises the cerebral corted. From N. Lassen, D. Ingver, and E. Skinhoj: Brain function and blood flow. *Scientific American, 239*:69-72, 1978. Courtesy of W.H. Freeman and Co., S.F., Calif.

in a front to rear fashion. These lobes are designated brain areas which perform particular large-scale specialities for the human species, such as the occipital lobe discussed earlier which processes a good deal of visual information. All rational thought is processed through this left-right and front-rear organization.

One artists's conception of the vertical arrangement of nerve cells in the five millimeter layer of the neocortex can be seen in Figure 14. While just a representative number of neurons are shown in the six-layer arrangement of cells in the human cortex, we must image the spatial compactness of ten billion or so neurons with their rich interconnections of dendritic networks to influence the human as composer and comprehender at all levels of literacy.

Tucked inside the rational brain is the first layer — the brainstem — which governs our most primitive behavior followed by the second layer — the limbic system — which automatically regulates different organs and glands of the body as they are needed in different situations, especially regarding the experience and expression of emotion. According to MacLean, the first layer or reptilian brain and the limbic system, the old mammalian brain, contain structures common to our animal ancestors and interconnect with the cortex to influence human behavior in ways that people are not even aware of. Thus, we each possess a triple, or triune brain, each with its own mode of perceiving and responding to the world. Figure 15 shows MacLean's conception of the evolution of the human forebrain while retaining the basic features of three formations that reflect our ancestral relationships, the reptiles, early mammals and recent mammals (1967).

Especially important in the brain stem is a concentrated nerve network the size of a human pinky called the reticular formation. The reticular formation is primarily responsible for alertness or our state of wakefulness. Wakefulness is the state of optimal "cortical tone" necessary for the implementation of all organized mental activity (Restak, 1979). When that tone is lost, we can remain in a coma or in a state of sustained sleep. When that tone is out of rhythm with the conscious, goal-directed behavior of the third brain — the cortex — we may often see behaviors usually associated with learning disabilities such as distractability, impulsivity, and hyperactivity.

Because the reticular formation enables us to focus our attention on particular elements of the environment and to screen out extraneous stimuli, its link-up with the lateral geniculate nucleus may be nature's

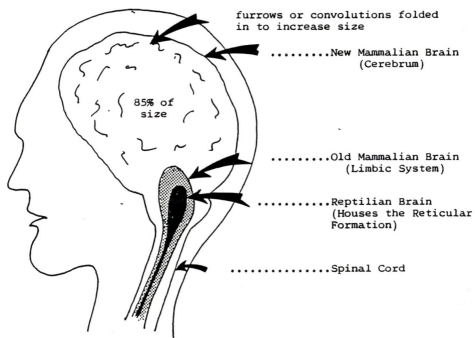

furrows or convolutions folded
in to increase size

.........New Mammalian Brain
(Cerebrum)

85% of
size

.........Old Mammalian Brain
(Limbic System)

...........Reptilian Brain
(Houses the Reticular
Formation)

.............Spinal Cord

Figure 15. Three levels of brain formation which house our ancestral past.

way of insuring that critical visual information reaches the brain rapidly. In other words, the eye may see "danger" but the reticular formation tells the conscious brain to act immediately on that visual information.

According to Restak (1979), the second brain layer — the limbic system — exerts a profound influence on human and animal behavior especially regarding the proportion given to our emotional state. Brain and behavior experts have linked the interconnecting parts of the limbic system to hormones, drives, temperature control, reward and punishment centers, and part of the hippocampus, to memory formation. The limbic system can be thought of as the controlling center for four basic survival behaviors — feeding, fighting, fleeing, and sex behavior. MacLean (1978) suggests that instead of explaining experience in terms of predisposition for compulsive or ritualistic behavior as is the case in considering the reptilian brain, or in terms of abstract thinking as is the case with the cerebral cortex, the functioning of the limbic system seems to involve a process whereby information is encoded in terms of emotional feelings which influence its decisions and its course of action.

Thus, activation of the limbic system due to emotional stress causes us to miss a key turn-off on a familiar highway while driving home from work. Under duress or threat, it is the limbic system that takes over our mental state and causes our much larger conscious giant to shut down. Since we may not even be fully aware of how imperceptibly the limbic system influences our behavior, one psychobiologist was heard to state during a panel discussion on brain behavior, "Schools teach the cortex; TV, the mid-brain." Think of television commercials and how powerfully they can influence our actions, even more so without dialogue. We will see why this occurs in the next chapter.

Because the neural pathways connecting the lower, more "irrational" brains to the rational brain mature slowly during childhood, parents and educators need to consider the vast impact of their own behavior and systems of learning delivery upon the minds of children. While grown-ups might earnestly believe that their content and modes of presentation are perfectly rational, the youngsters might think otherwise. Educators must fully realize that presenting intellectual content is not enough because the lower brain systems which control youngster's alerting, emotional, and motivational systems function at all times. The content has to be motivational, desirable, brimming with excitement and anticipated pleasure. Yes, pleasure is a key concept since once aroused with a specific learning activity, it becomes associated with the idea of that activity in the future. So, if a youngster prefers to write by first arranging picture stories, it means he or she enjoys it now and can anticipate enjoying it in the future. Affective forces, once mobilized, alert and motivate the thinking brain — the 85 percent cerebrum — in a conscious desire to learn the specific content.

The problem encountered with many educational programs designed for young children is that they lose them in rational rules, procedures, and sequences of instruction before the youngsters actually experience what they are supposed to experience. Should we be telling young children, for instance, the rules of language or should we be capitalizing on the aspects of visual literacy to bring children naturally to reading and writing. Witness the opening of an article entitled "Why Children Don't Like to Read" written by a well-known child therapy team, Bruno Bettleheim and Karen Zelan. They write:

> A child's attitude toward reading is of such importance that, more often than not, it determines his scholastic fate. Moreover, his experiences in learning to read may decide how he will feel about learning in general, and even about himself as a person. . . A child takes great pleasure in becoming able to read some words. But the excitement fades when the texts the child must read force him to reread the same word endlessly (1982, p. 56).

When learning of any new content such as writing or reading is approached from a holistic and natural way such as outlined in the last three chapters of this book, the child's whole mind will be energized for learning. When learning is delivered that has the qualities of meaningfulness and pleasure, it is more likely that the two lower brain systems will cooperate in the learning enterprise and more likely that the learning will be remembered. As neurologist, Restak writes "putting on a happy face" is an outward sign of a healthy, balanced brain and visibly demonstrates that learning is enjoyable.

Teachers need to capture the minds of children by appealing to their natural curiosity and desire to learn. From the child's point-of-view "putting on the happy face" during learning means that the learning is registering at the time of presentation and, more importantly, will want to be repeated when the adult suggests it the next time. From the teacher's point-of-view, the happy face is a manifestation of the teacher's attitude toward the content to be learned.

We will pause at this point to consider how the brain hemispheres and brain systems respond to verbal and nonverbal learning. At the end of Chapter Six, brain findings will be integrated with additional contributions from the area of learning style.

CHAPTER FIVE

THE DISTINCTIVE FEATURES OF VERBAL AND NONVERBAL LITERACIES

IN THIS CHAPTER we will come to better understand how verbal and nonverbal message forms differ from one another and how the two brain hemispheres respond to these differences. This is a key chapter for the educational specialist and media specialist. They both deal with learning input, a large majority of which is delivered through the visual processing system as was noted in the last chapter. However, a good deal of confusion often results about the understanding of "visual," which often leads the educators of written literacy modes to erroneous conclusions. For instance, is reading really a visual experience? Does the whole word approach to teaching beginning reading reflect a visual approach as compared to an auditory emphasis through a phonic-oriented approach? Do these dichotomies really exist or are they invented to sell particular program products? Furthermore, why do media specialists often report great interest and attentiveness by their learners once they become involved in filming and understanding visual stories as opposed to written visions of the same experience? What is inherent in the power of the visual media? The answers to these questions will continue to unfold in this chapter as we take a close look at the distinctive features which separate the verbal and nonverbal codes of learning.

Essentially, there are three major features that distinguish verbal from nonverbal literacies. These distinctions lie in the way that the communication forms of each are grasped, processed, and retained in human learning (see Figure 19).

SEQUENTIAL VERSUS PARALLEL MODE OF PROCESSING

First and foremost, as we have seen in previous chapters, such visual literacy representational modes as art, film, graphics, gesture and body language are generally considered nonverbal modes of communication with distinct types of message forms. Ruesch and Kees, as early as 1956 had categorized the three distinct forms of sign, action, and object language. Comprehending and composing these nonverbal message forms are not generally subject to the time and sequence constraints necessary for verbal communication. For instance, when we look at a scene or a picture of a particular scene, all the essential features of the scene are captured in a single eye fixation and perceptually recorded in the brain based on that one intake. Of course, we may miss a number of details in the scene which we could pick out with subsequent fixations. However, if the content of the scene was already recorded in our visual experience of the world's structure, then in that single instant, we would comprehend the overall meaning of that scene. This occurs, for instance, while waiting to be called into an office for a meeting, we sit outside in the waiting room rapidly turning pages of popular magazines, taking in visual chunks of familiar information presented in ads. If we observe a picture, however, that is further and further removed from representing reality or not in our mental schema for representing reality such as occurs when we view some impressionist or abstract painting, then we must look and examine the picture more closely. We attempt to reconstruct the content of the unknown to match a perceptual understanding we have of the natural world.

During transmission of the oral and written modes of communication on the other hand, we need time to comprehend what is being told to us or what we are reading about. Understanding is dependent upon our retaining verbal memory each meaningful chunk of information previously decoded, integrating it with information being delivered to the eye or ear at the moment of intake, and anticipating through the flow of language what new information will most likely be delivered. This verbal processing demands increments of time and the processing of several levels of memory unique to linguistically structured input before comprehension occurs (Perfetti, 1977).

How fast can a listener listen or a reader read to equal the speed of comprehension achieved through the single eye fixation of the visual literacy mode of communication? During the reading process, no matter how fluent the reader or wide his span of recognition for letters or words, no more than about five chunks of information reach the brain in a single second (Smith, 1971 and 1982). In roughly one fifth of a second intervals, comprehension of the whole becomes clearer. The reader relies on each subsequent eye fixation to transmit additional information about the topic, which is transfixed in the printed mode. A similar processing time exists for the listening experience as well. One quick glance of nonverbal forms, however, communicates the same amount of information that may have taken many fixations to process during textual reading or many minutes to listen to during conversation.

Foveal Fixations and the Acquisition of Meaning

Gilber (1976) has suggested that fixation pauses in reading serve three functions. The eyes momentarily halt along a line of running text to achieve maximum functional efficiency and give the visual cortex an uninterrupted period to process noncompeting visual stimuli. These prerequisite events allow time for ideas and relationships to be recorded and understood. These relationships need from a quarter to a sixth of a second from beginning feature processing to meaning identification (Geyer and Kolers, 1974; Smith, 1982). Saccadic movement carries the eyes in a smooth left to right sequence across a text and swiftly back across to the beginning of the next line of print. In fact, this is how we train young children to read and is probably a practice reinforced through oral reading activities.

While Ekwall (1977) has calculated the reading speed of the most efficient reader under ideal conditions as being 864 words per minute, Lawson (1968) has established the physiological limit as being 720 words per minute. Ekwall's research also showed that the time to fixate varies amongst individuals with the average time for good readers running between one-quarter to one-sixth of a second. It also takes from 1/25 to 1/30 of a second for the eye to move from one fixation to the next, and it also takes another 1/25 to 1/30 of a second for the eye to sweep from the end of a line of print to the beginning word on the next line. Within the fixation's span of recognition, the average first grader only sees about half a word, the average college student sees little more than a single word, while the most efficient reader may be able to see no more than three words.

We can represent this linear, time-consuming relationship that occurs during the reading act for the average college student in the following figure:

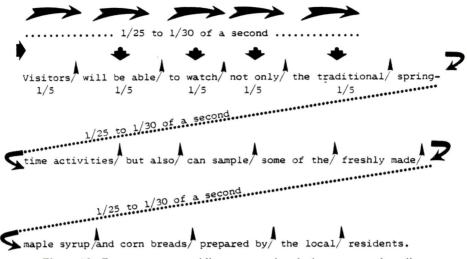

Figure 16. Eye movements and linear processing during contextual reading.

The dotted line represents the saccadic eye movements while the bars between the words represent the boundaries for each separate fixation where meaning processing occurs. Note that the reader needs about a fifth of a second to process each meaning cluster within the brain, needs 1/25 to 1/30 of a second for each saccade to be accomplished by the eyes, and needs the same amount of time to project the eyes to the next line. The less mature or beginning reader would be spending even more time at the process since his/her fixation pause would be taking in less than whole words. Now we may be able to appreciate the labor the young reader goes through as he/she attempts to group whole relationships of meaning as partial bits of information are initially picked up by the eyes to be sequentially transmitted to the brain. We can see, then, that verbal language processing does not directly translate to meaning but depends upon linear process alterations in which raw sound or printed configurations are converted into meaning. Since increments of time are needed in these process changes, the left hemisphere presides.

How does the reader acquire information during a fixation pause? Sources of information are constrained by the written language code and the reader has to abstract relevant information from linguistic forms of this code within the span of the fixation pause. At least three sources of linguistic information — grapho-phonemic, syntactic, and semantic — contribute to the acquisition of meaning during reading (Athey, 1977; Pearson, 1978; and Smith, 1982). Experience, linguistic competence, and intent determine how well the reader can shift among the three contributing levels. However, the more knowledgeable and efficient the reader, the more syntactic and semantic information is utilized to reduce the reliance on visual and phonemic processing. Yet, it is not over-simplifying to note that in the momentary act of fixation, it is through word efficiency that cues relating to higher order processing reach the brain.

The initial stages of the fixation pause appear to have an attention focusing purpose, leading to subsequent coordination with stored knowledge. Perfetti (1977) has proposed three levels of memory processing which might be helpful to associate with the three sources of linguistic information available from print. This suggests that a linguistic memory exists for language forms. At the highest level, semantic-syntactic information is integrated and interpreted to make sense with information from previous sentences. While the second level requires competence with linguistic structures, the highest integrative level demands synthesizing fragments of information, thinking about the relationships implied, and applying a sentence level meaning to the meaning of the context as a whole.

Seemingly, the first or surface level of memory processing is akin to a short-term memory which can hold only so many items for a short period of time before fading occurs. Its efficiency would partially depend upon the word clue information gathered during fixation pauses, how rapidly meanings were assigned to words, and how well clusters of meanings became accessible through familiar syntactic structures. A bit later we will see how the right hemisphere helps to reduce some of the burden of linguistic memory.

What factors influence the rapid integration of all three memory processing levels? At the surface level, the reader's cues are the visual and phonological characteristics of words. Words may be either recognized immediately or decoded through word analysis techniques. This distinction is quite important to note in reading proficiency. Automatic word knowledge suggests that during fixation pauses, maximum efficiency will be achieved in translating visual features to meaning identification in the quarter second processing limits. On the other hand, if the span of recognition narrows to focus on orthographic-phonetic properties within words, meaning efficiency is lost. Decoding in context requires attentive effort and takes time, the same time limits assigned to meaning processing. If the focus of attention is switched from semantic-syntactic processing back to word analysis, forgetting of previously read content may occur. Most important, the periphery becomes dysfunctional as maximum visual effort is focused on letter-sound features.

During fixations, the field of the perceptual span is restricted to foveal vision, the center of the span of recognition. The text within foveal vision is most clear, subtended by a 2° angle and extending over an area of seven to ten letter spaces for mature readers. When decoding occurs in context, the span narrows to analyze the grapho-phonemic features of that word. At a memory level, attention is now focused on a matching task, either matching the whole word perceived with a word already in the reader's long-term memory store or recalling phonemic properties that match graphic cues. Since phonological representation competes with automatic meaning representation, meaning gained from previous sentences has to be held in memory. Furthermore, since the span of recognition has narrowed to "decode" the unknown, fewer cues that may influence later fixations reach the brain from the peripheral area.

Item-by-item foveal viewing is characteristic of younger and less mature readers who need to engage in detailed word analysis. Taylor (1966) presented data which indicates that not until the 6th grade do readers begin to read more than a single word in an average span or recognition. First, second, and third graders appear to take in half a word in their average recognition span, which indicates that about two fixations are necessary per word. College students read an average of 1.3 words of 10 point type.

The Influence of the Visual Periphery

How can mature readers process more words during fixation stops given the limitations of intake during the span of recognition? Secondly, how does the fluent reader become even more fluent? These questions lead us to examine the powerful effects of peripheral vision during reading. In fact, Gibson and Levin reported in 1975 that the new techniques investigating the functions of peripheral vision in reading promised to yield new information about eye movements and reading for the first time within the last 50 years (1975).

The reader may recall that in the discussion of the visual information system found in Chapter Four, we noted that some neural cells respond to pattern recognition and special features of the environment. According to Lindsay and Norman (1977), these cells extract special features from visual signals such as line segments of certain orientation, angle, light contrast, movement, and color. Other neurons recognize spatial frequencies or certain spacings in the contour of images. The visual system, in fact, extracts an enormous amount of detailed information about specific features in the visual image. Due to the influence of the peripheral field in reading, more information is extracted from the total span of visual recognition than is needed for meaning acquisition. Recall that in the eye, the mass of neural cells were found in the region of the fovea, and it is apparently the influence of the cells outside the fovea that guide the decisions the periphery makes during reading. Let's see how this happens for both the fluent and nonfluent readers and how time once again is used during decision making.

We just noted that physiological limits exist ranging from 720 to 864 words per minute for the number of words that could be read silently in one minute. These limits are based upon the actual reading of words within the span of recognition, however, and does not take into account the influence of the peripheral field in reading. However, there is evidence to indicate that the movement plan from fixation to fixation need not follow a linear pattern. Information acquired during an earlier fixation may influence where the eyes are to be projected during ensuing fixations (McConkie and Rayner, 1976). Hochberg (1970) has also suggested that information acquire in the peripheral area outside of the distinct span of recognition may influence the decision the brain will take in projecting the eyes during the next fixation. This would appear to be the processing decision made during very fluent or "speed" reading where fixations are directed by an involved reader intent on abstracting meaning in the least amount of time. Word identification problems, difficulty with syntactic structures, and conceptional difficulties with content can impede this level of saccadic movement.

In two experiments investigating the perceptual span with skilled, silent readers, McConkie and Rayner (1976) produced data indicating that different types of information are acquired at different lengths into the periphery. Word length pattern appears to be picked up at least 13 to 14 character positions from the fixation point and this information may be used to guide the eye across the line. Visual shape of words and letters is ascertained from 10 to 12 character positions from the fixation point. Actual identification of the word's meaning occurred no further than 4 to 6 character-positions to the right of the fixation point. Figure 17 shows this relationship and indicates that to get beyond "words" of 5 character length, the reader must make efficient use of the periphery.

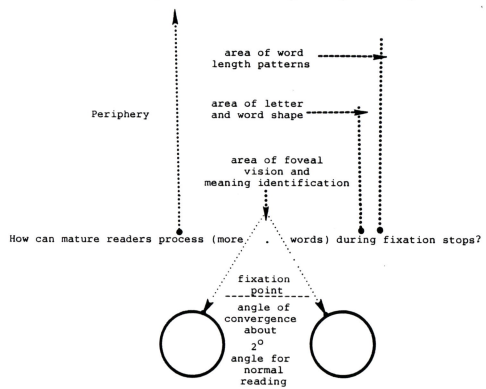

Figure 17. Information gathered through the eyes during the span of recognition in normal, fluent reading.

The influence of the periphery in fluent reading behavior seems clear. With knowledge of what the text is about coupled with conditions of textual redundancy, the mature reader may gain enough visual detail to project his/her eyes farther into the text to corroborate his/her anticipated meaning hypothesis. Hochberg (1970) has suggested that information picked up by the visual periphery-like word shape and spacing makes subsequent foveal processing more efficient.

Implications for young, immature, and disabled readers are likewise most important to note. If there are language constraints such as unknown words or grammatical patterns not familiar to the reader, then peripheral vision may become less efficient. Furthermore, peripheral processing of beginning readers would be influenced by the nature of the words taught. Too many words rapidly introduced may confuse the reader, especially if the words have similar configurations or letter shapes in particular positions. When a partially known word is encountered in context where syntax or semantic cues could predict an alternative word, a miscue could result from cues supplied by the peripheral processing.

Fisher argues that the disabled reader also has an overload problem. The disabled reader cannot resolve the competitive information supplied during foveal and peripheral processing and is forced to deal strictly with foveal processed text (1978). This reduced limit minimizes the capability to process semantic-syntactic information at the sentence and paragraph levels. Without the periphery to guide and inform the eye to possible meaning alternatives, the rate of comprehension must remain at a word processing level.

In oral reading activities, teachers often note the behavior of word-by-word readers and the effects of attention at the decoding level. Attention has not been focused at the semantic-syntactic level of sentence meaning even though the words have been called out. When the word-by-word reader finishes the sentence, meaning has been lost. The paradox for the beginning reader is that while syntactic and semantic information is stored away in the head, this information cannot be processed in contexts until words become automatic. In the beginning stages, it is words that appear in the focus of the fixation and it is the sequential, digital nature of words that require time to process.

Nonverbal Visual Processing

The nonlinear aspect of nonverbal communication needs to be fully understood by the reader to appreciate the fixating power of visual messages. Visual messages that reach us through such devices as pictures, ads, television, movies, or video games, are not "decoded" or broken down into smaller component parts before comprehension occurs. The reverse process occurs.

Paivio (1979) points out that in the visual system, simultaneously given information can be processed over a wide area of the retina. Because of simultaneity of functioning, the defining property of the visual system is that it is spatially parallel and is viewed accordingly as a parallel processing system. This means that visual language forms that impinge on the eye during visual, artistic, media, and aesthetic inputs reach the right brain holistically, all-at-a-time, as a single unit of perception. Now we can see why the age-old adage "the picture is worth a thousand words" rings with some truth. The visual message is perceived as a whole with all its component parts seeking equal recognition by the brain. This aspect of simultaneous processing that occurs during visual recognition can be represented in Figure 19 and contrasted with the mode of linear processing as shown in Figure 17.

Of course, the brain "fills in" meaning needed to conceptualize the information taken in by the eye during perceptual intake. Because visual language forms such as pictures represent the natural world, the viewer has a conceptual storehouse bond in schema relationships with which to enrich the intake. As noted earlier, the visual world does not simply imprint itself upon the retina. Rather, the brain as an extension of the eye, actively reaches out, explores the object, and interprets the part it sees with what has been visually experienced before (Arnheim, 1954). Thus, since television at least can be credited with reducing the boundries of the world, we each have a veritable nonverbal storehouse of events, of peoples, and of impressions lodged in visual memory.

Figure 18. Simultaneous, parallel processing that occurs during viewing.

DIGITAL VERSUS ANALOGIC MODE
OF CODIFICATION

The second distinguishing feature between the verbal and nonverbal literacy modes concerns the way their language forms are represented or codified. Nonverbal communication forms, particularly those of object language, are codified in a distinctly different way than the way verbal language forms are codified. Nonverbal literacy forms are essentially represented through analogy or analogic codification while written language forms are represented by a digital mode of codification. In analogic codification symbols, pictures, material objects, scaled devices represent the actual life situation itself. The material representation of a model ship, for instance, may be viewed as being analogous to the ship itself. A photograph is a concrete replica of a natural event or place. The two language representations of analogy and digits require differing brain operations to manipulate the features of each code.

An important characteristic of analogic forms is that they can capture an impelling immediacy (Ruesch and Kees, 1956). Just picture a page in **Sport's Illustrated** or **Time**. You see the quarterback grimmacing with a sense of urgency, arm poised to deliver a strike to a downfield receiver, as two earnest tacklers are within hands length of smashing him to the turf. Without seeing the actual outcome, you read from the picture all the drama and skill of the sport. Almost transported to the immediate scene, you realize that in all probability the ball was passed and the quarterback was sacked. The momentary event was captured in picture form by the single flicker of a camera shutter. Its meaning was comprehended during viewing just as rapidly with a single glance. The picture, however, becomes an analogic historical record of that sports event and will cause the event to be just as accessible to future generations of viewers.

Digital codification, on the other hand, deals with discrete step intervals. According to Ruesch and Kees (1956), its two primary examples are the number system and the phonetic alphabet. No continuous transition exists between any one letter of the alphabet and the next, or between any one number in the numerical system and the next. Information transmitted through a digital system is necessarily coded through various combinations of letters of digits that when put together a certain way will mean something like a word. Words or a series of words are sequential, serial forms of communication that require a discrete period of time to report or decode. Furthermore, they have to be spoken or written according to mutually understood rules to convey particular meanings. To put it another way, words are bound by context. In explaining meaning they are bound by what comes before and what comes after their particular position.

Not so with analogic forms. Their meaning is instantaneously and holistically conveyed. Thus, words lack the compelling immediacy that analogic representation can convey and cause some like Postman (1979) to regard analogic codification as exemplified in the television medium as the most compelling way modern society can gain the attention of youth. Within a matter of minutes countless images are flashed before the eyes of its participants, and these images do not need to be analyzed, decoded, or internally rehearsed in order to be understood. In fact, the television industry has figured out that the viewer only needs to see so many frames of an image before boredom sets in and attention starts to wander. That's why we think that television commericals in particular are running along in a rapid, seemingly disconnected pace but in actuality they are serving their primary purpose of attracting and holding attention.

Within digital codification, Elkind has indicated that letters have two more aspects of difficulty than the representation conveyed by numbers (1975). Like numbers, letters have ordinal and cardinal properties. The ordinal property is based on the position of the letter in the alphabet, and the cardinal property is represented by the name (A, B, C, etc.). Letters become even more complicated to learn than numbers because in addition to the two above properties, they also have phonic and contextual properties. A letter can represent one or more sounds and a sound can be represented by differing letters — combinations that offer hosts of confusions for youngsters. Elkind maintains that to manipulate the combinations necessary in phonics the child must be able to perform logical operations at the concrete operations stage of Piagetian mental development.

Postman (1979) also points out that the meanings of analogic forms arise from man's capacity to copy how nature is structured while meaning of digital forms are abstract and have no direct correspondence with the material world. One must learn both word meanings and the rules and conventions of the semantic code that allows words to be joined together to form grammatical sentences. Thus, all systems of digital symbols consist of small meaning units that can be arranged in different contexts and moved about in different positions. I, myself, am always amazed that given all the content and function words in the English language, only 12 basic sentence patterns exist (Dawkins, 1975) allowing us to form all the infinite variety of sentences possible to convey ideas from words.

Besides the abstract and sequential nature of language, Postman points out other important notions about digital forms of information. While object language forms are representations of reality, words are representations of ideas about reality. A word designates a category of things, a concept about some referent in the natural world. More and more words have to be added to a statement to clarify any particular idea or concept one wishes to convey. Sometimes in the act of communication, we cannot relate or describe successfully the exact event we want the listener (or reader) to imagine. Then we might be apt to say, "Remember the picture of . . . " or "Do you see how what I'm trying to say looks like . . . " We shift from the logic and abstractness of the verbal code to the concreteness of the analogic code so that the listener can call to mind the exact image we have difficulty describing.

The written language, on the other hand, can offer two additional levels of abstraction beyond the levels of digital codification and word meaning to cause comprehension difficulties. Moffett (1983) suggests that comprehension difficulties also arise as a result of increased rhetorical distance between the reader and writer and of increased use of abstraction in the level of language used by a writer to describe or symbolize an experience. Rhetorical distance increases as one moves from the telling of a personal experience such as occurs in journal or diary writing to the generalizing of events or processes such as occurs in the expository writings of science and social studies. In other words, a writer will find it easier to describe what is happening at the present moment in a personal journal since the occurrences are still fresh in his/her own experience. Moreover, if the writer knows that his/her readers have shared the same experiences, the writer has further reduced the rhetorical communicative distance between himself and the reader. Exposition, on the other hand, is the generalizing of something that may not have occurred in either the author's or reader's experience. So the conceptual distance between the two is enlarged due to unfamiliarity with the topic. Furthermore, the level of language used by the writer to describe the experiences of generalization could be removed from the language experience of the reader, creating in a way, a double comprehension bind for the reader.

An increased use of abstraction can occur when the author's style becomes more difficult to read such as when sentence structures and arrangements are used that are more and more removed from how we actually speak in the oral language. This is why even having familiarity with the topic may not be enough. One author writing on the same topic as another may just be more abstract and thus more difficult to read. If a reader has to deal both with a lack of experience with the content and a lack of familiarity with the language forms used to describe the content, loss of comprehension will undoubtedly occur.

Since nonverbal forms of communication generally represent actual life situations, it is unlikely that immediate understanding would not occur while viewing pictures or other visual media unless, of course, the content of the visual experience was totally foreign to the viewer. Once again, television can at least be credited with reducing unfamiliarity of the natural world making information in a nonverbal, representative way, more conceptually accessible to all. Postman highlights the communicative distinction of the analogic system (1979, p. 54).

> . . . this is not the case in analogic systems. Pictures, maps, and photographs are not reducible to vocabularies. The meaning of a line or contrasting areas of light is entirely dependent on the total context in which it appears and therefore a captive of that which is, in reality, being depicted. Analogic symbols have no meaning-units comparable in their constancy and portability to what we possess in digital systems. Thus, the meanings of digital forms have their origin in complex human conventions and binding human agreements.

AUDITORY-MOTOR VERSUS IMAGISTIC MODE OF RETRIEVAL

The third unique feature separating the literacies lies in the way their forms are retrieved from memory. The reader can recall that visual intake of a scene or picture was based upon multiple sensory impressions simultaneously presented to the retina and that these impressions were recorded in parallel within the brain. The retrieval process, which we call visual memory, occurs quite the same way in that the image is recalled holistically, all at a time. Furthermore, this image is a faithful representation of the original impression. Haber's (1970) experiments showed that the capacity for pictorial memory is virtually unlimited. His subjects could match with about 90% accuracy, over 1,250 pictures they have viewed on a previous day. Other experiments conducted by Haber showed that visual recognition memory remained strong when time was reduced from 10 seconds to one second per picture or when the visual orientation of pictures was reversed.

Visual imagery can be considered a symbolic system specialized for parallel processing of information (Paivio, 1979). Image and imagery as defined by Paivio refer to concrete imagery, meaning nonverbal memory representations of concrete phenomena or nonverbal modes of imaginative thought in which visual representations are actively generated and manipulated by an individual. Bower (1972) distinguishes between remembering in imagery versus remembering in propositions. During imagery we re-present to ourselves the appearances of past events we have witnessed while propositions are descriptive accounts about what is being remembered.

Paivio points out that the major neurological distinction of verbal memory is the activation of the auditory-motor speech system. Verbal processes are considered to be auditory-motor in nature, even when the verbal input is visual as occurs in the act of reading. Remember that visual input here is based on the sequential nature of the written language code which does not have a one-to-one correspondence with meaning. Particularly during the beginning or nonfluent stages of reading will the less efficient auditory-motor system be activated.

Now, when a reader achieves fluency in that graphic arrays of whole words within phrases and sentences are immediately processed for meaning within that fifth-of-a-second processing limit we spoke of earlier, the auditory-motor speech system is probably not activated. That is because the meaning of that phrase unit may have been directly translated to its visual representation or image. This feat was accomplished by rapid callosal interchange of information from the language center in the left brain to its nonverbal representation in the right brain. If, however, the reader needs to slow down due to deep conceptual input in the text (the rhetorical distance), or if sentence structure is difficult to wade through (the level of abstraction), or if unknown words are presented (meaning representation), then the reader will undoubtedly activate the auditory-motor speech system. Logical, sequential analysis of groups of words or letter parts occurs as the reader verbally manipulates language to gain meaning. We may even see lip movement occur or hear vocalization of the speech chords if the need to slow down is so great.

The reason we slow down when the auditory-motor speech system is activated is because the speech system is much slower than the visual chunking system. Remember our top reading speeds were about 725 to 850 words per minute. The fastest professional television or radio announcers speak about 150 to 160 words per minute, while the average person speaks about 135 words per minute (Judson, 1972). Therefore, the person who is subvocalizing during reading, consisting of tiny movements of the lips, tongue, or throat muscles, has severly limited his/her reading speed. Unwittingly, educators may force learners to activate the slower system every time they present words and reading contexts beyond the capability to the reader. If the reader can't turn the graphic input into visual meaning quickly enough and can't relate it to previously stored experiences, speed of comprehension bogs down.

Thus, visual memory can be clearly distinguished from verbal memory because of the processing distinctions involved. While the visual system is characterized by its spatial properties, the auditory perception system is a system specialized for handling stimulus patterns organized in a temporal or serial way. Because of its linkage to the auditory-motor speech system and since the verbal system by its very nature is syntactical in nature, the verbal system is sequentially organized. We saw that with digital coding, letters had to be arranged in a particular, sequential way for meaning to emerge. Moreover, words had to be arranged according to conventional, grammatical rules where position indicated meaning. Grammar, then, necessitates a temporal ordering of its units. Paivio concludes that the major difference between the two systems is the capacity for spatial representation and parallel processing of the imaginal process and serial representation and sequential processing of the verbal processes.

Haber (1970) verified the two types of memories from his pictorial memory studies. In the case of pictures, the image was stored permanently in pictorial form. Where printed words were concerned, the initial step of memory was to take the digital code out of its visual form, code the digits, and extract their meaning. The letters forming a printed word were not remembered as an image of distinct letters on a page, they were stored and recalled as the word itself and the idea that the word generated. Thus, memory evoked during the reading of words goes through several stages before an image is produced akin to the one directly produced through pictorial input.

RIGHT HEMISPHERE PARTICIPATION DURING READING

One of the key roles the right hemisphere plays during reading is based on the periphery's feature extraction. Pirozzolo and Rayner (1977) determined from their research that word identification is a multi-stage process, with visual feature analysis carried out by the right hemisphere and word identification and naming by the left hemisphere. Using the split-field tachistoscopic procedure, they found abundant evidence that a word presented to the left visual field (right hemisphere) must cross the corpus collosum to be named by the language center.

Reading, they suggest, involves parallel processes in which the reader is interpreting the sematic content of the information processed in foveal vision while featural information is being processed from parafoveal vision. The meaning identification process would be carried out by the left hemisphere, while the featural analysis of soon-to-be-fixated words is done by the right hemisphere.

We see then that the right hemisphere participates during two highly critical stages of the reading process. Its input begins during the initial fixating stage that occurs for lines of print and the other occurs during the ongoing aspects of comprehension. We noted that the right hemisphere is influenced by the spatial characteristics of letters outside the area of meaning identification. This is where the periphery of the eye tells the brain where to direct the next information-gathering fixation based on featural extraction. Now, in our discussion of imagery, we see that once foveal fixations have occurred and meaning has been identified due to the abstraction of syntactic-semantic cues obtained by the left hemisphere, meaning relationships can cross to the right hemisphere to be visualized as mental pictures or schema connections.

To summarize, we can see that visual, artistic, media and aesthetic inputs are characterized by nonverbal parallel processing, analogic codification, and concrete imagery. In that the visual perceptual system is involved during intake and recall of images, these literacies are learning modes where holistic, instantaneous recognition and meaning occurs. Its processing mode is distinctly different than that of the verbal system. Verbal learning is characterized by sequential, segmented processing in which a digital code has to pass through several levels of recognition and interpretation before meaning can occur. Figure 19 presents a summary of the distinctions that operate between the verbal and nonverbal communication modes.

These processing distinctions have important consequences for us in the literacy training of all our students in modern technological cultures, but especially for those learners identified by research as having distinct cognitive or learning styles. Research has verified that holistic, visual/spatial learning appears to be a function of the brain's right hemisphere, while sequential, segmental learning is the processing mode of the left hemisphere. Other research, as we will note in the next chapter, tells us that learners exist in our classrooms who are decidedly right hemisphere preferent.

Postman (1979) maintains that a "generation gap" exists in the think-

THE DISTINCTIVE FEATURES OF
VERBAL AND NONVERBAL LITERACIES

Left Hemisphere Processing Style		Right Hemisphere Processing Style
Verbal		Nonverbal
	1. Mode of Processing	
sequential		parallel
takes increments of time to compose and comprehend		simultaniety of processing in holistic way
	2. Mode of Codification	
digital		analogic
needs various combinations of letters or numbers to represent meaning		represents the actual life situation itself like pictures, scaled objects, gestures
	3. Mode of Retrieval	
auditory-motor		imagistic
requires serial integration and sequential processing of auditory-motor perception systems		image is recalled in parallel, all-at-a-time and image is faithfull representation or original

Figure 19. The distinctive features of verbal and nonverbal literacies.

ing processes of modern youth due to a conflict in hemispheric conditioning. On the one hand there is the language-centered view of the world championed by the schools, and, on the other hand, there is the twentieth century image-centered view dominated by the media, particularly television. The generation gap exists because the nature of language learning and of scientific enquiry depends upon linearity of thought and the step-by-step presentation of ideas and evidence. Television, however, depends on nonlinear, nonsequential transmission of information and its content need not be subject to rational and deliberate thought.

It would seem, therefore, to balance the holistic, rapid, emotional appeal of the electronic media, we need to tame it with the logic and conceptual deliberation of language. If, however, the schools continue to prod the more deliberate, analytic left hemisphere of youngsters in unimaginative ways, they may be unsuccessfully competing with television's mode of engaging instantaneously the mind of youngsters, in unfortunately, mindless tasks. The challenge is to capitalize on the image-centering powers of media presentation without falling prey to the passiveness of entertainment and to use other nonverbal modes to assist in the processing of verbal information. Fillion (1973) warns about the dangers of separating the two literacies. However, he suggests that in our attempt to introduce serious visual education into the print-dominated schools, we should not put print against nonprint or visual against verbal. The task is to let the strength of one merge into the other. If, for instance, content is too abstract for concrete visual imagery to occur or if it is too far removed from the life experience of readers as often occurs in Science and Social Studies texts, a picture, a drawing, a graphic representation may be that means to fill in the unknown before reading begins. In essence, nonverbal prompting can "fill in" or expand one's conceptual schema to enrich the content of verbal messages. This is a key concept for those learners who experience perennial written literacy failure and for those whose learning style is identified as stronger for nonverbal modes of learning.

CHAPTER SIX

A LEARNING STYLE VIEW OF
VISUAL LITERACY

IN THE PREVIOUS two chapters, we saw that the human brain is composed of two distinct modes of organization and that, for most of the population, the particular brain hemisphere will tend to be activated that is most adept at solving the processing demands of any given task. If an analytic, linear problem needs to be solved, the left hemisphere will tend to dominate while if the thought process is holistic, intuitive, and synthetic, the right brain undoubtedly will excel. However, for many learners a task need not be processed by a brain hemisphere best suited for the thinking demands of a task. We noted earlier that because wide ranges in hemispheric thinking are possible throughout the general population, some thinkers can be highly verbal and others can be highly nonverbal in their habitual mode of processing. The question posed in this chapter goes a bit further. Are their learners who **prefer** to think and learn through the mode of visual literacy rather than through another mode, particularly that of written literacy?

We do know from split-brain studies that a hemisphere not specialized for a particular function may be able to accomplish that function, albeit more slowly and less efficiently. Levy and Trevarthan (1976) found that their split-brain patients did not always use the hemisphere that was specialized best to perform a specific task. They proposed a "metacontrol system" of hemispheric activation, allowing for a bias toward one hemisphere over the other regardless of the processing demands of the task. This bias is controlled by one's aptitude or predisposition to behave in particular ways according to one's established values, expectations, and contentions. Levy and Trevarthan conclude:

> . . . that a particular hemisphere's dominance over behavior depends only indirectly on specialization of capacity. We suggest that the hemispheres are

also specialized with respect to intentions to act in particular ways, and that these dispositions are independent of, though usually correlated with, differential aptitudes. It is dispositional lateralization, and not aptitudinal lateralization, that determines cerebral dominance for a task. Once behavioral control is gained, it is the aptitudinal specialization that determines how well some tasks will be done.

Das, Kirby, and Jarman (1975; 1979) have applied the brain functioning system of Luria (1973) to present a mode of information processing and integration that helps explain how biases and planning come into being. The model is helpful because it extends the three-tiered brain system proposed by MacLean and accounts for use of the most complex area of the human brain — the prefrontal cortex.

SIMULTANEOUS/SUCCESSIVE PROCESSING AND LITERACY CHOICE

Like MacLean, the Russian neuropsychologist, Alexander Luria, proposed an interrelated system among three basic units of the brain. He developed his model of how the brain works as a result of his 40 years of clinical experience with brain damaged individuals. The first basic unit, concerned with motivation, attention and arousal, is composed of the same brain matter identified by MacLean as the Reptilian Complex. An important system located within the first basic unit is that of the Reticular Activating System (RAS). This system alerts the third level of brain, the executive and command level, to receive incoming information. If the incoming information is as important for the young child as the visual form of a new word, the RAS will filter out all other competing stimuli that try to reach the executive brain through the senses. While the youngster focuses on the visual features of the new word, he or she is not receiving interference from such sources as classroom sounds, light reflecting off the desk, or stomach reminders that lunch is soon. If, however, the ascending and descending nerve fibers that connect the RAS with the executive brain have not neurologically matured, a young child may be quite hampered in his/her attempts to learn.

The second unit of brain according to Luria is concerned with the reception, the processing, and the storage of sensory information. This unit is quite important in children's early life learnings since the features of the outside world are being integrated in the brain in the form of sensory memories. The second unit also processes information in terms of wholes or in sequence. Sequence can be considered as time ordered events which occur one after another even if the time lapse goes unnoticed. For instance, speech is linked by sequences of sounds, by sounds that make words and by words that make sentences. Beginning reading is often marked by the matching of sounds to letters that have to be sequenced to identify a word. At this second level of brain, the role of the two hemispheres becomes more sharply defined.

The final level of brain described by Luria is concerned with conscious, goal directed thinking and represents the highest level of brain development in the animal kingdom. This third unit, encompassing the prefrontal cortex, is that unit we associate with thinking as "planning" or "willing." When we plan or intentionally decide to take one of several alternatives, we activate the third functional unit.

Das, Jarman, and Kirby in their Simultaneous and Successive Cognitive Process Model make a distinction between brain coding and brain planning. They propose that the two modes of information processing generally associated with left-brain sequential, successive processing and right-brain parallel, simultaneous processing are available to any one learner at all times. Two major conditions contribute to use of one or both processing modes when engaged in a learning task. The first is the learner's usual way of processing information as influenced by genetic factors and the way the learner has been shaped by the social and cultural environment. The second is the processing demands inherent in the task.

The model is a bit different than consideration of the processing capability of each hemisphere considered in isolation. The key to whether a learning task will be processed in simultaneous or successive fashion or both is determined by the frontal lobes. The third unit of brain uses the coded information of simultaneous or successive input and determines the best possible plan of action. The plan is willed or projected into the future and how the brain processes sensory information is determined by **how** the information will be used.

Of particular relevance to parents and educators of young children are the three author's comments on testing, particularly intelligence testing. They suggest that since such testing does not tap the brain functional unit which comprises a full one third of the brain area, the meaning of I.Q. tests does not show the full potential of brain. Such a model is particularly important to advocates of Visual Literacy because the ability to think through the nonverbal mode is generally not formally tested nor championed in the school setting.

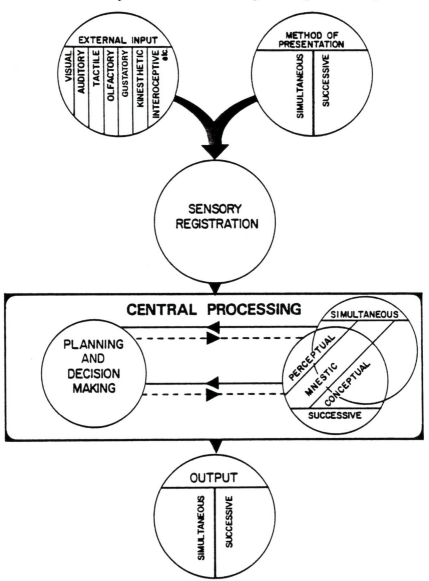

Figure 20. Model of simultaneous/successive information integration. From J.P. Das, J. Kirby, and R.F. Jarman: Simultaneous and successive synthesis: An alternative model for cognitive abilities. *Psychological Bulletin, 82*:87-103, 1975. Courtesy of American Psychological Association and J.P. Das.

Note Figure 20 which indicates a schematic of how their model works. Information integration occurs as a result of the combined action of four basic units: the input, the sensory register, the central processing unit, and the output unit. Let's note briefly how information is received and processed at each unit level.

An input can be presented to any of the sensory receptors which in turn transmits the information through a particular sense modality. We investigated in Chapter Three, the mode of information transmission through just one receptive system — the visual — and saw how the raw data in the form of light waves is converted into a coded pattern recognizable by the brain. The input presented to any receptor system can also be presented in a parallel (simultaneous) or serial (successive) fashion. Thus for instance, a picture could be presented piece by piece as in a puzzle situation. The latter provides a condition where the viewer mentally constructs the whole as the whole is being constructed.

The stimulis input is then accommodated by a sensory register. The authors suggest that the sensory register acts as a buffer between the input system and the all-important central processing unit. There are two ways that the relationship between the sensory register and the central processing unit can be conceptualized. The central processing unit questions the buffer to determine what information is to be transmitted and allows a transmission to be made. By the same token, the sensory register can interrupt the central unit and force it to accept information. This may occur more frequently perhaps because sensory information cannot often be detained.

The central processing unit is composed of three interrelated components. One component processes separate information into simultaneous catagories, a second processes bits of information into successive series, and the final, acting as the executive decision-maker, integrates and uses the information transmitted by these two components. An important feature to note is that the processing mode of the three components within the central processing unit is not affected by the form of the initial sensory input. Thus visual information which may have been received as a whole can be processed in a successive, serial way and auditory information delivered in discrete intervals can be processed in a simultaneous way. The planning and decision-making component could be considered synonomous with the activity of thinking, especially causal thinking. It uses the coded information from the other two components and decides on a best possible plan of action.

At the responding level, the output unit determines and organizes the systems necessary for responding. Once again both simultaneous and successive processing can be involved at the response level. An important consideration here is task requirement. The task requirement may be conditioned by the instructions given prior to the task. The instructions pose a "mind set" on the learner and predispose that person to act a certain way on that information even if that way is not his/her habitual mode or if the processing mode is not best suited for the task. For instance, a person may be handed a series of pictures in mixed-up order and be told to put them in the order that makes the best sense. This making sense dictates that the person reconstruct all the parts which are, in turn, visualized in wholes so that the larger meaning unfolds. If the person's preferred mode of processing was the oral language mode, she/he may produce a better outcome if he/she were allowed to verbalize the components of the task even though the task would appear to require simultaneous visual input.

The simultaneous/successive model lends a meaningful perspective to our next topic — that of learning style. It also allows us to understand why some learners may be more visually oriented and others more verbally oriented. For some, according to the model, either the simultaneous or successive component at the central processing unit level is stronger than the other. This component strength may then dictate how the executive planner intends to use information or solve a problem through the output mode. This notion has particular relevance to the visual literacy mode of information processing and will help us to understand preferences for visual learning.

LEARNING STYLE: CONCEPT AND IMPLEMENTATION

Learning style examines how a learner learns and processes information in everyday life. This view presents quite a different focus than on what one learns. As a concept, learning style has extensive merit because it seeks to determine how individual learners processes information. Strengths determined in the assessment (the how) will help the learner learn any curriculum content (the what). For example, if a learning style assessment of a group of learners shows that some prefer to learn cognitive skills through a particular delivery system, educators can present the content — the what of the curriculum — in that frame of reference. Thus, rather than be concerned about adult notions of what reading approach is best for youngsters, what perceptual modalities youngsters should use in learning to read, or how the room environment should be arranged for reading, learning style practitioners can inventory the youngsters directly to determine their learning style preferences and present reading instruction to match those preferences.

Kirby (1979) noted that the term "learning style" has emerged rather recently on the American educational scene (the early 1970's) and serves as an umbrella term for the concept of style. Prior to the 70's, the major focus was on the cognitive view of style, prompting a great deal of research into the singular dimension of cognitive, mental set. The most renowned view of cognitive style assessment, the field dependent and field independent construct of Witkin and his associates, probably has been the most extensively studied and has had the widest application in the field of education (see review by Witkin, Moore, Goodenough, and Cox, 1977). Kirby (1979) describes 18 more cognitive style models, almost all of which were operational prior to consideration of the more expansive views of learning style begun in the early 1970's. While Messick (1976) presents some 20 dimensions of cognitive style in his review, Claxton and Ralston (1978) discuss 11 models of cognitive style and analyze in-depth three models relevant at the college level.

What makes the focus of learning style more expansive than the singular dimension of cognitive style? Kirby (1979) feels that cognitive style constructs generally focus on one element of style with two polar extremes; i.e., one is either more field dependent or field independent. Cognitive style constructs are generally expressed in "either-or" extremes while learning style models are composed of a number of elements which are not necessarily bi-polar in nature. The learner may or may not have one or another element of style, and the absence of one element does not necessarily mean that other elements will take its place. In learning style assessment there are varying strengths and weaknesses. Thus, if a practitioner assesses learner's perceptual modality preferences, he would find that some youngsters will show a marked preference for visual learning, a moderate preference for auditory learning, and a negative preference for tactual learning. In Kolb's four-stage experiential learning model (1981) a learner can be more adept at bringing one set of learning abilities, such as active experimentation, to bear on a learning task but the learner may have some degree of proficiency in the three other elements of concrete experience, reflective observation, and abstract conceptualization.

Secondly, learning style enthusiasts tend to regard cognitive style as just one dimension of the overall learning process. They look beyond cognitive concerns in attempting to meet students' individual physical and social needs of a more practical nature (Kirby, 1979). According to Dunn, Dunn, and Price (1979, p. 53) "learning style is the way in which responses are made because of individual psychological differences." Keefe, research director of The National Association of Secondary

School Principals (NASSP), also views learning style in its larger context, as "cognitive, affective, and physiological traits that serve as relatively stable indicators of how learners perceive, interact with, and respond to the learning environment" (1982, p. 44).

FIVE TAILORINGS OF STYLE

Just five of the many dimensions of learning and cognitive style will be presented here. These five are highlighted because they have some compatability with the area of visual literacy. However, one sour note is sounded. These five generally assess style through pencil and paper procedures. Therefore, the dimension of written literacy is generally an entrance requirement in these style-assessment procedures. The next section will look at other ways that visual literacy researchers can determine preference or nonpreference without the intermediary stages of the oral or written literacies.

An Experiential Learning Model

Kolb (1981) was impressed with college students who subsequently failed in their career choices because the disciplines they chose to study were incongruent with their personal styles. As a freshman advisor at a leading university, Kolb frequently encountered learners pursuing disciplines which they did not have the cognitive set to enjoy and understand. He undertook the task of inquiring further into the nature of learning styles and how specific university disciplines demand specific cognitive functioning. Kolb's four-stage model enables a college student to know his/her process of cognition, the type(s) of learning style most preferred, and the academic disciplines or careers most concomitant with the student's thinking processes and style.

He called his model — the Experiential Learning Model — for two main reasons. The first he attributed to a historical perspective and the second was to emphasize the important role that experience has in the learning process. He notes that the experiential emphasis differentiates his approach from other cognitive theories of the learning process. "The core of the model is a simple description of the learning cycle of how experience is translated into concepts which in turn are used as guides in the choice of new experiences" (1976, p. 2). How experience precipitates the model is reflected in Figure 21.

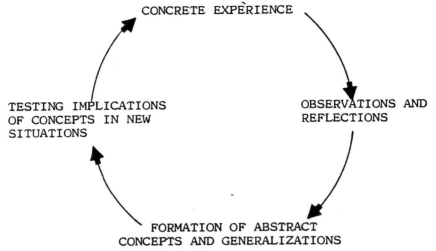

Figure 21. The experiental learning model of David Kolb (1976).

Learning, according to the Kolb model, is conceived to be on a four-stage cycle. Immediate concrete experience becomes the basis for observation and reflection. These thoughts form new concepts and generalizations which can be tested in various situations. To be an effective learner the four following kinds of abilities are needed:

Concrete Experience Abilities (CE);
Reflective Observation Abilities (RO);
Abstract Conceptualization Abilities (AC); and
Active Experimentation Abilities (AE).

Kolb asks two questions. Can a learner be equally skilled in all four abilities and secondly, are the abilities necessarily in conflict within many individuals? Answering these, he points out that there are two primary dimensions to the learning process that are represented by the poles of his model. The first dimension represents the concrete experiencing of events at one end of the learning process and abstract conceptualization on the other. The second dimension shows reflective observation at one end and active experimentation at the other extreme. However, in the process of learning, the learner can move in varying degrees from active participant to observer, from assimilator of observation to practical applicator, and from practical applicator to risk taker.

The Kolb **Learning Style Inventory** (1976) presents a nine-item inventory which requires the reader to rank order four words on each item row. A "4" is assigned to the word on the row that best describes the person's learning style, a "3" to the next word that best characterizes the person's style, a "2" to the next most characteristic word, and finally a "1" to the word that is the least characteristic of the person's style. One word in each item row corresponds to each of the four learning modes in the model; for instance, the word "feeling" relates to the dimension of Concrete Experience while the word "doing" relates to Active Experimentation. By adding up the ranked numbers according to the four scales, a profile can be plotted showing a strength or weakness learning style mode.

The completed profile can be compared with a normed profile provided in the **Self-Scoring Test and Interpretation Booklet**. The normed profile was based on the results of 1,933 adults ranging from 18 to 60 years of age. Approximately two-thirds of the normed group was male and two-thirds were well educated, having a bachelor's degree or higher. A wide range of occupations and educational backgrounds were also represented including teachers, counselors, engineers, salespeople, managers, doctors, and lawyers.

The following figure prepared by a St. John's University Graduate Student, Alejandro Villalba, summarizes Kolb's model and style imple-

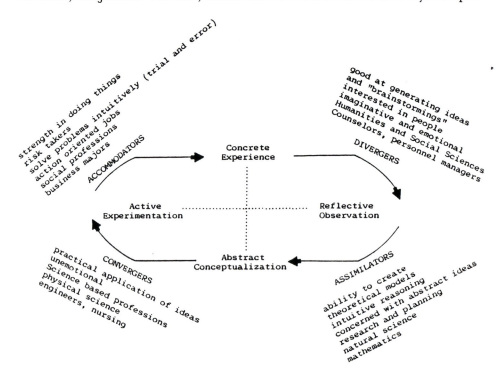

Figure 22. The four major learning styles in Kolb's model and types of performance generated.

mentation. The figure shows the four main learning styles that emerge from completion of the scales on the Kolb **LSI**, the type of thinking generated by each style, and the type of job occupation or profession that most correlates with each style dimension.

Verbalizer/Visualizer

A second procedure for evaluating style, also appropriate for the older learner, is the Verbalizer/Visualizer Questionnaire (VVQ) of Alan Richardson (1977). Richardson reported six studies conducted with high school and college students on the continent of Australia in which he formulated the development of his VVQ.

The questionnaire consists of 15 items to which the reader responds true or false. An item which may have a high visualizing component might be, "My daydreams are sometimes so vivid I feel as though I actually experienced the scene," and an item which may have a high verbalizing quality may be, "I read rather slowly." In the validation studies reported, Richardson (1977) indicated that the cut-off scores for defining habitual verbalizers and habitual visualizers produced extreme groups ranging between 15 and 25 percent in each. He suggests that for research purposes, it is best to use the 15 percent rather than the 25 percent criterion. Richardson also cited the work of Walter (1953) in reference to the cut-off scores. Walter concluded, after assessing the EEG characteristics of 600 normal people, that two thirds are of the mixed type, and the remaining third fall into about equal numbers of habitual visualizers and habitual verbalizers.

A Hemispheric Assessment of Style

E. Paul Torrance (1982), along with a number of research colleagues, has developed a self report, pencil-and-paper procedure for assessing style of information processing based on hemisphericity. Four different forms for adults (A, B, C, and M) and three different forms for children and adolescents (Forms A, B, and C) have been developed of the "Your Style of Learning and Thinking" (SOLAT). All forms consist of multiple-choice items which were selected base upon the results of interdisciplinary research on the specialized cerebral functions of the left and right hemispheres. Torrance notes that because the assessment of hemisphericity poses problems for the educational psychologist (a number of these problems were posed in Chapter Four), he has chosen to use a self report instrument based upon the findings of hemisphericity research in other disciplines. He also notes that the items selected for use on the SOLAT showed a high degree of internal consistency and that rather extensive norms, reliability data, and validity information have been compiled for Forms A, B, and C for college and adult subjects. Complete copies of Forms A and B (Torrance, Reynolds, Riegel and Ball, 1977) and Form M (Schwartz and DiMattei, 1981) have been published in open sources. Furthermore, reliability studies have been conducted and summarized in the preliminary norms technical manuals (Torrance, Reynolds, Ball, and Riegel, 1978; Torrance and Reynolds, 1980).

Each item on the alternate forms of the SOLAT (Form A consists of 36 items and the others, 40 items) is aimed at presenting the learner with three choices — one a left hemisphere function, one a right hemisphere function, and the other an integrated way of processing information. Torrance (1982) notes that measures of creative style such as reflected in the SOLAT have made possible a host of exploratory studies regarding the role of hemisphericity in creative functioning despite the shortcomings inherent in self-report instruments.

At this point, we should also note that because the SOLAT has been most used with creative and gifted populations, it may be more than reasonable to suggest that these populations were quite literate and could read and relate the thrust of each item to his/her own personality.

An Aural Learning Style Assessment

Harry Reinert (1976) has developed a procedure for assessing learning style profiles which has the visualizing component of the VVQ (Richardson, 1977) but does not require the ability to read. The **Edmonds Learning Style Identification Exercise** (ELSIE) will yield a profile showing whether a learner has a strength or weakness in visualization, the written word, listening, or activity. In this procedure, the listener will hear a list of fifty common English words read one-at-a-time at ten second intervals. The listener is required to respond to each word heard by marking one of four columns on a prepared answer sheet. The marking is done in the following way: column one is circled if the word evokes a mental picture of some object or activity, column two is circled if a mental picture of the word appears spelled out, column three is circled if no mental picture appears but a focus on the word's sound, and column four is circled if some physical or emotional feeling is triggered by the word, such as the tightening of muscle or a feeling of sorrow.

The 50 items have been coded by high and low regularity of occurrence in each of the four categories. For instance, the word "pool" has had a high visualizing response rate while a low response to the sound category. The word "truth" has had a high sound categorization but a low visualizing one.

After completing the 50 items, the listener tallies his/her total responses for each of the four categories of Visualization, Written Word, Listening, and Activity. The raw scores for each category are then transferred to a learning style profile chart which visually displays a high or a low response rate to any of the four categories. The listener's scores in all four category areas are relative to stanine scales constructed on the chart (0 is the median and $\pm$ 4 is the range). The stanine scale is arranged on bands above and below the median. The scale was based on norms derived from analysis of 909 persons who comprised the pilot group. No other reliability or validity data are reported.

Reinert (1976) notes that very seldom will an individual stay within the median range (0 band) on all four categories. The basic assumption made in interpreting each profile is that the further the individual varies from the median in any of the four profile areas, the more or less pronounced will be that mode of learning for that individual. For instance scores at the extreme of the stanine bands ($\pm$ 3 or $\pm$ 4) may be construed to mean a strong or weak influence for that particular mode of learning.

For followers of Visual Literacy, two profile categories will identify learners with high and low visual/spatial preferences. The category of Visualization indicates the relative importance of actually seeing objects and events in order to learn, and the category of Activity represents the relative importance of involvement in physical activity in order to learn.

Visual Learning: One of 24 Elements

Kenneth and Rita Dunn's conceptual framework grew out of their direct observations of youngsters engaged in varieties of learning tasks. The Dunns noted that some youngsters when faced with a problem, did not go to the teacher but preferred to work with a peer. Some preferred not to sit in their chairs during problem solving while others liked to nibble on food while they independently worked a problem to its conclusion. Because their model is observational, they have tended to expand their elements of style based on what learners have demonstrated about their learning preferences. In 1972, the Dunns' model was composed of 12 elements of style; in 1975, they expanded to 18 elements, (Dunn & Dunn, 1975), and in 1978 and in 1981 with Gary Price, they were assessing 24 elements of style. A major review is again planned for 1985-1986.

The **Learning Style Inventory** (LSI) of Dunn, Dunn, and Price (1978 & 1981) is a self-report instrument based on a rank-ordering of choices for each of 104 items. Students respond "true" or "false" to each item on a score sheet submitted for computer analysis to yield a learning style profile. As students respond, they indicate their preferences or non-preferences for 24 elements of learning style grouped into four major classification areas of environmental, emotional, sociological, and physical stimuli.

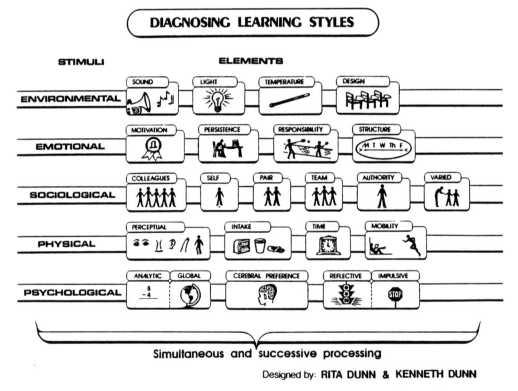

Figure 23. The learning style model of Dunn, Dunn, and Price (1981). Figure of model designed by Rita and Ken Dunn, St. John's University, Jamaica, N.Y. 11439. Courtesy of the Dunn's.

Dunn (1982) indicated that most learners show strong negative or positive preferences from six to fourteen of the elements. Learners indicate they are affected by:

a. Environmental stimuli such as sound, light, temperature, and the need for either a formal or informal design;
b. emotional stimuli such as motivation, persistence, responsibility and the need for either structure or options;
c. sociological stimuli such as learning alone, with peers, with an adult, or in a combination of social contexts;
d. and physical stimuli such as perceptual strengths and preferences, need for intake, time of day energy levels and need for mobility in learning. Within this area are found the four elements of Auditory, Visual, Kinesthetic, and Tactile preferences.

The 1978 **LSI**, a revision of an earlier instrument, was administered to a random sample of over 4500 subjects from several states and Canada (Dunn, Dunn, and Price, 1981). Using a factor analysis procedure the present LSI was obtained containing 24 elements. Its overall reliability obtained on students from grades 3 through 12 was equal to or greater than .60. Two additional studies conducted by the authors to measure the reliability of the **LSI** indicated that most of the reliabilities were quite high.

Ohio State University's National Center for Research in Vocational Education published the results of its two-year study of instruments that identify cognitive and learning styles and verified that the LSI had "established impressive reliability and face and construct validity" (Kirby, 1979, p. 72).

The **LSI** also provides a consistency score for each learner as a check on whether he/she read and answered the questions carefully. This consistency score comes from a sub-score provided by a number of questions that are repeated throughout the inventory. The **LSI** has an easily administered format, a far easier reading level than the other instruments mentioned earlier (it has been normed as low as third grade), and can be paced with highly distractable students if delivered orally. Furthermore, modification of the curriculum or of the learning environment can readily follow after **LSI** assessment and individual profile plotting.

Learning style and its relation to exceptionality at both the high and low ends of the curriculum has been undergoing intensive investigation (Dunn, 1983). A major feature in such inquiry is the selection of populations with polar likes and dislikes for particular, even singular, elements of style and then subjecting these population groups to particular read-ing and learning methods. Reviewing a number of studies, Dunn (1983) reported that the most important characteristic for the underachiever appeared to be his or her tactile and kinesthetic preference over an audi-tory or a visual one.

Unfortunately for those wishing to use the **LSI** in Visual Literacy re-search, the weakest reliabilities reported for all 24 elements were for the visual preference area (Dunn, Dunn, and Price, 1981). The reliabilities for Tactile preferences were far stronger ranging from .59 to .73 for all populations while Kinesthetic reliabilities were also respectible with a range of .51 to .64.

The forthcoming revision of the **LSI** (Dunn, Dunn, and Price, 1985), will feature a change in testing format, a reduction of elements from 24 to 22, and renorming. Students will no longer be faced with the forced-choiced, true-or-false answer format. Third and fourth graders can answer "T" if they agree with an item statement relating to anyone of the 22 elements, "F" if they disagree, and "U" if they are unsure or unde-cided about the preference of that item. Students in grades 5 through 12 will respond on a five point Likert scale ranging from Strongly Disagree (SD) to Strongly Agree (SA). The reliability for the Visual Preference area using the new Likert format for 1046 subjects in grades 6 through 12 was .26. While stronger than the earlier 1978 and 1981 editions, the problem for the inventory authors in assessing the visual area may be the joining of items that measure both verbal and nonverbal likes and dislikes. The authors define the Visual Preference learner as, "a learner whose primary perceptual strength is visual and can recall what has been read or observed: such people, when asked for information from printed or diagramatic material, often can close their eyes and visually recall what they had read or seen earlier" (1985, p. 4).

LIMITATIONS IN THE ASSESSMENT OF STYLE

We have seen that even the most sophisticated of learning style in-strumentation generally elicits voluntary information through pencil and paper procedures. Because this information may be thought out, weighed, and rationalized by the learner, the left hemisphere is un-doubtedly a heavy contributor to the response mode. Even Joseph Hill (1971), who systematically worked out a cognitive mapping procedure based on three sets of 64 elements, noted that his reporting procedure may be incomplete. As a more thorough backup procedure, Hill recommended gathering corroborative data through teachers' observations of individual in different instructional settings (Radlike, 1973). The notion of directly observing behavior to determine learning preferences will be explored in a later section of this chapter. For the present, let's see how brain functioning has been equated with style.

BRAIN LATERALIZATION PROCEDURES AND STYLE DETERMINATION

Researchers have attempted to correlate one or more of the brain lateralization procedures discussed in Chapter Four with constructs of learning or cognitive style with various types of learners. By correlating certain elements of style with known findings from brain research techniques, researchers hope to obtain greater evidence that particular constructs or elements of style involve the activation of one brain hemisphere more than the other. Generally, Witkin's model of field-dependence/field-independence has been the one dimension of cognitive style most researched while the EEG and the lateral eye movement procedures have been the brain research techniques most utilized. A connective link between cognitive style research and lateral eye movements would tend to bolster both constructs, since they both attempt to account for individual differences in preferential modes of cognitive-perceptual functioning and both suggest neuro-physiologial involvement (Goodenough & Witkin, 1977). While Hoffman and Kagan (1977) suggest that future studies should link other measures of brain lateralization (such as dichotic listening and split-field tachistoscopic tasks) with both eye-movement behavior and cognitive ability, existing investigations looking at the cross-section of both fields have produced rather ambiguous results (Otteson, 1980). As noted earlier, this ambiguity undoubtedly results from problems with brain research methodology, testing procedures and subject selection, and the methodological constraints of each cognitive style construct. Only one study reported to date has compared a verbalizer/visualizer component of learning style with a brain lateralization technique to determine their interactive effects.

EEG Recordings and Style

A few investigators have sought to determine if cortical activity as measured by the electroencephalogram (EEG) would show changes in alpha rhythm when thinking style was being measured. Most researchers base their work on Galin (1979) who is a strong advocate of the EEG technique as a natural way of measuring hemispheric engagement of normal and disabled subjects during every-day learning tasks. In a pioneer study, Galin and Ornstein (1972) studied the EEG asymmetry of 10 normal subjects recorded at the left and right temporal and parietal areas of the scalp during two verbal and two spatial tasks. They found characteristic EEG patterns of activity and nonactivity during the differential task processing. The verbal tasks were writing and mentally composing a letter; the spatial tasks included block design much like the **Block Design** subtest of the Wechsler Scales and one requiring the subject to decide which of five figures was represented by a number of sectioned parts.

Doktor and Bloom (1977) pursued earlier EEG and eye movement findings with high ranking personnel in the management field to determine if there were cognitive style differences between occupational groups. Using the verbal-analytic and spatial-intuitive tasks proposed by Galin and Ornstein (1974), they made EEG recordings on eight high-ranking executives, either Presidents or Chief Operating Officers of large corporations, and six Operations Researchers. The operational assumptions were that Operations Researchers were analytically trained individuals who would construct mathematical models to help solve complex problems while the executives would be more intuitive and "right brained" in problem solving styles.

The results supported the predicted hemispheric dominance of the Operations Researchers. That group revealed a consistent alpha ratio shift on the EEG tracings for verbal-analytic and spatial-intuitive tasks while the executive sample evidenced an opposite mental shift. Although only half the executives demonstrated a right-brained style of problem solving for both type tasks, the authors concluded that selective lateralization of cognitive style might fruitfully be related to occupational group.

The implications of this type of research for followers of visual literacy are clear. During selected visual, verbal, creative, and artistic tasks, EEG tracings would reveal if hemispheric shifts occurred. Secondly, these tracings could be compared with learners' self-reported perspectives of their own style. The latter could be done with any of the five instruments mentioned earlier in this chapter.

Metcalf (1975) focused on the field articulation construct of Witkin and hypothesized that either the field-dependent or field-independent cognitive style would correlate with the brain hemisphere activated to solve a task. In a very ambitious project involving 22 batteries administered to normal functioning adults and adolescents, Metcalf measured brain wave activity occurring during tasks of cognition and laterality. Each subtest was administered simultaneously during EEG recording while attempting to hold to a minimum the production of excessive eye movements, muscle activity, or other distractors that might interfere with the EEG analysis. The cognitive style battery included ten subtests, three of which had been used successfully in previous research on cognitive. The laterality battery contained twelve subtests designed to elicit either left or right cerebral activation.

Contrary to the findings of Galin and Ornstein (1972), Metcalf found that his normal subjects did not show consistent use of one hemisphere or the other for any task. Metcalf suggested that variation may have resulted from the way he analyzed his data (in four second intervals as compared to Galin and Ornstein who analyzed in larger units with a more global averaging of data). He did find that arithmetic tasks almost always resulted in left hemisphere activation, and that the most powerful stimulator of right hemisphere activity was a "mental trip" task. During that task, the subject was asked to take a journey with eyes closed and to visualize that journey.

Eye Movements and Style

Most of the investigations comparing differential hemispheric functioning and parameters of style have focused on the lateral eye movement procedure. Of all the brain lateralization techniques noted earlier, the eye movement procedure demands little in terms of special equipment and training. Although eye movements can be measured by a monitor and recorded by oscillograph, most researchers in clinical settings use an observational technique — watching the first eye movement shift a subject makes in solving either a visual/spatial or verbal/sequential problem. An example of a verbal-sequential problem is, "Susie is taller than Mary and Mary is taller than Jane. Who is the tallest? An example of a problem that requires parallel, visual processing is, "In which direction does George Washington face on the quarter?" The direction of eye shift during questioning is contralateral to the brain hemisphere involved in the solution of the problem.

Research generally indicates that the direction of leftward or rightward eye movements is a function of both problem or question type (Kinsbourne, 1972) and of individual differences in cognitive style (Bakan, 1969). Gur (1975), and Gur, Gur, & Harris (1975) have revealed, however, that when an examiner faces the subject during question delivery, individual differences in cognitive style preference seem to prevail over question type. Hence, subjects tend to shift their eye movements according to their preferred way of solving mental problems. In the face-to-face situation, subjects can be classified as either "right movers," who habitually activate the left hemisphere or "left movers," who prefer to use the right hemisphere. The face-to-face technique is thought to be more anxiety producing for the subject, predisposing him/her to activate the hemisphere habitually used rather than the one best suited for the processing demands of a given task. That motion is entirely consistent with the metacontrol system concept discussed earlier. A bias to behave in a certain way under anxiety is conditioned by one's attitude or predisposition to act rather than by the type of problem.

All that is required in the examiner-facing-subject condition is a trained examiner and an equal number of verbal/sequential and visual/spatial questions. It is easy to see why this procedure has been the most widely used in the clinical setting. The most extensively used instruments to measure style have been the **Embedded Figures Test** and the **Rod-and-Frame Test** which assess the field-dependence/field-independence construct (Witkin). A number of similarities have been noted between the field-independent (analytic) individual and the right mover, and between the field-dependent (global) person and the left-mover (Hoffman & Kagan, 1977).

Richardson (1977), whose Verbalizer/Visualizer Questionnaire was discussd earlier, correlated his 15 items with the eye movement procedure. He concluded that his 15 item Verbalizer-Visualizer Questionnaire provided a stable index of an individual's cognitive style and could be used with reasonable confidence in the study of the sequential and parallel processing of cognitive events.

Two critical reviewers (Ehrlichman and Wienberger, 1978), on the other hand, have issued a word of caution regarding the interpretation of studies using the eye movement procedure. They have found that the evidence linking lateral eye movements to hemispheric asymmetry to be equivocal. The questions designated for left-and-right hemisphere activation registered favorable results in only half of the studies reviewed.

These reviewers conclude that further research on the direction and extent of eye movements and cognitive-affective processes is necessary before reliable inferences about hemispheric function can be drawn from studies of eye movements.

STYLES OF DIVERSE LEARNERS

Other studies, while not using a direct brain measurement procedure, appear to reveal that distinct populations and sets of learners have unique learning styles that differ from the mainstream. These studies show that specific thinking strategies are employed by these learners who are often considered "failures" by mainstream standards. Included in this grouping are culturally different groups, urban inner-city learners, and the learning disabled. Quite interestingly, the thinking style employed by many learners within these groups is often the same as that of the gifted, talented, and creative.

Lesser (1976), for example, asserts that people who share a common cultural background also share in varying degrees, common patterns of intellectual abilities, thinking styles, and interests. He cites studies that reveal strong correlations between learners' cultural group backgrounds and the type of intellectual strengths and weaknesses they display; these regularities of behavior seem to persist as students advance educationally. Perrone and Pulvino (1977) point out that different cultures do educate their youth in different ways, some focusing on one hemispheric processing style more than the other. These researchers concluded that it is extremely important to discover the representational systems and consequent learning preferences of diverse individuals to design appropriate educational offerings. Ramirez and Castañeda (1974) found that the processing style of Mexican American children was field-sensitive as compared to a field-independent mode for dominant culture children. They believe that this conflict in style of information processing poses a major dilemma for Mexican American children in mainstream schools. Cureton (1978) maintains that there exists a Black, inner-city learning style in which motivation is the key factor that separates the inner-city from the middle-class child. Intelligent children labeled the "other gifted" (Alexander, 1982), the "creatively gifted disadvantaged" (Torrance, 1979), or the learning disabled have been shown to favor a right hemisphere or simultaneous mode of information processing.

Zelnicker and Jeffrey (1976) modified the procedure of the **Matching**

Familiar Figures Test (MFFT) of Kagan (1965). They developed a secondary set of visual problems demanding global analysis of contour differences rather than the detailed analysis of internal features required in the MFFT. Kagan had termed youngsters who were slow but accurate in matching drawings "reflective" while those who were fast but inaccurate were "impulsive." When Zelnicker and Jeffrey (1976) administered their own visual problems to a previously determined group of impulsive and reflective middle-class children at the third, fourth and fifth-grade levels, they found that the errors of the reflectives increased while the errors of the impulsives decreased. The reflective children were more accurate than the impulsive children on problems involving matching figures by their details, but no differences were found between the two groups on comparable global problems.

Wittrock (1978) suggests that an important educational implication of Zelnicker and Jeffrey's findings is that impulsive children need not be inferior to reflective children in problem-solving ability when global strategies are used appropriate to the solution of the problem. These findings also imply that learning can be difficult when a mismatch exists between students with global cognitive styles and curriculum and instructional tasks that emphasize analytic scrutiny. Coleman and Zenhausern (1979) add that the Zelnicker and Jeffrey results are consistent with the belief that impulsives process in the holistic style of right-brain preferents while reflectives process in the sequential, left-brain style.

In a number of studies, Rosalie Cohen (1969) examined the conceptual styles of middle-class and educationally disadvantaged, low-income group youngsters. She revealed how conceptual style, in part, is conditioned by the environment. Style, in turn, becomes a rule-set or mind-set for the selection and organization of sense data. She identified two mutually incompatible styles of reality organization, termed analytical and relational, and examined how the relational learner suffers in the analytically oriented learning environment of the school.

In face, the dichotomy between the highly relational and the highly analytic styles can best be seen in the schools. Indeed, Cohen believes that the explicit intent of school tests, curricula, and methods is to teach the analytic rule-set. Intelligence and achievement are measured by the school, in part, by how well pupils have learned how to analyze. What is less obvious is that the same analytic rule-set is also embedded in formal school organization and in the social settings where teaching and learning take place. For analytic children, the school's formal organization acts as an additional reinforcer of analytic thinking. For relational youngsters, however, the school's impact on conceptual development is disorganizing and contrary to their shared-function orientation to roles and responsibilities. The school's requirements for social participation and even its climate lack the cues necessary for relational types since the cues are generally delivered in a parts-specific way. Since tests of intelligence and achievement measure analytical skills, children with a relational cognitive style may score below norm or fail on school tests.

What Cohen describes as analytical style parallels quite closely the processing mode of the left hemisphere and the relational style, that of the right hemisphere. This would appear to be an especially fruitful area of research, and may be supported by the use of a new assessment tool, the K-ABC (Kaufman and Kaufman, 1983), whose merits will be discussed shortly.

INVESTIGATING THE STYLE OF
THE LEARNING DISABLED

Another highly fruitful area of inquiry has been the investigation of the processing style of the learning disabled. The term **learning disabled** may be a misnomer in our culture. Disabled learners very often are neither deficient in use of the oral language nor in the whole realm of nonverbal processing. Indeed, they may be more creative in modes of synthesis and visuospatial creation than their linguistically able peers (Sinatra 1980: Sinatra and Stahl-Gemake, 1983).

Traditionally, learning disabled youngsters have been categorized based on a written-language deficit model. This model acknowledges that written literacy is the prized academic pursuit of our culture. Those of average intelligence without evidence of mental retardation, physical abnormality, or emotional difficulty who do not achieve grade level standards in reading and writing must be, in fact, disabled. Geschwind highlights the plight of learning disabled youngsters in our culture (1972):

> We happen to live in a society in which the child who has trouble learning to read is in difficulty. Yet, we have all seen some dyslexic children who draw much better than controls; i.e., who have either superior visual-perception or visual-motor skills. My suspicions would be that in an illiterate society such a child would be in little difficulty and might do better because of his

superior visual-perception talents, while many of us who function well here might do poorly in a society in which a quite different array of talents was needed to be successful . . . As the demands of society change, will we acquire a new group of "minimally brain-damaged?"

Vellutino and his colleagues (1975a; 1975b) did find that while significant differences existed between dyslexics and normals on verbal tasks, they did not exist on nonverbal processing tasks. In three studies by Marcel, Katz and Smith (1974), Marcel and Rajan (1975), and Pirozzolo and Rayner (1979), good readers were found to be superior in left hemisphere processing for the task of word recognition but poor readers were consistently as good as or superior to the good readers in right hemisphere processing tasks. Witelson's investigations using the perceptual modalities of hearing, vision, and touch indicated that spatial functions are found in both hemispheres of dyslexic children in contrast with normal children's spatial specialization in the right hemisphere. Witelson proposed that the dyslexic population, mainly male, shows a deficiency in the phonetic, sequential, and analytical mode of information processing because of an overdeveloped use of the spatial, holistic mode (1976 & 1977). She hypothesized that two neural correlates operate for the learning disabled: one a deficiency in the linguistic, sequential mode of information processing and two, an intact or over-developed use of the spatial, parallel, holistic mode.

In this regard, Bannatyne (1971) had suggested that many learning disabled males have a visuospatial organized brain with an "executive control" center in the spatially oriented right hemisphere that dominates the whole brain including language functioning. Fadley and Hosler (1979) hypothesized that dyslexic children may look at a word in the same way they look at a picture with eye movements designed to catch the most important aspect of the word to translate it wholly into imagery as quickly as possible. Imagery, as was discussed earlier, is a specialty of right hemispheric functioning.

A rather remarkable study showing the right-brained processing strengths of linguistically deficient students was conducted by Symmes and Rapoport (1972). Fifty-four disabled readers, only one of who was a girl, were considered a group of "unexpected reading failures" since they showed good verbal skills (as reported by their parents). The group had a mean Wechsler (WISC) intelligence score of 114 and performed at a superior level on six tests of spatial visualization. The group's poorest WISC scores were in Digit Span, Coding, and Arithmetic, all tasks of linear sequencing, the processing mode of the left hemisphere. On the other hand, its highest verbal scores were in more "global" functions; i.e., where meaningful discourse is involved in tasks of abstract use of language and in verbal comprehension. As suspected, their average Preformance IQ of 116 was measured higher than the verbal at 110.

Guyer and Friedman (1975) have also explored the relationships between the field articulation style proposed by Witkin and his associates and differential hemispheric processing in normal and learning disabled males. These researchers employed a number of tests chosen for their association with particular brain hemispheric specializations. Right hemisphere-related tasks were visual sequential memory for nonsense forms, visual recognition, and visual closure (the latter the ability to perceive a Gestalt upon presentation of random bits of a picture). Left hemisphere-related tests were a **Portable Rod-and-Frame Test** devised by Nickel (1971), an auditory sequential memory tests, a verbal recognition test, and a verbal closure test.

The investigators found on the **Portable Rod-and-Frame Test** that 63 percent of the learning disabled boys were field sensitive as compared to 37 percent of the normal functioning boys. Another interesting finding was that the Visual Closure results were positively related to reading vocabulary and mathematics calculation for the learning disabled group but not for the normal boys. If the Visual Closure test is truly a task measuring right hemispheric processing, the results suggest that learning disabled boys tend to use the right hemisphere, or a nonverbal processing mode, in trying to solve academic tasks.

USING INTELLIGENCE PROFILES
TO ASSESS STYLE

Many investigators have also used various groupings of the Wechsler Intelligence Scale profiles with both learning disabled and academically proficient students to form hypotheses about their learning and cognitive styles (Galvin, 1981). The Wechsler Intelligence Scale for Children (1949; Revised, 1974) and the Wechsler Adult Intelligence Scales (Wechsler, 1955) have been historically used in the psychoeducational assessment of learners experiencing school, social, and learning difficulties (see Kaufman's three-part series in the October, November, and December 1981 **Journal of Learning Disabilities** for an up-to-date perspective).

Levy (1974) indicated that as early as 1955 and 1964 in studies by

Reitan and Arrigone and DeRinzi respectively, the verbal and performance scales of the WAIS measured what were considered left and right hemisphere functions. In most of the 20 studies reviewed by Kaufman (1981), he found that the Verbal/Performance scales of the WISC-R have shown a greater degree of intelligence discrepancies for learning disabled youngsters than for normals. Learning disabled students have been found to be equal to or superior to normal functioning students in visuospatial tasks (primarily the Performance Scales) but decidedly inferior to normals in tasks requiring linear sequencing (Rugel, 1974; Vance and Singer, 1979). Cordoni et al. (1981) have suggested that in order to assist learning disabled young adults in choices of post-secondary education, their cognitive profiles should be determined especially to see if changes are noted when compared to the well-documented profiles of younger learning disabled students. Consistent with earlier clinical and empirical findings for WISC-R testing, Cordoni et al. found that the most marked deficiencies for young LD adults was on the Sequential Factor, a factor which represented one of the recategorizations of the Weschsler subtests.

In another context, Kaufman (1979) noted that the impressive amount of research gathered on the field-dependent/independent construct of Witkin and his associates (1977), merits interpretation from both cognitive style and brain hemisphere perspectives. Field-independent subjects have been found to be far superior to field-dependent subjects on the three Wechsler subtests of Picture Completion, Object Assembly, and Block Design.

A new intellectual assessment tool — the **Kaufman Assessment Battery for Children** (Kaufman & Kaufman 1983) — may provide an exciting perspective in Visual Literacy and simultaneous/successive research. The **K-ABC**, developed by a husband and wife team on the clinical psychology faculty of the California School of Professional Psychology at San Diego, measures the intellectual strengths and achievement of youngsters from 2-½ to 12-½ years old. The theories of both Luria and of the brain researchers regarding left and right brain processing modes were most influential in its development. Young children from age 7 and under can be measured by 7 to 13 batteries which show their strength proficiencies for either sequential or simultaneous processing or both.

In the Sequential Processing Scale, the youngster solves each problem by mentally arranging the stimuli in sequential or serial order. In the Simultaneous Processing Scale, the problems are more spatial or analogic in nature. This means that through such tasks as face recognition, the picture of a face is presented to the child. In the Simultaneous Processing batteries, the child must simultaneously integrate and synthesize information to solve particular problems.

The impact of the new test instrument on the educational system needs time to develop. However, we are finally witnessing ways that a child's stronger mode of processing can be assessed so that the most efficient teaching strategies for that child can be programmed. This means that if a youngster has a stronger processing mode for simultaneous processing, he or she could be taught through that mode, specifically through the visual literacy strategies enumerated in the third section of this book.

THE STYLE OF THE GIFTED AND TALENTED

There exists quite a bit of documentation on gifted and talented populations to know somthing about how they prefer to learn and would best profit from instruction. When six samples of adults were administered a number of measures designated to assess either creative style or ability, Torrance (1982) found that there was a "consistent tendency for the measures of creative style to be positively and significantly related to the right hemisphere style of information processing and negatively and significantly related to the left hemisphere style" (p. 36).

Studies measuring the learning style of gifted school-aged youngsters have shown that they preferred to learn alone, are more persistent in their learning behavior, and are **less** teacher motivated than those identified as non-gifted (Griggs and Price, 1980; Price, Dunn, Dunn, and Griggs, 1981). In a large-scale review which looked at the preferred learning styles of gifted and talented students in grades 4 through 12, Rita Dunn (1983) found that these learners are independent, internally controlled, self-motivated, persistent, perceptually strong, task-committed, and nonconforming. The studies, which used either the Norwicki-Strickland **Locus of Control, The Learning Style Inventory** (Renzulli and Smith, 1978) or the **Learning Style Inventory** (Dunn, Dunn, and Price, 1981), also verified that the gifted strongly prefer to learn through independent studies and projects rather than through lecture or discussion. A recent doctoral dissertation has revealed, as well, that the gifted and highly gifted showed a highly significant preference (at the .001 level of confidence) for right hemisphere and integrated cerebral processing as measured by the SOLAT (O'Connor Cody, 1983). Furthermore the right hemisphere preferent individuals, most of whom were gifted in this study, disliked the learning style element of structure and were not adult motivated.

Torrance and Ball (1979) also studied the relationship between participants in a state honors program and their teachers' perspectives of their creative behavior. Creative application of students' learnings were compared with the students' dominant style of learning as measured by an adolescent form of the **SOLAT**. It was found that students with a right hemisphere style of information processing made more creative applications of learning than those identified as left hemisphere preferent learners. Those in the middle with an integrative style did not differ substantially from the right preferent group.

These studies suggest that gifted, creative learners are signaling to educators that they prefer learning situations in which they don't always need educators to be present, that their own motivation and drive will carry them through the tasks, and that learning climates conducive to right hemisphere incubation of imagery and synthesis would be in order.

Believing that much of the learning experienced in school is peripheral to higher thinking, Wiles and Bondi (1980) identified 20 skill clusters of creative thinking within the middle grades. Of the 20 creative thinking skills, four were in the nonverbal constructive skills area and included the following:

(1) Compacting perceptions to symbols;
(2) Imagery manipulations;
(3) Model building; and
(4) Symbolic thinking.

Note that one-fifth of the thinking skills are firmly established in the visual literacy mode. Many of the strategies and literacy-building techniques that will be offered in Chapters Seven, Eight and Nine will incorporate the thinking style of the constructive skills area.

SUMMING UP

Because so much information has been offered in these middle three chapters, the summation section which follows will integrate findings from the brain research and learning style areas. A particular focus will be on the Visual Literacy mode of thinking and seeing how these harmonize with brain, style, and written literacy consideration.

1. Differing brain organizations exist for verbal and nonverbal thought.

Brain researchers have shown educators that differing perceptual, cognitive, and aesthetic inputs demand different processing strategies from the brain. Some may require more left hemisphere processing and some more right hemisphere processing. Most important, however, is the notion that if some learners do not do well with certain tasks delivered in a prescribed way, as often occurs in the teaching of written literacy, it may be more fortuitous to change the delivery strategy to capitalize on the strengths of another literacy mode. Furthermore, the very nature of dual distinctive features within the literacy modes indicates that one mode more than the other may match with the preferred processing strength of a learner. We now have enough evidence which shows this notion to be more than just speculation. Witelson found, for example, in her carefully designed studies with over 200 normal and learning disabled boys and girls (1976 and 1977) that there were different patterns of brain organization during tasks involving the sensory modalities of audition, touch, and vision.

As noted by Sperry, the nonverbal can dominate the verbal (1973). A complete mirror switch in which the right dominates the left should leave little effect on cerebral performance — except for the problem of getting along in a predominantly right-handed world. Sperry adds that the differential strengths between the right and left hemispheres' processing modes in different individuals makes for quite a spectrum of individual variations in human intellect — from the mechanical or artistic geniuses on the one hand who have difficulty expressing themselves in speech or writing to the highly articulate who think almost entirely on a verbal level.

2. Verbal and nonverbal literacies have distinctive features inherent in their very modes of communication and these distinctive features are generally processed differently by the two brain hemispheres.

Inherent in the communication forms of nonverbal modes (visual, artistic, media, and aesthetic literacies) are distinctive features different from those that exist for the verbal literacies. The processing style of the individual in verbal or nonverbal tasks depends, to some extent, on the processing demands dictated by the task (Bogen, 1977). It is erroneous to think that everything nonverbal, in pictorial forms, or in visual/spatial arrays such as the **Group Embedded Figures Test** will be processed by the right hemisphere (Cohen, Berent, and Silverman, 1973 and Zaidel, 1979). The ability to perform such tasks rests on the ability to analytically dismember the parts from the whole, a task specialized for left hemisphere processing.

3. **Cooperation rather than competition between the two brain hemispheres is the prevailing mode in most learning** (Restak, 1982).

If 99 out of 100 people initially activate the right hemisphere when presented with a nonverbal task, the hundredth person may take a verbal orientation to the solution. Although possibly a bit more slowly, he or she would arrive at the same conclusion but through a different processing style. Hellige (1980) suggests that it is more accurate at the present time in discussion of such global functions as "language processing," "verbal processing," and "visuospatial processing" to think of partial rather than absolute hemispheric specializations. Indeed the dual processing modes of the hemispheres are beneficial to the full range of human thinking (Sperry, 1973; Nebes, 1974; and Levy, 1977).

Furthermore at more global, meaningful levels, both hemispheres cooperates in literacy processing. EEG studies in reading with very young children (Kraft et al., 1980) and in writing with college undergraduates (Glassner, 1980) tell us that learners use the right hemisphere during recall and composing processes. Using the EEG during two modes of writing — one focusing on the writer's ability to convey a message to another and the second focusing on the writer's ability to express his/her thoughts about a personal experience — Glassner found that while writing presents itself as a product in a linear form, its processes incorporate nonlinear, nonverbal modes of thought. Zaldel (1979) adds that while the right hemisphere has been characterized as synthetic, gestalt, visuospatial, and nonverbal, the labels are merely descriptive and often erroneously applied. He has found that the spatial ability to do embedded figures lies in the left hemisphere, and that receptive vocabulary, auditory comprehension and reading share the cooperation of both hemispheres. Blood flow mapping in each of the hemispheres has also shown that reading aloud activates seven discrete cortical regions on the surface of each hemisphere, while silent reading activates four areas (Lassen et al., 1978).

4. **Educators need to alter the reinforcement procedures for those learners who have not achieved with conventional learning programs or methods**.

In actuality, brain researchers are supporting a concept that educators have known about all along. Brain researchers are suggesting that if a task can be delivered in another motivational or configurational way, possibly more concomitant with the information processing strength of the learner, the task may be better learned. Yet Fagan (1979) maintains that effective teachers have traditionally used holistic methods such as word games, creative writing assignments, and graphic representations, long before the current focus on brain hemispheric specialization confirmed the efficacy of such methods for many students.

In the area of remedial education, in particular, the student is generally submitted to a great deal of repetition rather than to an altered or redirected approach. The repetition generally means more of the "same," and the same is delivered in the same information processing mode as the original learning. Especially in the elementary grades do youngsters fall prey to the same routine instructional patterns. Witness how the so-called basics are repeated without meaningful content year after year. For instance, when a youngster fails in reading, he or she is generally pulled out of class during oftentimes interesting content instruction and subjected to piecemeal reading instruction using the very same rationale that was employed in the original methodology in which the youngster failed. Let's look at young Jason's profile, submitted from a local agency, to see how he might best profit from a redirected, more holistic learning approach. Jason was 8 years and 7 months old at the time of evaluation and already had spent two years in the second grade. Also, note that a psychologist indicated with a (W) the areas in which he perceived Jason to be weak but **never** used an (s) to suggest a thinking/learning strength.

We can see that in traditional school related tasks such as Information and Arithmetic, Jason is quite low. In Digit Span and Coding, both of which require linear, sequential processing, he is also quite weak. In truth, all four of these tests have something in common; they are related to verbal memory and the ability to relate information in sequence. This type of linear thinking is strongly tapped in many reading programs that emphasis the "decoding" or sounding-it-out aspect of reading. But in parallel, holistic processing and in nonverbal thinking Jason's no misfit. In fact, he is achieving, in some cases, as well as a 14 year-old youngster. So, if all the 8 year-old kids in Jason's school were competing in the drawing of architectural plans for a new school, Jason might emerge as the "gifted" one in that task. Schools should take greater notice of what the strength profiles are telling them about the nonverbally gifted Jasons (not the IQ scores) and use that information to plan educational strategies that will intellectually activate the right hemisphere to strengthen reading and writing acquisition. Levy (1983) calls this a "gateway" approach in which arousal of one hemisphere can be the initial strategy for whole-brain learning.

Wechsler Intelligence Scale for Children (R)

1. Verbal Scale   — *95*
2. Nonverbal Performance Scale   — *117*
3. Full Scale   — *105*
4. Subtest Profile:

	Scaled Score	*Test Age*
Information	7 (W)	7-6
Similarities	10 (W)	8-6
Arithmetic	7 (W)	7-6
Vocabulary	12	9-6
Comprehension	10 (W)	8-6
Digit Span	9 (W)	7-6
Picture Completion	13	11-6
Picture Arrangement	13	11-6
Block Design	15	12-6
Object Assembly	15	14-2
Coding	6 (W)	7-0
Mazes	13	11-2

5. Educators need to continue study of the operation of both brain hemispheres during all stages of literacy learning in natural learning contexts.

From an educational perspective, we need applied level of research to determine if what is done in the laboratory setting with normal and split-brain subjects can increase learning productivity in the classroom. As expressed by Wittrock (1978), studies are needed to examine the facilitation of learning that may occur when analytic or holistic strategies are intentionally presented to students learning school subjects. Epstein (1978) is quite clear on this point as well. He notes that because of the anatomical evidence of his brain growth stages, a working implication is to present intensive and novel inputs to youngsters during these time periods.

Our children don't walk around with damaged brains, with severed corpus callosums, occluded visual fields, plugged ears, or bound hands. Information is rapidly moving from one hemisphere to the other via the corpus callosum, so that integration of visual/spatial perceptions with verbal, analytic reasoning occurs almost instantaneously in single acts of perception. Restak (1979) adds that if each fiber within the 200 million fiber network of the corpus callosum has an average firing frequency of twenty impulses a second, the corpus callosum is handling something like 400 billion impulses a second as this sentence is being read.

It becomes quite difficult, then, to set up procedures to isolate the functioning of just one hemisphere or the other for normal functioning human beings although two procedures, blood flow and electrophysiological recordings, allows learners to be studied in natural learning contexts. According to Galin (1979), EEG methods provide a more direct and sensitive means of investigating disorders of laterality than such measures based only on hand, eye, or ear dominance. The EEG procedure allows the actual engagement of the two hemispheres to be measured during a wide variety of naturalistic cognitive tasks, including contextual reading and composition writing, and is not subject to the very narrow restrictions on task and content that occurs with dichotic listening or tachistoscopic split-field testing.

Recent EEG research conducted by Glassner (1980) with older students to determine which hemisphere was engaged during the writing of two types of discourse can become critically important in our teaching of composition. Equally important is EEG research which tells us that for young primary learners interhemispheric processing appears to be more efficient than greater left hemisphere processing when retrieving and performing logical and/or inferential operations about experiences previously seen, heard and read about (Kraft et al., 1980).

6. **Because maturation of the fibers between the brain systems continues through the childhood years, the nonverbal literacies — visual, artistic, media, and aesthetic — can aid the neural development responsible for the verbal literacies.**

The implication of EEG research with young children and that noted from myelin development is that interhemispheric integration can be facilitated when the right hemisphere is given a commanding role in stimulating the verbal. The less nonverbal experience a child has had, the less will be the schemata formed, and by extension the less the verbal reenactment of those experiences. The more the nonverbal experience a learner has coupled with association of all the varied ways that nonverbal experiences can be represented at the fourth level of literacy such as through drawing and painting, body movement, music, sculpture, pictures, filming, maps, flowcharts, etc., the more will be the schemata developed, and undoubtedly the richer the verbal accounting of those experiences.

The purpose of such parent training programs as The Institute for the Achievement of Human Potential described by Richard Norton and Glenn Doman (1982) is to teach parents, particularly mothers, how to maximize and extend their children's potentials. Every procedure taught at the institute is aimed toward direct positive influence on brain development so that greater thinking potential will result. Working with parents and young children from newborn to seven years-of-age, the authors have drawn the following rather startling conclusions from their program:

a. The growth of intelligence and the rate at which children are capable of learning (taking in raw data) is nearly an inverse function of age

b. Every newborn has a large neurological potential which often remains untapped

c. Every child is capable of much higher levels of function than normally occur

d. Parents are the best source for tapping the neurological resources of their children

e. Central nervous system growth diminishes beyond the age of six, and

f. The quality of being "gifted" is primarily a product of the environment and is a level of intelligence which can easily be reached by nearly every child

Through the early pre-school years, it is especially important to allow young children to explore their environment and to provide kinesthetic, tactual experiences to force communication between the hemispheres. Since the commissures continue to myelinate well into the elementary school years, concrete, visuospatial activities should also be a regular ingredient of the daily curriculum diet. Then, as youngsters move through the stages of literacy development and integrate strategies from each they will be meshing nonverbal and verbal modes of learning through maturing neural conduits that allow this integration to successfully occur.

7. Educators need to acknowledge the powerful influence of the subcortical systems on cognition by making literacy learning meaningful and enjoyable.

Teachers and parents cannot forget the emotional and motivational importance of the two subcortical brains — the reticular formation and the limbic system — acknowledged by MacLean (1978) as the first and second brains. Our most subtle feelings have a physical basis within the limbic region, making it extremely difficult to separate emotions and consciousness with actual contact in the outside world. Frostig and Maslow (1979) and Restak (1979) exhort us not to forget the impact of these two brain systems which govern our alerting and emotional systems respectively. Since the neural pathways between the cortex and the reticular and limbic systems function all the time without our conscious awareness, educators must realize that curriculum content cannot be approached solely by intellectual reasoning. The systems regulating feelings, emotions, and attentiveness are tied to the very learning of information. Furthermore, teachers' attitudes toward the reason for learning certain disciplines and towards the learners themselves may have more impact than the content itself on how well it will be learned. Some keys to motivation may be to present challenging ways to solve a problem that are more closely aligned to the learner's affective state and the tone of the classroom climate. Such changes can act as compelling forces in activating the brain sub-systems responsible for alertness and emotional tone.

Thus, the classroom learning climate should not be matter-of-fact, coldly aligned to the learning of segmented pieces of written literacy in such activities as drill pages for sentence analysis practice and work sheets to practice decoding and word attack skills. Rather, the climate should be based on a meaningful need to know in which the learning of the three "R's" is bound to the learning of the natural and artistic world and which eagerness to know forms the emotional basis of the classroom learning atmosphere.

CHAPTER SEVEN

CONSTRUCTS OF VISUAL/VERBAL LEARNING

W E SAW IN THE previous three chapters that the brain is organized to respond to visual and verbal learning in quite different ways and that prevalent in our culture are learners who develop a preference for learning information through one literacy mode more than another. The purpose of this chapter is to look at how theoretical constructs, models, and programs have dealt with visual/verbal dichotomies in human learning. We will see how some programs fused visual and verbal learnings so that the best of both influenced each other.

This chapter also begins to emphasize the theme of the latter third of the book. That theme, how to use visual literacy ideas and strategies to enhance verbal learning, will be explored from a number of perspectives in these final three chapters. Chapter Seven will return to the discussion raised in Chapter One and Two regarding the essential importance of concrete experience in human learning. We noted that inherent in the concept of the primacy of visual literacy were the processes of seeing or visualizing and manipulative exploration. How these natural processes can be brought to the classroom is the subject of this chapter. In the subsequent chapters, we will explore how visualization and nonverbal, representational modes can extend experiential learning to provide the basis for many creative ways to learn verbal literacy.

THE NONVERBAL CORE TO WRITTEN LITERACY

The written literacy movement has been involved in its own internal conflict since the mid 1970s. We examined that conflict a bit in Chapter Two, and saw that it rested on how the written language should be presented to learners — in wholes or in parts.

145

Undoubtedly, as Samuels (1980) concludes, the adverse relationship between holistic and parts approaches to literacy learning need not exist. The holistic approach advocates beginning with the larger unit and moving to smaller units while the parts or subskill view is that of beginning with smaller units and moving to larger and more complex units. Both approaches recognize the whole and related parts. A major feature distinguishing the two approaches, especially during the beginning stages of literacy learning, is that of sequencing. According to Samuels, this means looking at which tasks and which unit size teachers would use to start instruction and how programs and skill sequences would be implemented as students increase in skills.

However, does the notion of holistic mean more than just presenting the whole language unit first and then working down to the part? Is there an underlying conceptual core to the whole and if so, what is the nature of this core?

At this point, let's examine the insightful model of Moffett and Wagner (1983) to review the conceptual foundation of literacy modes.

	CODING	
CONCEPTUALIZATION	experience into thought	NONVERBAL
VERBALIZATION	thought into speech	ORAL
LITERACY	speech into print	WRITTEN

Figure 24. The three levels of coding from Moffett and Wagner (1983). From James Moffett and B.J. Wagner: *Student-Centered Language Arts and Reading, K-13: A Handbook for Teachers*, 3rd ed. Boston, MA.: Houghton Mifflin Co. Courtesy of Houghton Mifflin Co., 1/31/85.

The three levels of coding model shows that the four traditional components of the language arts — listening, speaking, reading, and writing — are firmly anchored in a common, holistic core. Language, like the nonverbal media of communication, communicates some raw experience which has to be coded into the particular way messages are transmitted in that medium. Thus, in the oral language, phonemes signal distinctive differences amongst sounds that reveal particular words used to describe an experience while in the written language, graphemes are the means used to code the same raw experience. Yet, the content of messages whether identified by the oral or written language is based on nonverbal experience. This means that before people code an experience into any particular message form, such as in speech, writing, or even drawings, graphs, and flow charts, they have to focus on the raw experience they wish to present and organize it, probably without the use of words, in some form in the mind. This focusing is the stage of conceptualization or incubation of ideas which is conceived holistically, all-at-a-time. The three levels of coding clearly indicate how literacy — the interpretation and use of written forms of language — is based on a nonverbal genesis.

Moffett and Wagner maintain that the real basic skills are thinking and speaking with nonverbal thought at the core and not the "basics" construed by many to be spelling, punctuation and word recognition. They remind educators that reading and writing occur last in the acquisition of coding skills, generally after proficiency in oral speech and after considerable acquisition of nonverbal experience. Their three levels of coding — conceptualization, verbalization, and written literacy — indicate that experience has to be encoded into speech, and that thought has to be translated into speech before speech can be represented as writing. Since each level of coding is basic to the next, it is erroneous for parents and educators to think of reading and writing as the "basic skills."

Written literacy is often seen as the first or basic skill since reading and writing occur early in the school framework and lay the foundation for all subsequent book learning. But more than being basic itself, reading and writing depend upon the learning acquired through the two prior codings. Written literacy forms merely add a secondary visual coding procedure for understanding language beyond the real basic levels of coding.

Moffett and Wagner further suggest that when students experience difficulty at the third or literacy level, teachers make an erroneous assumption that the learning difficulty lies at that level. That is, because a problem arises in tasks of reading and writing, the problem appears to be one of difficulty with the written literacy level. However, the learning difficulty may not reside at that level. The real difficulties may lie at either the underlying conceptualization or verbalization levels or at all three levels at once. The authors add that by asking students to compose and comprehend orally, thereby ruling out word recognition and transcribing skills needed to perform at the written literacy level, teachers can determine if difficulties do exist in the conceptualization of experience or in the verbalization of thought.

Moffett and Wagner provide a concrete way to help us conceptualize how to bring a holistic literacy approach to the classroom. The approach fuses the three levels of coding in the structure and intent of the communication situation.

They use the term **discourse** to designate a whole unit of language used for a specific purpose. A **discourse** then could be a conversation, a lecture, a letter or journal, a poem, a short story, an ad, or even a label on a particular product. It is the largest unit of language in which a complete message exists between the sender or receiver. Thus, for a group of 11th graders in an electronics class, a line drawing representing a circuit, communicates a whole, meaningful context or nonverbal discourse which is immediately comprehended by all who have the relevant schema. According to their holistic view, composing and comprehending words, sentences, and paragraphs should be done within the context of a complete discourse. When substructures alone are used as learning units, readers and writers lose a sense of relevance and connectedness with the overall purpose of the message. If **discourse** is the superstructure of the communication context existing amongst sender-receiver-message, the paragraph, the sentence, and finally the word itself with its letters, syllables, phonemes, morphemes, and affixes are the substructures within. The paragraph or stanza, like the other substructures, is governed by the kind of discourse in which it is a part. This means that a number, sequence, and composition of paragraphs depend upon the discourse mode in which they occur and on the particular organization determined by the intent and content of the communication situation. Traditionally, the four modes of written discourse — narration, description, exposition, and persuasion — can dictate how the paragraphs within will be structured.

Sentences will also vary in style and complexity according to the kind of paragraphs in which they are used. Sentence structure is the set of relations amongst the words within the paragraph. Sentence level relationships are governed by the rules of grammar which consist of word function, word order, and word endings. Moreover, the structure of any given sentence governs the structure of each word within that sentence and how it will be punctuated. Thus, individual word meanings are dependent upon their locale in the sentence of which they are a part, and individual sentence meanings are dependent upon the paragraph in which they are a part, and individual paragraph meanings are dependent upon the total intent of the written discourse.

Global comprehension and creation of verbal and nonverbal works occur at the whole discourse level. It is at this level where essential meaning is grasped holistically as synthesis occurs to establish relationships. Furthermore, it is also at this level where emotions and feelings are tied to the meaning transmitted through the message.

VISUAL THINKING AS A STRUCTURE OF THE INTELLECT

A second model which illustrates the relationship of visual learning in the overall context of learning is that of Guilford's Structure of the Intellect Model (1967). The reader can image that model by visualizing a block construction of 120 square blocks. The blocks will be laid side by side to make a base of 5 blocks by 4 blocks or a total of 20 blocks packed into a neat rectangle. On top of those 20 would be stacked 5 more rectangles to total 120 blocks. Each of these blocks in Guilford's Model represent an area of intellectual functioning. Thus, rather than conceive of intellectual functioning as measured by 11 or 12 subtests as is often done on the Wechsler Intelligence Scales, intelligence is composed of 120 discrete but related components.

Guilford attempted to illustrate the multifaceted nature of intelligence by classifying cognitive abilities into the three categories of operations, content, and products. Each category is represented by a separate vector on each block, making all three intellectual abilities inherent in each of the 120 structures. There are four content categories, five operations categories, and six product categories.

Content refers to the nature of information or material. Figural information deals with content that is concrete, meaning that which can be seen, heard, or felt. Information in the form of secondary symbols such as letters, numbers or words is symbolic content. Semantic content refers to the meanings or ideas that the symbols represent and behavioral content refers to information regarding our behavior and others, including thoughts, desires, feelings, and intentions.

Within the figural content area of intelligence are the two additional parameters imposed by the vectors of products and operations. Products of information are concerned with units, classes, relations, systems, transformations, and implications. The second parameter of figural content has to do with modes of intellectual operations that can be carried on with the six forms of information. These are classfied as cognition, memory, convergent production, divergent production, and evaluation. A specific figural ability could be conceived of as "memory for figural classes" or "convergent production of figural transformations." Practical tasks such as drawing a figure, doing picture arrangements, or assembling blocks on a block design test would tap a number of these figural abilities.

Kleinfeld (1973) demonstrated that particular cultures, namely the Eskimo culture, do surpass the Causcasion in a number of figural abilities. He ennumerated 10 such figural abilities gleaned from anecdotal accounts, empirical studies, and analysis of the demands made by artic hunting. In actuality, he used the Eskimo culture as a cultural illustration to argue that research based on a multifaceted intellect model would identify strengths in culturally different groups. If the Eskimo could surpass the Westener on 10 Figural Ability tests, would not other cultures demonstrate similar strengths in thinking relative to the style of their upbringing? We also noted that in the Wiles and Bondi (1980) creative-skill cluster model, one fifth of the skills were concerned with figural-type thinking.

MAKING EXPERIENCE WORK IN THE CLASSROOM

Two models can be used by the teacher and administrator in the classroom setting to capitalize on the power of experiential involvement in language development. The first developed by the author in 1975 and 1977 required that physical activity initiated through sports, arts, and science content form the basis of reading and writing lessons.

The populations for each of these programs were considered reading "failures" but in each program run over short periods of time, youngsters learned a large number of new vocabulary words. The essence of each program required that both natural experience and the language arts be fused together in integrated projects focusing on a central theme. In other words, the arts or science teacher didn't demonstrate and orally discuss one project while the language arts teacher conducted reading and writing activities in another.

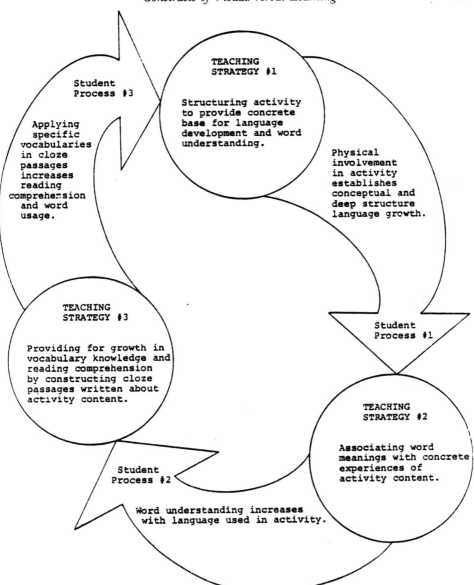

Figure 25. Model showing how to increase conceptual understanding through the structuring of experiential activities. From Richard Sinatra: The cloze technique for reading comprehension and vocabulary development. *Reading Improvement*, 1977, *14*, 80-92. Courtesy of Project Innovation, Chula Vista, Calif.

In the first summer program, over one thousand Black youngsters from grades one through eight participated in an outdoor camping program in which they learned to read 175 vocabulary words associated with the camping experience (Sinatra, 1975). Seven activity areas provided the natural context for the learning experience and for the learning of the new vocabulary words. In each activity area, teachers and counselors "acted out" or concretely presented the meaning of new words as students learned to read and write them. For instance, during Field Mathematics, when the new words "pace" and "pivot" were introduced, the teacher demonstrated how to use these words in outdoor math calculation, had the children act out the words, and then had them use them in reading and writing exercises.

In the second summer program (1977), 44 remedial reading youngsters completing grades one through five learned to use a significant amount of new vocabulary words in reading comprehension exercises. They participated in actual sensorimotor experiences prior to using the new words in reading and writing activities. During the regular school year these youngsters were taught reading through a synthetic phonics approach in which they put words together based on spelling pattern consistencies. In the summer program, new vocabulary was holistically introduced when children participated in meaningful activities under the direction of activity specialists such as in Drama, Science, Arts and Crafts, and Indian Lore. After participating in an actual "hands on" activity, the youngsters then made experiential-visual-verbal connections with the new words during reading and writing exercises that followed. The figure shows this interaction model of learning in which nonverbal experience provided the foundation for verbal learning at both the oral and written levels.

Notice how student thinking processes were shaped due to particular teaching strategies in the cycle. When a concrete activity was used as a basis for learning as indicated in Teaching Strategy #1, students conceptualized at the nonverbal level — the visual literacy level — and begin to establish deep structure verbal meanings with actual physical activity. As the new words were verbally used in more and more activities associated with the actual experience, students' understanding increased. Finally, they were able to apply the words appropriately at the written literacy level in reading passages based on the cloze format. During reading, students were given a whole discourse — the complete reading passage — with specific vocabulary parts deleted. As students read the passage and used the new words correctly in a number of deleted slots in the passage, they demonstrated that they had mastered both the sight reading of the new words and their semantic use in specific reading contexts.

Dale's "Cone of Experience" model (1969) provided a second profitable way to show teachers how to build concepts and vocabulary for learners of all ages and all ability levels. Dale's model is based on the premise that learning new concepts evolves from the concrete to the abstract. Activities of action provide the concrete base for the abstract use of symbols which explain and define the activity of action. While Dale formulated his model for the learning of new concepts, teachers have been asked to construct vocabulary building lessons in the areas of science, social studies, health, mathematics, the fine and creative arts, drama, cookery, and nutrition. The culminating literacy activity of each lesson is one in which their students use the new vocabulary in written compositions or reports. This kind of activity indicates that students have conceptually understood how to apply the new vocabulary in the written mode.

The key to use of the model whether teaching the vocabulary of the theater, the human skeleton, the parts of the plant, or of geometric shapes is to implement the model from the bottom up, from the concrete to the abstract as indicated in Figure 26.

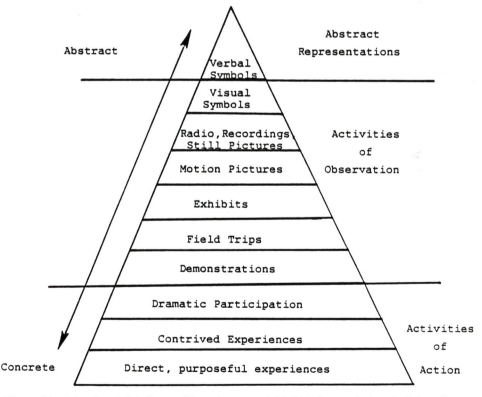

Figure 26. Adapting Dale's Cone of Experience model (1969) for vocabulary building. From Edgar Dale: *Audio Visual Methods in Teaching*, 3rd ed. New York: Holt, Rinehart and Winston Inc., 1969. Courtesy of Holt, Rinehart, and Winston and CBS College Publishing, 7/13/82.

Here's how the model works. The teacher must first focus on the particular grade level or age level of the students he/she will teach. Next, the teacher must zero in on a manageable aspect of the curriculum, generally one rooted in a natural content area such as music, home economics, shops, science, social studies, gyms, or health. Within one of the content areas, the teacher plans one or a series of discrete lessons which will follow the hierarchical application of the model. Thus, for second graders learning the parts of a plant, the parts of a microscope, and how to plant a garden are three separate lessons.

The key to each successful lesson is to merge the three bottom bands, labeled "Activities of Action," into one "hands-on" kind of effort in which totally new vocabulary words will be taught to eager learners. They won't even realize they are being immersed in new learning because the whole approach is so natural. Once the action activity is complete, the teacher can use as many bands of the observation activities that lend themselves to the specific lesson. For instance, in some cases a local exhibit or place to conduct a field trip may be known. In others, the teacher may know of films or still pictures that relate to the topic. Finally, students use the new vocabulary at the abstract level. They can use the words within the nonverbal, representational mode of charts, graphs, maps, diagrams, drawings, etc., and in written literacy representations of reading and writing.

From the dozens of excellent lessons done by teachers of students from kindergarten to high school and including many in special education groups, a few have been selected to illustrate how the model works. Notice how the model illustrates the true meaning of a holistic approach to learning and how the major components of literacy learning are brought to bear upon one learning experience.

One kindergarten teacher, Miss Jo Ann Di Giulio from P.S. 149, East New York used a cooking lesson to teach her kindergarten youngsters some 15 new words as well as some new concepts. The youngsters were to make Three Bears Porridge. The new words selected to be taught were recipe, ingredients, rolled oats, tablespoon, teaspoon, chopped, powdered milk, bubbles, simmer, covered saucepan, porridge, raisins, half-cup, honey, sunflower, and stir. To establish her direct, purposeful experience, she set up on a large table a display of cooking utensils and ingredients for the porridge recipe. She cleverly labeled each utensil as well.

She involved the children in one of the major sensory systems to establish brain associations for the word meanings. Children used sight and touch as they were allowed to handle the utensils; tablespoon, teaspoon, measuring cup, and saucepan. The sense of hearing was stimulated when various ingredients for the recipe were put in covered containers and children had to guess what was inside as they shook each container. Within separate containers were rolled oats, honey, sunflower seeds, raisins, powdered milk, and apples. Next, the sense of taste was incorporated as the rolled oats, sunflower seeds, raisins, apples, and honey were tasted from separate dishes. Later, smell was brought into the experience when all ingredients were simmering in the porridge . . .and of course, taste was the culminating activity when the children ate "the experience."

An important part of the model application in the use of the oral language synchronized with the events of the experience. This means that the new word is tied to the concrete experience as the experience is being lived. Notice how Miss Di Giulio had children hear the words as they were experienced. Children gathered around the table while the porridge recipe was being prepared. A large bowl was on hand to receive the various contributions.

These were the stages and directions as children stood about the table:

1. Have three children assist in adding the **rolled oats**. Ask the group, "How many **tablespoons** do we need of the rolled oats."
2. Have some children add the **sunflower seeds**. Ask, "How much **sunflower** seeds do we need?"
3. Add **raisins**. Ask, "Do we need the same amount of **raisins** as we do of the **sunflower** seeds or **rolled** oats? Do we need more or less raisins?"
4. Chop the apples. Place the apples on the cutting board. Chop apples, put apples in a one teaspoon measure. Ask, "Do we have enough apples? How did I **chop** the apples?
5. Add the **powdered milk**. Have a child measure out the powdered milk. Ask, "Do we need the same amount of **powdered milk** as we do of the **chopped apples**? Do we need one **tablespoon** of any other ingredient?"
6. Stir in the hot water. Measure out ½ **cup** of hot water. (activity of observation)
7. Place all the **ingredients** in a **covered saucepan**. Have the children check the saucepan to see the bubbles forming. Ask, "What

do you think is happening to the porridge when you see the **bubbles?**"

8. Stir in ½ **teaspoon honey** and have a child measure out the honey. Ask, "Do we need more honey or more rolled oats?" The last step in the recipe is to eat the porridge when "just right!"

At this point a large chart was made visible which illustrated the steps of Three Bear Porridge. Visual inspection of the chart helped children answer questions which involved conceptual understanding of the new words.

Figure 27. Visual sequence for kindergartners' Three Bear Porridge.

Finally, children used the new words in verbal exercises and some children experienced their first reading activities. The teacher contributed a language experience story that followed the flow of steps in the actual recipe and which were exemplified on the chart. As one of her final activities, she used the following cloze passage which some children were able to read and most were able to respond to orally:

First, we add the _____. Then we add the _____. Next, we add the _____. After, we add the _____, we add the _____. Then

we add the _____ and stir in the _____. Next, we place the
_____ on the stove and look for the _____. Then, we let the
porridge _____. At last, we add the _____ and eat the
_____, when it is _____:

Vocabulary

rolled oats	hot water
sunflower seeds	covered saucepan
raisins	simmer
chopped apples	honey
powdered milk	"just right"
bubbles	porridge

Use of the Dale Cone of Experience is not just appropriate for the early grades but for the middle and secondary grades as well. Any new body of vocabulary that can be taught through the experiential model will be better understood and remembered. One middle grade teacher taught the vocabulary of types of government by forming different types of governing bodies within her class. A small group of noblemen were selected, while a peasant in debt was brought before a mock trial. By the end of the lesson, the class had visible evidence of the meanings of "tyranny, representation, debtor, resistance and monarch."

A very important conceptual application of the model is that at the abstract representation level, visual symbols or nonverbal representations precede the use of verbal symbols. This is important conceptually for both teacher and student. Students have just experienced a "three dimensional" source of learning, and now they will be asked to reproduce it or understand it in a "two dimensional" form. Teachers are placed in a position where they must visualize how the experience can be represented at the second stage of visual literacy. This forces them to conceptualize if the experience can be best represented through a diagram, a chart, a graph, a map, etc. Students are then encouraged to produce that representation as it captures the "three dimensional" experience. By so doing, they have reconceptualized the event, comprehended it, before they have to put words to it. This is the conceptual base of thinking and literacy as expressed in the earlier model of Moffett and Wagner (see Figure 24).

In Chapter Nine, we will return to the use of nonverbal representation and how its many forms extend mental connections. However, at this point we can see how both stages of visual literacy — the primary, visual-seeking level and the representational conceptual level — can be insightfully woven in one tasteful lesson.

PICTURES: ANALOGUES OF
NATURAL EXPERIENCE

Pictures, as analogues of experience, are one step removed from actual events. Pictures, films, and illustrations strive to capture the immediate, the concrete to make information more readily available than by coding it in a written language form. Duchastel (1978) has commented on the three roles that illustrations serve in texts: first, pictures serve an attention role in which the illustration is used to attract and motivate; secondly, illustrations serve an explicative role in which that which cannot be explained or described is illustrated; and finally, illustrations serve a retentive role whereby the purpose of the illustration is to facilitate recall and memory.

This section will investigate the rules of picture use. We need to consider the interesting questions of whether a syntax exists in picture communication and how pictures communicate literal and interpretive levels of meaning.

Levels of Picture Communication

Becker (1978) maintains that there are two levels of meaning in picture communication. The first level occurs from the representation that the picture literally conveys, that is, most objects depicted are meaningful in and of themselves. The second level of meaning occurs through the organizations of pictures. Certain arrangements or juxtapositions of pictures cause viewers to infer symbolic content. The point, especially in filming and the TV industry, is that the ordering of what is seen is done by someone other than the viewer. The viewer has not directly imposed his/her schema on the picture ordering but reconstructs visual material that has been previously organized by someone else. How these various levels affect the composing process for both visual and verbal literacies will be considered in more detail shortly.

The viewer's intent also has a great bearing on how visual messages will be interpreted. Tversky (1973) has found that both verbal and visual information are acquired and retrieved differently depending on the learner's perceived use of the information. Thus, for picture recognition, if the viewer accepts the organization of a visual sequence as representing the natural order of things, a different interpretive thinking mode will be employed than if symbolic content is presumed lurking in the visual message. If a deeper meaning is presumed, then more complex thinking and possibly more visual scrutiny will undoubtedly be involved. This occurs for the author, for instance, when a Ingmar Bergman movie is about to be seen. Because of prior encounters with Bergman films, a presumption of deeper symbolic content other than a representation of Scandanavian life is expected. When viewing a new film by the same master, a high arousal and expectation level causes greater visual scrutiny to occur in order to gather all the signs of deeper meaning.

Viewer experience and intent coupled with the picture organization influence the verbal and written language that will be used to explicate a viewed experience. This phenomenon has been revealed to the author many, many times in his work using visual arrangements to improve the writing process. This is also why use of picture arrangements and visual compositions can not have "canned or programmed" scripts. Language is brought to the sequences by the individual perceiver. Picture sequences provoke both convergent and divergent thinking dependent upon the experience and intent of the perceiver . . . to limit divergent written language production in a canned format would be very counter-productive to the thinking generated through nonverbal/verbal interaction.

One good example would suffice to show the healthy conflict between teaching intent and student intent and how perceived symbolic content can influence students to react beyond the literal. The author's intent was to project 35 MM slide sequence to a group of reluctant high school adolescents to motivate them to write and to learn a particular type of writing style. The group viewed a sequence about skiers who ascended via a mechanical tow to a mountain top and then descended in various skiing configurations to meet again on the bottom. The intent was very straightforward and literal and most of the group reacted in that way. They wrote at a very literal level revealing in their paragraphs and organization a narrative and descriptive style. They noted the sequence of events and described various aspects of the winter scene they viewed.

However, one Black sophomore turned in a very emotional composition on the social issues separating Blacks and Whites. At a later class period with another 35 MM slide composition, he demonstrated once again a deeper conceptual involvement than other members of the class. He saw a short slide sequence of people visiting a famous, historic monument of ancient Greece. His third draft appears:

> The little people approaching the old buildings escape the tall grass and go inside. The stone tower is seated and watching over the trees and grass, its flowers swaying back and forth in the sunlight. The people in general are falling apart getting older and older. Making way for the new is a little girl who is approaching, taking her place in life. The new is creeping on the old slowly, cautiously moving foward invading the ancient.

From the teacher's perspective, all initial levels of written production evoked from such picture stimulation need to be regarded as acceptable. The initial efforts represent the levels of language, conceptualization, and intent that each student brings to the task. While teachers may not be able to influence the levels of conceptualization and intent that each student contributes to the meaning, teachers can help students polish and repolish acceptable uses of language. Thus, even though 17 year-old Lydia creates some interesting visual pictures in her first few sentences describing the traditional bullfight, the teacher needs to help her during the editing and revising process. Lydia wrote,

> "There are all coming out to the crowd represent there self, late on they start coming back in side so they can start the game. . . "

Using single pictures and picture arrangements to stimulate writing will mean different things to different viewers at different times of their lives. Just as in reading, meaning conveyed through picture arrangement is influenced by prior learnings, intent, and implicit and explicit composition factors (Howie & Sinatra 1982). Metz (1980) has also suggested that the interaction between language and visual forms cannot represent a complete explanation of one for the other. However, one function of visual input is that it can both inspire and be inspired by the language used to describe the visual experience and that one function of language is that particular words can be used to name the parameters that vision delineates and distinguishes.

The Grammar of Pictures

Use of picture arrangements presents another dimension in approximating direct meaning. In the written language we use particular sentence structures and sentence arrangements to state the exact meaning we wish to convey. The explicit sentence meanings are made known by both position and use of signal words which serve a highly important function in expressing sentence relationships. Becker cites Pryluck (1973) who suggests that content works differently for visual and pictorial signs than it does for verbal ones. Visual communication is "structurally inductive" while language is "structurally deductive." Pryluck feels that the two contextual factors of sequencing and juxtaposition are quite important to consider in pictorial communication because relational devices between picture ideas do not exist as they do for language.

Bower (1972) has suggested, on the other hand, that pictures do have a "grammar," in that scenes can be parsed into subpictures which can be "decoded" further into objects and contours. He speculates that a common base grammar underlies our verbal production of sentences and our pictorial analysis and generation. Gestalt laws of perceptual organization, specifically the principles of spatial proximity and similarity, are the phrase-parsing rules of the picture grammar. There are various perceptual organizations that lead to strong associations; these being, the spatial relationships of "is a constituent of, is composed of, is a surface of, is a part of (1972, p. 86)," and these become the basic relational predicates of a picture grammar.

Verbal relational devices are function or signal words which indicate in the oral or written language that ideas will be related and coordinated in some important way. With picture stories, coordination between ideas has to be inferred through the very selection, sequencing, and juxtaposition of the individual pictures that make up the arrangement. Because the "go-betweens" are missing in picture sequencing, students telling or writing of the meaning in picture compositions may be apt to produce more inferential, divergent compositions.

This phenomena can be noted when youngsters use the Photo-Story Discovery Sets published by the Education Markets Services of Eastman Kodak Company (1983). The 30 or so pictures in each set can be arranged by students to create any number of stories. Adding or dropping one picture from a "first draft" photo story alters either the meaning or tone of the story. When pairs of youngsters stand at their desks and arrange and rearrange meaningful stories, one can listen to the insertion of the relational devices that show the direction and creativity of their thought.

How verbal and nonverbal relational devices interact in the two literacy modes is illustrated in the following figure:

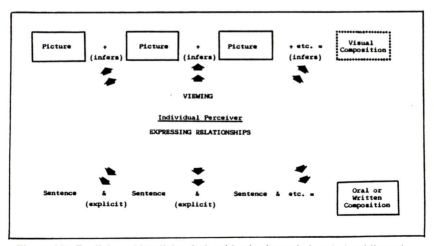

Figure 28. Explicit and implicit relationships in the verbal and visual literacies.

The figure indicates how a sequence or arrangement of pictures allows a perceiver to infer a visualized whole — a visual composition. The visualized whole is made up of a series of separated components called pictures, juxtaposed by theme and content to each supply a continuous thread of meaning that is woven into the overall whole. Individual pictures stimulate thinking and language production, essentially prompting the thinking mode of synthesis. Individual perceivers who will tell or write compositions search for connectedness within the picture composition and compose and connect sentences to explain the relationships they perceive. Notice that the relational devices — the thread that connects the pictures — is inferred while the words and phrases used to connect the sentences are explicit.

Since many students have difficulty expressing relationships between ideas, a good technique to use in simulcast with picture arrangements, is to provide them with transition words and phrases. These transition words are generally the relative pronouns and coordinating and subordinating conjunctions that make the relationships within language explicit. The author has arranged in two earlier sources lists of these function words. In the first source the most frequent connector words in the written language have been arranged in lists to parallel their use in three types of picture story presentations for ESL learners (Sinatra, 1981). In the second arrangement, the connector words were arranged by function and relationship with respect to specific types of sentence construction (Sinatra, 1983a).

Specific lists of connector words and transitional phrases appropriate to particular organizational arrangements can be distributed after students have viewed a visual composition and have begun to write their verbal accounts. The connectives help them organize relationships perceived in the visual presentation and achieve smooth coordination between sentences. For instance, to aid reporting and sequential writing, it is helpful to provide students with transition words and phrases, such as "next . . . meanwhile . . . furthermore . . . besides . . . in addition to . . . therefore . . . consequently" which carry the direction of thought forward. Spatial connectors such as "nearby . . . across . . . above . . . below . . . here" help students organize features as they record descriptive scenes and relate details in proximity to each other. Coordinating conjunctions such as "but . . . however . . . although" will help students contrast ideas as they persuade and theorize. Specific techniques using pictures and spatial configurations to build fluency with connector words will be presented in Chapter Nine.

ANALOGOUS RELATIONSHIP BETWEEN VERBAL AND PICTURE COMPREHENSION

Both Sigel (1978) and Sinatra (1980 & 1983) have suggested that picture comprehension is analogous to reading comprehension in that cognitive processing is involved. During reading and picture viewing, the perceiver must transpose either digital or analogic coding cues to appropriate meaning. While comprehension of the written language and of pictures involves comparable cognitive processes, Sigel maintains that each representational code has a different rule system. He illustrates these two rule systems for comprehension of pictures and of the written language in the following way:

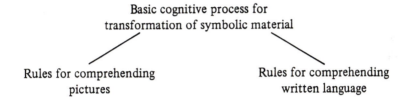

Basic cognitive process for transformation of symbolic material

Rules for comprehending pictures

Rules for comprehending written language

Although a different set of rules governs picture literacy than verbal literacy, the rule common to each is the understanding that objects and/or events can be represented in alternative ways such as through words or pictures. According to Sigel, comprehension of a picture occurs when meaning is extracted from the picture, and when one can relate to the picture as a representation of a referential object or event experienced in the past or projected in the future.

He proposes that a "conservation of meaning" exists with regard to how objects or items can be represented. Conservation of meaning occurs when the meaning of an object remains despite the transformation of the media in which the object is presented. Thus, an apple keeps its identity as an apple whether it is represented by a wax model, a picture, or a word. Changes in media presentation create a different surface representation of the apple, but they do not alter the apple's basic meaning. Variation in the media presentation will of course influence the cues available for appropriate identification. A replica provides more cues than a picture and a picture provides more cues than a word. Sigel concludes that the ability to comprehend picture stimulis is developmental in nature and emerges in children as they acquire the principle of the conservation of any quality.

The development of the conservation of meaning occurs over time and is an acquired knowledge experienced by the youngster as he/she acts on objects. These actions or engagements using motor, haptic, and visual inputs yield knowledge and information. Information, as such is self constructed in that during the course of active engagement, the child comes to learn the rules by which to deal with object constancy and diversity. These rules yield more information that guide the youngsters' subsequent relations with objects or the representation of objects. The conservation of meaning is then "an outcome of the child's interaction with the object world" (1978, p. 107) and is knowledge "constructed through experience with proximal and distal instances" (p. 106).

The concept of the conservation of meaning helps explain the dual relationship that exists in the comprehension of verbal and nonverbal material and the way that the mind can act upon information experienced in the past or envisioned in the future. Conservation of meaning makes use of the two interacting systems discussed at length in Chapter Five, one that deals with sensory, nonverbal information and the other which deals with labeling, verbal behavior. In essence, one cannot really separate picture comprehension from the larger imaginal system of which it is a part. This is because the neural connections establishing pictorial inputs and visionary reflections and projections are found within the same half brain. However, because of the rich interconnections between the verbal and nonverbal systems, we can use words to describe pictures, use words to describe our imagery, and evoke imagery to assist in the selection of words (Bower, 1972).

An analogous relationship between imaginal and verbal literacy which preserves the principle of conversation of meaning may be expressed the following way:

READING: WRITING: VIEWING: VISUAL COMPOSING

Reading and viewing are alike in that both require active, receptive processing of information, while writing and visual composing necessitate selective, often personalized, expressive functioning. Transmitters of information, such as writers and visual composers, encode messages to engage the credibility of receivers while receivers of information, such as viewers and readers, reconstruct those messages to achieve understanding and appreciation. Furthermore, visual composers and writers both strive to achieve unity and coherence in presenting messages to engage the senses, affect, and credibility of audiences. Just as the writer selects words that have emotional connotations, the picture maker conveys images that work on many levels to suggest humor, irony, or symbolic commentary (Eckhardt, 1977).

The analogous relationship can be rearranged to achieve a powerful model of learning for learners of all ages. The model is reflected in the following figure:

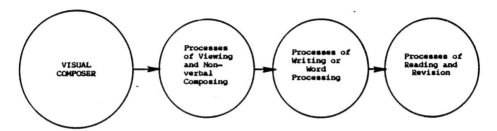

Figure 29. The power of visual composing for literacy learning.

The visual composer is anyone who uses objects and media to design and create meaningful nonverbal messages. Notice that explication of the meaning of the nonverbal can be accomplished through writing or word processing. Secondly, reading and revision naturally occur as a consequence of the creative challenge to use the best language to capture the meaning of the nonverbal. The key to the model is the sensual engagement of the visual composer so that language is precipitated. In it's easiest and most economical form, the model may be implemented with the use of a simple camera.

When students are shown how to compose through the selective, visual eye of the camera, their overall thinking and literacy levels can be improved. This occurs because composers of visual messages can be compared to writers in their roles as transmitters of information. The visual composer learns to combine objects, space, light, angle, and mood to suggest a particular message or effect just as the writer uses words, sentences, and paragraphs to achieve a particular style. The visual composer will also learn that the world often looks a little different through the view finder. The most commonplace object can assume a delightful countenance if photographed under the right conditions and if juxtaposed with the right associative details. Those who start squinting at details of their environment are almost always delighted with the exquisite colors, shades, and textures that materialize before them and suddenly begin to look at the world with an entirely fresh and dynamic point of view (Cameron, 1980).

As composing through the camera's eye heightens one's awareness of the nonverbal, visual world, composing through written language helps one to become a better reader. Moreover, when students become active participants in nonverbal, composing strategies that incorporate verbal strategies as well, they will intellectually benefit from the dual involvement of both brain hemispheres. Both brains will be activated through the visual composing, the imagining and the real and anticipated use of language.

The end product for the visual composer is the completed visual and/or verbal composition. While use of the visual composition strategy to improve writing development will be developed in greater detail in Chapter Nine, the author has suggested elsewhere that of the four ways that visual compositions can be prepared, the most intellectually rewarding way is when they are photographed by the individual student (Sinatra, 1983b). This is not as simple as it appears in popular TV commercials. Rather than providing students with cameras and turning them loose to shoot indiscriminate subjects and events, they must be trained beforehand to compose a central theme. This means they have to visualize the whole effect of their visual story before they start shooting the individual parts. This mental activity will help them when they come to the task of writing the composition based on the organization and content of the visual composition.

SOME SUCCESSFUL VISUAL COMPOSING PROJECTS

Let's turn our attention to a few visual literacy projects in which groups of learners were trained to become visual composers. Many more visual literacy curriculum strategies will be enumerated in the final chapter and Appendix A will list a host of visual literacy resource guides. The object here is to focus on the results of a few large-scale programs in which visual composing made a difference in subsequent verbal literacy growth. In Project Beacon (Kodak Education Market Services, 1976), minority children in one experimental first grade class in Rochester, New York made dramatic gains in reading after involvement in a reading program using motion picture cameras. The Project Beacon experimental youngsters averaged 50 percent higher in reading than the test scores for a control class and they performed better than fourteen other first grade classes, including six classes with exceptionally low student-to-teacher ratios and two from high socioeconomic areas.

By the year's end several children in the experimental class were reading at third grade level or better, and the average gain for the entire class was one year and six months growth in reading.

How did these Black, inner-city children achieve such great success? They essentially made their own movies as a primary learning experience before reading occurred. The technique followed this nonverbal/verbal interaction:

1. The children suggested a theme or topic for a Super 8 movie they wanted to make. Under the teacher's guidance, the youngsters developed an experience vocabulary which were the words necessary to develop and describe the theme.
2. The teacher then reviewed the experience vocabulary list with the word list in their basal reading book. Any other words listed in the basal which pertained to the movie topic were added to the experience vocabulary. Using this completed word bank, the story action was planned, and large cue cards were written to help direct the action of the film sequence.
3. Children were next assigned to camera and actor roles.
4. The movie was rehearsed for sequence and length. During this phase, body and gesture language were linked to verbal language.
5. The cue cards were filmed along with the live action that the cue cards told about.
6. The completed film was projected and reviewed by the whole class.
7. Finally, the children proceeded to read many of the words that were used in the visual story presentation in their basal reading selections.

In a second project also aimed at low functioning youngsters, photography and the ability to "read" photo-stories were the key curriculum components (Fransecky, 1969). In this visual literacy project over 100 migrant youths in grades one, two, and three were randomly assigned to experimental and control classes. The project concern was to discover if migrant children whose experiential level was limited and based on a farming way of life would demonstrate differences in literacy learning when instruction was based on photo and visual training materials as the primary curriculum source. Little if any traditional reading materials such as books, reading kits, or basal readers were used in the reading program in the experimental classes. Rather, a visual/verbal notebook was the major source of reading material.

In the first and second grades, a significantly larger percentage of pupils in the experimental classes achieved from five to nine months growth in Reading as measured by the **Wide Range Achievement Test** compared to the migrant students in the control classes. In the third grade, 8 students in a class of 13 experimental students made from five to nine months in reading growth where in the comparable control class only 2 pupils out of 14 demonstrated a similar gain.

Two project implementations deserve special attention. The first was that the youngsters' photographic stories were processed rapidly to insure quick feedback and to sustain high motivation. The second was that the visual/verbal notebook was the source for the recording of the meaning in the photographic stories and for other visual experiences. The notebook, like a personal visual/verbal diary, was a successful way to achieve coordination between the pictorial representation of experience and the oral and written modes of language.

A rather large-scale visual communication program has been described in a three-part series in **Audiovisual Instruction** (Fransecky and Ferguson, 1973). The Milford, Ohio Visual Communication Project, K-12, involved elementary and secondary school students in a series of visual communications activities integrated with the district's ongoing language arts, science, mathematics, and social studies programs. Some of the visual communications activities were drawing, use of Photo Discovery Sets, use of pictures or slides to describe a process, use of the camera, and use of the slide projector. The goal for the student was to become capable of producing and receiving a broad range of discourse forms and visual/verbal language structures through a series of five phases implemented through the grades. Research results revealed that for 314 second, third, and fourth graders involved in the visual literacy project, a significant interaction emerged for visual literacy treatments by grade level and reading achievement.

A final project, conducted in Wilmington, Delaware, focused on the ability of the inner-city child to improve in communication skills and self concept when involved in filmmaking activities (Hairston and Cooper, 1973). A major objective of the program was to improve the self-concept and the ability to communicate and evaluate ideas of fourth and fifth grade inner-city children using the motivational forces of filmmaking with cultural experiences. Results comparing 71 students in the experimental group with 56 students in a control group showed that for the experimental group a significant ($p > .02$) self-concept emerged.

Furthermore, improved personal and group relationships, improved self-expression, and improved class attendance were observed in experimental students involved in the filmmaking activities. A listing of their activities included the following: planning, researching, and script writing for filmmaking; story boarding; role playing; artistic creation for props and scenery; filming; viewing unedited film; learning to edit, evaluate, and re-film; recording of dialogue and selection of accompanying mime, and final editing of a film.

THE VISUAL VALUE OF PRINTED TEXT

Braden (1983) raises an interesting point about the complementary value of words to images and vice versa. When we think of illustrations in text, we usually think of nonverbal representations in the form of pictures, photographs, or drawings. But what about the visual value of text itself? Braden maintains that when verbal language becomes visible in written form, certain text features such as typography, typographical cuing, printing conventions, format, and layout aid understanding. Typographing cuing and page layout, for instance, are used for their visual input, to enhance the meaning of certain parts of text for readers.

A type of format that uses both verbal and nonverbal features to enhance meaning and audience impact is the outline graphic. Braden defines the outline graphic as "a form of visual display . . . well suited for use in instructional settings where complex verbal information is to be learned . . . and which provides concurrent access to both visual and verbal elements (1983, p. 153).

Every outline graphic has four basic characteristics that serve to enrich the correlation between verbal and visual literacies. The content of the outline is skeletal and its form, therefore, parallels the qualities of a written outline. Secondly, the display of information within the outline has a visual component which transcends the simple denotating of text. For instance, such features as spatial arrangement, border design, artistic spacing, and boxing-in to chunk or segment content are used to connotatively suggest or highlight meaning. Third, the outline graphic is orderly. As the graphic is used to enrich and organize verbal material, the nature of the subject matter will directly influence the type of order imposed. Some outlines will be linear in configuration, others will be hierarchical, and others may have a loose application of subtopics. A final important quality of outline graphics is that they are holistic. All of the verbal and nonverbal components are arranged in an orderly framework in which the relationships of components are visually made known to each other.

Two types of outline graphics constructed by Braden are illustrated in Figures 30 and 31. Each presents in graphic organization, the holistic effect of the same presentation. Figure 30 shows how the outline can be organized around a central element. The title of the design is abbreviated, another feature to draw attention to the center triangle. The triangle shape calls attention, as well, to the three-leveled nature of the topic, visual displays. The arrows allow the eye to focus on each of the three separate components that make up the whole.

The same information found in Figure 30 is arranged differently in Figure 31. Now the central meaning is housed in a circle and the subtopics and their components are arranged around the central figure. This layout tends to emphasize the relationship of the components to each other. While the overall effect is integrative, the size of the boxes and rectangles also implies a hierarchical relationship.

How the idea of graphic outlining can be used to help students organize and retain printed information will be reexamined in Chapter Nine. There we will investigate how the notion of semantic mapping integrates the theoretical constructs of schema theory with the practical

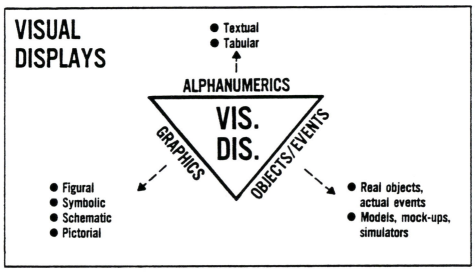

Figure 30. Outline graphics with component clusters. From R.A. Braden and A.D. Walker: *Visualizing the verbal and verbalizing the visual.* In R.A. Braden and A.D. Walker (Eds.), *Seeing Ourselves: Visualization in a Social Context.* Blacksburg, VA.: Virginia Polytechnic Inst. and State University, 1983. Courtesy of R.A. Braden and A.D. Walker.

application of graphic outlining. Some research also confirms that advance organizers in the form of graphic organizers, outlines, and even preparatory instruction assists in the structuring of forthcoming communication and aids the lower ability student (Allen, 1975). For now, the imagination of the reader can be stirred by noting that some schema theorists refer to the circles, boxes, and rectangles of Figures 30 and 31 as "concepts."

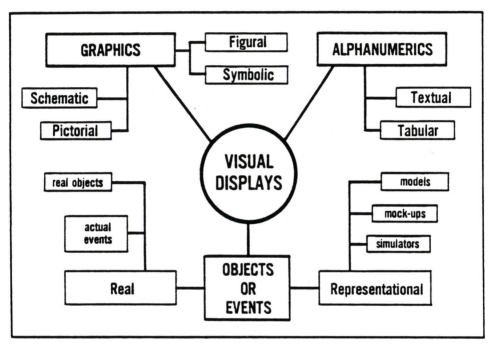

Figure 31. Intergrative outline graphic showing adajacent-component relationships. From R.A. Braden and A.D. Walker: Visualizing the verbal and verbalizing the visual. In R.A. Braden and A.D. Walker (Eds.), *Seeing Ourselves: Visualization in a Social Context*. Blacksburg, VA.: Virginia Polytechnic Inst. and State University, 1983. Courtesy of R.A. Braden and A.D. Walker.

CHAPTER EIGHT

THE VISIONARY ASPECTS OF COMPOSING
AND COMPREHENDING

THE ISSUES of comprehension and composition consistently remain at the forefront of education. Comprehending does represent the essence of the reading act as composition, the goal of transcribing. A pedagogical fallacy occurs, however, in that comprehension is abstracted from the reading process and transfixed as a separate skill taught in isolation. Accordingly, we are flooded with numerous skillbooks and discrete lesson pages designed to polish the "thinking" of reading comprehension. However, as discussed in earlier chapters, comprehension is conditioned by the discourse of which it is a part and becomes illuminated through relationships self-discovered within the whole. This self-discovery is stimulated by the thinking of synthesis, which is the thinking of connectedness and creativity.

Possibly the skills approach has served a short-lived purpose. It has allowed us to focus on the numerous components of written literacy and to try to define its parts. But now educators must realize the need to move beyond the parts perspective, especially for those learners who have experienced difficulty with the integration of parts. The parts approach repeated day after day in school after school and conditions learners, who are visually and verbally literate, what to look for and how to analyze but not how to think and to synthesize during vital times of communication.

Synthesis, the reader will recall, requires a search for connectedness. It becomes a discovery of the nature of relations among different things. This thinking occurs, for instance, during the reading of a story or novel in which the reader sees how the characters and plots interact with one another to bring about a feeling of enjoyment and fulfillment. It occurs during writing when the writer composes sentences with particular word arrangements that convey the intent the writer is visualizing. Synthesis requires the higher thought processes of evaluation, justification, classifying, grouping, and preceiving how things are alike or different. The individual thinker must perceive how parts are joined, related, or different without being told that they are so. Teachers can point out how a combination of sounds make a word, how the combination of functional parts make a sentence, or how many key episodes there are in a story, but the meaning and relationship of each part to the whole is not there until it is individually synthesized by each student. This visualization of relation, along with flashes of insight that often accompany synthesis, is a major function of right-brain thinking.

A similar issue has faced composition, regarded as the highest achievement in the expressive use of written language. Composition subsumes those visible parts of which it is composed such as agreement, spelling, punctuating, and handwriting. From discussion raised in Chapters Two and Seven, the reader will recall that the visible features of written language represent the tip-of-the-iceberg aspects of composition. The more important levels of composition, however, lie below the manifestations on the printed page and are based on the writer's intent and his/her ability to relate, to report, to record, to inform, to persuade, and to speculate.

The focus of this chapter is to explore not the visible but the visionary aspects of comprehending and composition. This visionary look forces us to turn inward to explore in greater depth the workings and contributions of imagery. We will see that many prominent writers and scholars in the field of education are propelled by the visionary nature of thought as they produce their own works.

Notice that the words discussed so far, "composing, comprehending, communication, and composition," are related by a prefix identity. The Latin prefix "com" means to bring together the parts into a related whole, and the recognizable relationship among these words is that they all involve similar synthesizing, integrating, and combining functions (Howie and Sinatra, 1982). In order to communicate during reading and writing, one must synthesize bits of information into meaningful, integrated text, defined as a group of related sentences which have cohesion, unity, and structure. The core of communication expressed through comprehending and composing has an internal visionary factor which often influences the very quality of the communication.

THE GENESIS OF COMPOSING AND COMPREHENDING

When does the ability to "com" begin in communication? It begins very early in life as discussed in Chapters One and Two when the youngster develops representational thought. We saw that for young children, representational thought can be expressed in a number of ways such as through gesture and body language, play, modeling, construction tasks, and even computer programming or flowcharting. The Russian psychologist, Vygotsky, claims that gesture of itself is the child's developmental stepping stone in the progress to written language. In his **A Prehistory of Written Language**, Vygotsky (1978) writes that gesture is "the initial visual sign that contains the child's future writing as an acorn contains a future oak." The child's earliest scribbles on paper are actually a form of gestural representation. These scribbles later become drawings of simple pictures and stick figures that represent the meaning of children's thought. A major breakthrough occurs, of course, when the child realizes that he/she can make pictures of not only things that represent the environment but also can **draw or make the figures** that represent speech. Adults call this latter stage, writing.

Let's look at some children's earliest attempts of composition. Kindergartner Michael was requested to write about something that was his favorite. Notice how in his selection of Spiderman, written "Sptman," he represented the strength of his favorite character with the illuminated biceps. Furthermore, that strength is further realized in the written message "Stop you NA." The picture here is the force, the energy of the text.

Figure 32. Kindergartner's composition in which picture is force of message.

Notice in the following two compositions of first graders how the picture is used as part of the text. There is enough discourse to obtain a meaning of why each child selected his/her favorite place. However, the picture still adds information that undoubtedly each child could not express yet in the written mode. A good amount of that information is affective in nature. The child on the left likes Trinidad because her nice cousins live there. In her picture, the reader can sense the warmth of the bigger and older cousins. The music room is selected as the second child's favorite place because of the feeling he has for the teacher. You can see the pleasant effect the teacher has on the youngsters in the room.

Figure 33. Two, first grade compositions showing affective nature of pictures.

The next child, however, is a bit further along in school. Her reasons for choosing the acquarium as her favorite place are quite clearly expressed. The written communication is full and can stand alone. The picture in this example is used to embellish text. It is added as a pleasant afterthought, left over from the days of the "Spiderman" period in which pictures were the generating force of expressive communication.

E. Paul Torrance (1979) writing on the topic of "Creativity and Its Educational Implications" goes one step further in the explanation of children's art. He believes that the power of such methods in which children's production of art leads to another form of expression lies in the belief that "creativity excites creativity." For instance, creative poetry can

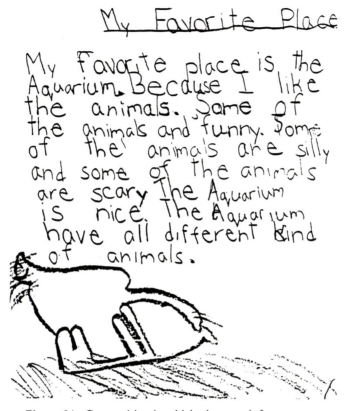

My Favorite Place

My Favorite place is the Aquarium. Because I like the animals. Same of the animals and funny. Some of the animals are silly and some of the animals are scary The Aquarium is nice. The Aquarium have all different kind of animals.

Figure 34. Composition in which picture reinforces text.

stimulate the scientist, and the discoveries of the scientist can mentally stimulate the creative imagination of the poet. Torrance explains that the more creative acts a person experiences, whether they be those of another or the person's alone, the more richly the person lives. Anything that makes such a person more alive is likely to facilitate and produce creative achievement. How does Torrance accomplish this with young learners? In setting the stage for the creative process, he has learners produce something like a drawing, a story, a papier-maché animal and do something with what they have produced. This something necessitates the thinking mode of synthesis, emanating in part from the nonverbal right-brain, and in part from the prefrontal corted, to result in a new mode of expression through another language form. This form can be written expression accomplished through paper and pencil or through word processing.

While Torrance focuses on art as a means of creative expression, the reader may recall that the art educators discussed in Chapter Two saw art as the sensory raw material of communication. The raw material provides the very basis of visions.

INNER VISIONS

This process of synthesizing is considered by many to be "visionary." Moffett feels that gazing and visualization are the precursers to this type of vision (1982). Gazing or staring, he maintains, is the young child's means of meditation and the main way he or she learns. By paying rapt attention through spontaneous gazing, the child receives direct knowledge without the necessity for discourse. Such was the thesis of Chapter One, explaining that Visual Literacy is the preemptive literacy of thought.

Visualization arises from gazing and may be considered synonymous with nonverbal representational thought of Figure 1. During visualization, the thinker or writer gazes inward where inner attention and imagination flourish without the necessity for verbalization. By suspending oneself in the inner vision, the writer can feel the strength of self. Moffett writes:

> Writing presupposes just such inner strength. A writer of whatever age has to feel full of herself and have a degree of confidence, belief that she has something to say, faith in her will, and control of her attention. Gazing and visualizing, finally, develop **vision** — seeing and perceiving in both outer and inner ways prerequisite for writing (1982, p. 236).

Another writer considers the visionary aspect of writing to be a process of discovery. Donald Murray (1978) suggests that the processes of writing as discovery are three: prevision, vision, and revision. Prevision encompasses the selection and limiting of a topic and use of any internal or external force that precedes the production of the first draft. The writer's previous experiences embedded in imagery, observation, previous writing, research, discussion, interviewing, reading, and picture viewing serve to assist the writer to preview one topic before writing about it. Murray uses the word "vision" itself to represent the first draft. The first draft serves as a discovery draft in that it is written so that its parameters can be viewed. Revision is what Murray considers to be the most important aspect of the discovery process. It is the clarification of self, originally captured in the singular vision of the first draft.

Unfortunately, revision is the least emphasized aspect of the writing process. This may be because many educators do not write themselves and therefore do not understand nor appreciate the need for clarification of thought that occurs during revision. Certainly, educators write reports and memos that are direct communiqués in their official lives. But the writing of composition which is invariably a major function of schooling needs to go through levels of discovery for teacher as well as student. In this way, teachers will shift from a first communiqué perspective to one where the labor of visions is rewarding through repeated drafts.

A second problem encountered in the understanding of revision is its confusion for editing and proofreading. When students are asked to revise their first writing efforts, they are generally conditioned what to look for in way of surface or "tip-of-the-iceberg" correctness. They are not conditioned in the search for discovery found in the message. Students need to believe that "writing is rewriting" (Murray, 1978, p. 85). During revision, editing and proofing are just part of the process. But it is the discovery aspect of revision that guides the mind's eye as it explores the most complete way to voice the message. Revision, then, fulfills the intuitive thinking of prevision and represents what Moffett (1982) considers the strength of self. It is the latter which needs to be rewarded during the composition process.

In Donald Grave's figure showing children's consciousness of the levels of writing, the reader can see that revision is the last category of which children become aware (1982).

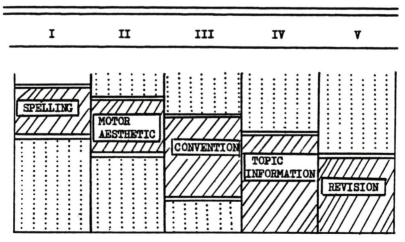

Figure 35. Child's consciousness of problem solving during writing. From Donald Graves: Research update: How do writers develop. *Language Arts, 59*: 173-179. Reprinted with permission. Courtesy of Teachers of English, Feb. 13, 1984.

The diagonal lines on the figure show when children consider the category important. For instance, in early writing children are most preoccupied with spelling because they can't show the message to anyone if it can't be read at face value. Then they are next concerned with being neat and then with the mechanics or conventions of written language. Graves suggests that some writers never get beyond the first three categories, and, moreover, dependent on the focus of the teacher and school, "the child will not learn to take ownership of the selection, the best means to solving issues in the first three tracks (I to III)" (1982, p. 178). The dots suggest when children are not aware or conscious of the category yet they may be involved in it. When the dots are above the category areas of II, III, IV, and V, the younger writer is just becoming or barely involved in that category and therefore is not fully aware of its importance. When the dots are found below as in tracks I, II, and III, the category is more automatic and it does not occupy the child's conscious mind.

Graves points out, however, that all five categories exist in the lives of writers whether they be six year old beginners or professionals. Furthermore, the writer must function in all five tracks each time they are involved in a written work. Children cite the importance of the categories as they appear in the figure because this is undoubtedly the way they are conditioned to regard the levels of writing. "What teachers emphasize in class becomes the center of child imbalance" (Graves, 1982, p. 178).

A vital aspect of revision is the momentary crystalization of flickers of imagery. During these flickers, the writer reviews images of the past or previews images projected out of the sensory, creative mind. We saw in earlier chapters that concrete imagery is a function of right hemisphere processing and could also be considered a basis of the "schemes" or schemeta a thinker holds in his/her imaginary store. During composing and revision, it is more than the nonverbal contributions of imagery that direct the thinking of the writer. The schemeta are also composed of the connective links that form among the categories of language interaction noted in Graves' figure and among the images themselves. For instance, a writer can visualize the relationship of the meaning of one image to another, but he/she needs the words, the means of writing or typing, the grammar, and the connection of meanings to harmonize a whole, a discourse.

The inner search for these harmonious relationships requires the thinking of synthesis, composed of both verbal and nonverbal interactions. Synthesis, moreover, is the energizing component of composing and comprehending. While both processes have been dichotomized into the more familiar fields of writing and reading, the underlying thought connecting both is similar. A number of educators, today are aware of this basic inner relationship between the two fields as evidenced in these journal articles: "Using a Writing Model to Teach Reading" (Trosky and Wood, 1982), "The Role of Writing in Developmental Reading" (Stotsky, 1982), "How Reading Affects Children's Writing" (Eckhoff, 1983), "Toward a Composing Model of Reading" (Tierney and Pearson, 1983), "Writing and the Teaching of Reading" (Wittrock, 1983), "Composing and Comprehending: Two Sides of the Same Basic Process" (Squire, 1983), and "Research on Reading/Writing Relationships: A Synthesis and Suggested Direction" (Stotsky, 1983).

Tierney and Pearson (1983) suggest that the reader tackle the reading process as the writer does the revision process, with the same discovery mind. They write, "If readers are to develop some control over a sense of discovery with the models of meaning they build, they must approach text with the same deliberation, time, and reflection that a writer employs as she revises a text" (1983, p. 576).

In Trosky and Wood's process model (1982), the writer initially builds relationships in writing before uncovering similar relationships found in other written sources. The model of Visual Composing found in Chapter Seven and redirected in Chapter Nine offers a nonverbal construct as the preliminary mode of involvement, followed by writing, then reading. The visual composition model may be more appropriate, then, for those youngsters who have difficulty with expressing themselves in writing, have difficulty with the conceptualization of ideas, or who are more nonverbally biased or motivated. The visual composition serves as the stimulus of prevision (one of the many possibilities noted by Murray), but it is still revision that guides the writer through the many stages of draft.

The Strength of Associative Learning

To return to the discussion raised in Chapters Four and Five, we recall that imagery is based on strong right hemisphere functioning, that it is fast, concrete, and vivid, and that it can be manipulated to stir and arouse creative imagination. We note further in this chapter that imagery is a strong component of the visionary aspects of composing and comprehending and can activate and embellish the verbal system during the very time of composing and writing. It is also important to emphasize that visuospatial images can be stimulated by the verbal system. Images representative of direct experience and its analagous forms as well as metaphorical representations of both can be associatively aroused through verbal stimulation. This is how we generate mental images during silent reading and how we can stir the imagination of youngsters during story telling and poetry. In fact, when visual imagery is aroused and associated with verbal messages, comprehension, retention, and production of verbal language is strengthened (Paivio, 1979).

Bower (1972) maintains that in most associative learning both the imaginal and verbal systems can be involved. Because the two systems have very rich interconnections between them, we can use words to describe pictures, use words to describe our imagery, and evoke imagery to assist in the selection of words. When words are to be learned, the verbal system is clearly involved and the imaginal system may be engaged based on the strength of the associative connections between the verbal and imaginal content.

Bugelski (1977), Becker (1978), and Paivio (1980) also affirm the existence of two richly connected information banks which cooperate during the thinking process. Becker (1978) suggests that while these are multiple communicative sources from which we gather information, we create meaning from information gathered simultaneously through aural and visual tracks and from interactions that have been sensed at different points in time. These past interactions should not be thought of as static according to Bugelski (1977). He does not equate the image as a noun or as a thing in itself. He sees imagery as a dynamic activity in which the image is an action or a reaction, probably neurally based, which generates other neural or motoric behaviors. A current neural reaction which may be based on the reactivation of an earlier lived sensory reaction can be fleeting and unconscious. Moreover, the language that may be associated with a dynamic image may be tied to the modality that was activated when the sensory activity was lived. In Paivio's view (1980) the dynamic and creative imaginal systems override language in human learning. He views cognition as an elaborate audiovisual system in which knowledge of the world is likened to an "elaborate film library with verbal commentaries" (1980, p. 296).

Several additional concerns arise in the discussion of imagery. Do we, for instance, have reasonably accurate proof that imagery is indeed a right hemisphere mode of processing? Secondly, what happens when imagery is provoked during reading or writing or as a conscious, goal-directed activity? Finally, what is imagery's relation to creative imagination and giftedness?

RIGHT HEMISPHERE ACTIVATION DURING IMAGERY

In the 22 separate batteries measuring laterality and cognitive style administered to approximately 45 normal functioning adults and adolescents, Metcalf (1975) found with EEG tracings that the most powerful stimulation of right hemisphere activity for almost all subjects was the "mental trip" task. During this task the subject was asked to take a journey with his or her eyes closed and to visualize that journey.

Using the electroencephalogram (EEG) with college freshmen, Glassner (1980) investigated which brain hemisphere was engaged during the writing of two types of discourse — one, a factual account of a process and, second, the recall of a closely felt experience. He found that interhemispheric interaction does occur even when the writer tries to focus on a factual account and convey a literal message to another. He noted that while writing as a human activity presents itself in a linear form, its processes incorporate nonlinear, nonverbal forms of thought. In other words, the writer is engaged in mental imagery as the pen or pencil is sequencing the thoughts in the act of writing.

That differential hemispheric activity goes on during differing cognitive tasks was also demonstrated in one landmark study with 18 young children (Kraft, et al., 1980). An individual electroencephalogram (EEG) was recorded on each child while he or she was engaged in essentially three types of tasks. The first task involved watching the visuospatial transformation of material based on Piaget's conservation tasks, the second involved using the oral language to logically explain what happened during the physical transformation stage, and the third involved reading about what had happened and then answering four questions about the reading passage.

It was found that greater right hemisphere activity was recorded during the transformation of material tasks which required a physical change of concrete form and during the silent reading of the passage. Furthermore, greater left hemisphere activation occurred when children had to talk about and justify what occurred during the physical change stage and during the time when they had to think about and answer the comprehension questions relating to the reading passage.

It was especially revealing that greater right hemisphere activation was indicated for the six-to-eight-year-old children during the silent reading of the passage rather than during answering questions about the content. Since the children read a passage about an experience they had just previously witnessed, they were undoubtedly engaged in imagery, a visual representation of that experience. When reading involves a spatial, thinking component as when information is recalled in parallel through the process of imagery, the right hemisphere is apparently activated. It is during the answering of questions, when the mind has to logically reformulate the information to answer what was specifically asked and then verbally express the answer, does the left hemisphere come into play.

PROVOKING IMAGERY DURING COMPREHENSION

While Glassner showed how imagery functions during writing (1980), Levin (1973) and Yarmey and Bowen (1972) reported the effects of visual imagery on reading comprehension. In the Levin study, one group of disabled readers having sufficient decoding skills but lacking organizational strategies was asked to imagine a picture for each sentence used in a story. This group scored 40 percent higher in comprehension than a matched group of disabled readers who were asked to read the story alone. Levin felt that the visual imagining aided the poor readers' organizational strategies unconsciously allowing them to integrate verbal and visual input. Yarmey and Bowen found that both educable retarded and normal children performed better in comprehension when they were asked to generate a visual image corresponding to each sentence of a story.

Will reading educators make use of the enlightening findings of the 1979-1980 national assessment of reading and literature (National Assessment of Educational Progress, 1982)? The 9, 13, and 17-year-olds who reported that they read fiction scored higher on reading comprehension exercises than those who read mostly nonfiction and those who reported they do not read in their spare time. The fiction readers are undoubtedly involved in experiences of the imagination and thereby reconstruct meaning to fit their lived and imaginary notions about the world.

What happens during the reading of fiction to influence the powers of comprehension, often believed to be a school-related skill or subject? During fictional reading, we imagine, we reconstruct, we represent the language of the author to conform to our schema. Of course, the more vivid, colorful, and exciting the fiction, the more we are apt to greedily rush along, taking big visual chunks to convert to mental imagery. The more we become involved and the more we enjoy, the more likely we are to activate the reticular formation and the limbic system to flavor the imagery with emotion and resistance to forgetting. Compare this mental processing with that of the reading often conducted in school in which information is to be remembered. If students do not have the schemata for some of the things they read about, how can they convert the information to imagery to reduce the verbal memory load?

PROVOKED IMAGERY DURING WRITING

Imagery can be intentionally stimulated by the teacher as a means of improving written content and output. Imagery can be aroused in a number of ways (Sinatra and Stahl-Gemake, 1983); however, some techniques are quite easy and can generate some rather good writing. Because illustrations are often used in young children's reading selections to help them concretize the reading experience, pictures and drawings can be used initially to expand imagination. Students can be asked to close their eyes and "step into" the illustration. Youngsters are asked to describe what they feel, smell, taste, see, and hear as they move and interact with features of the illustration. Because students have read the selection up to the placement of the illustration, they have enough understanding of the storyline to write highly imaginative but plausible story conclusions.

When the imagination is stimulated for a pre-writing experience without the use of a concrete stimulus such as a picture, the student should be put in a restful, calm state while questions are posed by the teacher. The questions are not directed at the content of the topic, but are used to arouse sensual impressions. For instance, the teacher places a topic on the chalkboard such as "Tell About Your Favorite Place" or "Tell About Your Trip to Another Planet" while blank paper lies on the desk in front of each student. The lighting in the room is lowered as youngsters are asked to place their heads on their desks and close their eyes. With eyes closed and extraneous stimulation eliminated, students are asked to see the topic in their imaginations. They can be asked to focus on their topic just as they would focus through the lens of a camera or telescope. The teacher, meanwhile, delivers such questions as:

What are some of the things you see in your imagination?

Jot them down quickly on your paper.

What do you feel about the things you see?

Do you hear any sounds?

Are there ways you want to move when you see certain things in your mental picture?

Do you want to feel and touch certain parts in your picture?

Are there any certain smells or tastes?

Students compose their first drafts while in the dimmed light situation and while imagery-stimulating questions such as those above are proposed. The reader can see that third grade Veronica was enticed to write a coherent first draft that contains many imaginative and sensual words:

Tell About Your Imaginary Trip to Another Planet

by Veronica, 3rd grade

The planet I am visiting is very soft. It feels very weard it feels like the moon. You can hear alot of sounds like little creachers making little squeaks.

It looks like a place were they keep alot of spaceships and alot of creachers. It is high up in the sky and oter space. I like it there I would like to stay there for a hole day but I would miss my parents and if I stood there for a day I wouldn't know what to say to the creachers.

Here is another way that one imaginative, third grade teacher stimulated the visualizing powers of her students in an activity which integrated all aspects of the language arts. Mrs. Barbara Schrift Genen had been a former teacher of gifted children and turned her creative talents loose on inner-city, third graders, at P.S. 29, Bronx, New York. Of her 30 or so children, 18 had been holdovers at either first, second or third grade due to below level achievement in reading as measured by city-wide standardized testing.

Mrs. Genen's aim was to have the children produce a personalized, written composition by having them pretend they were a particular object. She developed the lesson and the children's visualizing, affective behavior in a nicely coordinated series of stages. Her lead-in was literature. After having children listen to the **Steadfast Tin Soldier** by Hans Christian Anderson, she developed the concept that a writer makes believe that objects such as the toy soldier and the ballerina can talk and have feelings since in real life these objects can't do these things. Then she had the children listen to a story that a young child had composed about another object.

The young girl, pretending she was a tree, gave the tree life and emotions as she wrote:

> Hi! I'm Tom Tree. I am very tall. I have many leaves on me. Sometimes children climb on me and break my branches. OO! That hurts! Other children use a knife to write their names on me. I hate that. Oh! Oh! Here come some men with a saw. They are going to cut me up and use me in a fireplace. Then I'll burn and that will be the end of me. Boo! Hoo!

Then, acknowledging some of Tom Tree's inanimate friends, book, pencil, car, and shoe, which were displayed on a picture of a tree subsequently produced by Mrs. Genen, she asked the entire group to select one of those friends and breathe some life into it. In a cooperative effort, seated in a circle with teacher in the middle, the children closed their eyes and assumed the character of their choice, Mr. Pencil. They thought of how Mr. Pencil looked, of what people did with him, and how he felt when people did certain things to him that made him sad. As children provided comments and sentences, Mrs. Genen developed a language experience story which the children heard read to them and which they read chorally and in some cases individually.

Finally, they were asked to become one of the three remaining objects or to select one object of their choice, and write a paper telling what the object would say if it could talk. They were asked to consider:

a. Who they pretended to be and how the particular object looked,
b. What people did with the object, and
c. How they felt when people did certain things to the object they pretended to be.

After individually writing their stories, they were asked to share them with the rest of the group. While one child read his personalized account, the others listened with the following critical set of criteria and reacted to the student writer at the end of his/her reading.

1. Did the writer tell what the object looked like?
2. Did he/she tell what people actually did to this object?
3. Did he/she tell how the object felt when these things were done?
4. Was there anything that the writer might have added to the story?

One of the many stories completed by the third grade class is printed below. The reader can note how Edwin remained faithful to the topic and was able to make his book seem sensitive and alive.

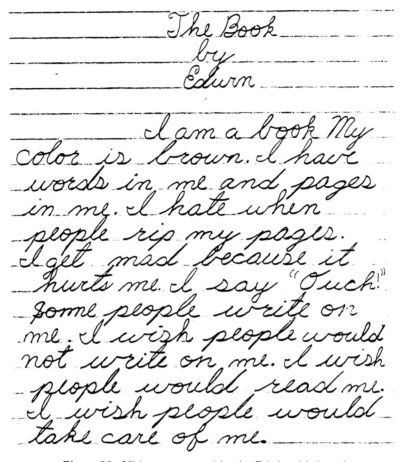

Figure 36. Visionary composition by Edwin, third grader.

The strengths of such an interactive approach are the following:

1. A transition was made from a literacy work written by a renowned author to a personalized account written by a peer.
2. Children began and worked at the whole discourse level. They heard several entire selections read and were asked to visualize certain things about an object as they wrote.
3. They cooperatively evolved a story and saw that story turned into a written form.
4. Finally, when children were asked to write their own accounts, there was no problem about visualizing what to write about. They had seen, listened to, and felt the experiences of other objects while the global characteristics of right brain functioning were supplying the images and textures to their individual objects.

When the imagery-stimulating technique was used with 20 adolescents in a state youth facility, their writing was as good as when they had slide sequences and lists of information relating to a topic to write about (Sinatra, 1984). Interestingly, their improvement over a prestudy composition was 36 percent for Imagery Writing and 40 percent for Report Writing. In Report Writing, a list of 10 to 12 randomly ordered sentence fragments appeared on a printed page and the students have to weave a coherent report based on the information. During Imagery Writing, all the information came from each student's imagination; there were no printed sources to which to refer.

IMAGERY, VISIONS, AND CREATIVITY

There exists ample documentation about the behavior patterns and mind processes of gifted and creative individuals to know how they thought when they processed ideas at the level of creativity. This documentation is found in many of the readings in the book **Educating the Ablest** (Gowan, Khatena, and Torrence, 1979) particularly in the writings of Gowan printed in that source and elsewhere (Gowan; 1978, 1979) and in the writings of Khatena (1977; 1978).

Khatena relates the activity of creative imagination with emotional energy as he writes:

> Much of brain activity relative to the creative imagination has to do with imagery on the re-experiencing of images. My recent research on the creative imagination led me to define the functions of the imagination as the chemistry of mental processing where interactive intellectual and emotional forces participate in stimulating, energizing and propogating the creative act (1978, p. 227).

This emotional input is much akin to the right hemisphere insights discussed by Ross (1982) and Levy (1983) in Chapter Four. They felt that the challenged brain demands more energy and that full and rich language comprehension requires right hemisphere contributions. Normal brains are made to be challenged and "they only operate at optimal levels when cognitive processing requirements are of sufficient complexity to activate both sides of the brain and provide a mutual facilitation between hemispheres as they integrate their simultaneous activation" (Levy, 1983, p. 70). Moreover, because the right hemisphere plays a large role in general activation, arousal functions, and emotion, when the student has the motivation and interest to learn a particular content or skill, both brain hemispheres will be activated, adds Levy.

Thus, regardless of the way the content or skill is being offered, motivation and arousal can supply a large energy source in the learning of that content or skill. This notion is consistent with the concept of the metacontrol system discussed in Chapter Six. If, for instance, a youngster is involved in word attack experiences or lists of arithmetic computation problems, which appear to require a left hemisphere processing mode, the right hemisphere could lead in the mental activation used in these tasks if the youngster **likes** and **gets enjoyment** from doing these activities. If, on the other hand, high-achieving, gifted youngsters find such rote tasks boring, then a good amount of their potential brain energy becomes dysfunctional. In this vein, Wiles and Bondi (1980) contend that many learning experiences in schools are either peripheral or actually detrimental to the creative thinking process and that enforcement of the discipline-of-studies perspective is at odds with creative skill development.

In discussing the conditions which favor the production of right-hemisphere imagery, Gowan (1979) indicates that for genius and normal people it can occur during daydreaming, fantasy, meditation, creative spells, relation, and even during sensory deprivation as long as consciousness and the ability to remember are present. Key components in the incubation of right hemisphere imagery appear to be lowering of sensory intake and ceasing of internal verbalization or the desire to think things through with language. In his accounts of the testimony of geniuses, Gowan (1979) related that when left-hemisphere thought process was abated, the right hemisphere resonated and could see clear mental images, models, or nonverbal symbols. Thus, Gowan concludes that right hemisphere imagery is the vehicle through which incubation produces creativity.

The right hemisphere imagery generated during this time of creativity was a solitary, non-social process. Thus, to extend this potential to the educational setting, many creative and gifted learners who have shown they prefer to work alone on idependent projects (Griggs and Price, 1980; Dunn, 1983) would profit from times of almost "solitary confinement" to mentally synthesize a complex learning task. The environment could be made conducive to the creative process as occuring in four components according to Wallas (1926): preparation, incubation, illumination, and verification. Based on the flow of steps that occur in the creative process (Gowan, 1979), educators might undertake the following if they wished to set the stage for visionary creativity:

    a. Provide intense study and analysis of a particular problem or situation.
       One function of this study is to supply the necessary vocabulary and ver-

bal descriptors so that the creative solution, when reached, can be shared with the rest of the world. Content study and serious concentration would be required here.

b. Contrive a means of placing the gifted or creative person in an environment which triggers emotion and fixed purpose so that right hemisphere imagery can flourish.

c. Once the images have appeared and have led to the generation of discovery and action (which may be translated into pictures, doodles, math equations, flow charts, non-verbal models or metaphors), to allow the creative person to **revel** in the intense emotions of awe, contentment, fulfillment that accompanies and follows the creative discovery.

d. And, to provide, once again, the space and tools so that the creative person can verbalize, computerize or record their discovery into a form to be understood and validated by others. At this stage, the creative person may need to have access to a colleague or mentor/teacher so that the creative experience is clothed in correct syntactical/semantic language descriptors or math equations.

In his model of the different stages of the creative process Gallagher (1975) adds that after the preparation stage of sustained study in which cognitive memory is the predominant mode of thinking, the stages of incubation and illumination are expected to occur. In these stages intellectual freedom, risk taking, and tolerance of failure and ambiguity are learning style characteristics required by the learner. The sloppy, often confused and incoherent forms of work produced during these stages are indicative of divergent thinking, the predominant thinking mode during periods of incubation and illumination. Finally, during the verification stage, convergent and evaluative thinking are the predominant thinking modes in which intellectual discipline and logic need to be the style to accomplish this important last stage.

Guilford (1979) suggests, however, that many high-IQ youngsters are poor in divergent production and for that reason, he calls them creative underachievers. Possibly these youngsters would profit from immersion in the four creative, constructive skills clusters identified earlier by Wiles and Bondi (1980). Through symbol and imagery manipulation, model building, and symbolic thinking, divergent production of creative thought could blossom. Note also that in the Gowan (1979) model of the creative process, the process of thinking style, alternating between convergent and divergent thought, is far more important than focus on content study alone. Through the four-stage process approach, the full potential of each hemisphere as well as its heightening effect upon the other will be allowed to flourish.

VISIONS STIMULATED THROUGH READING

Gifted and creative people find fulfillment in the very act of composing and comprehending. Furthermore, they often turn to reading during dormant periods in their creative cycles. Such periods in which a great deal of fictional and informational reading may occur, may set the stage for inner visions and creative outbursts that follow. Witness Charles Darwin's life story as captured by Irving Stone (1980). Darwin made a point of reading a great deal out of his field as he incubated between his many diverse experiments and explorations. As he worked on an experiment or a report later on, he found that visions from his earlier readings actually influenced his work. Thus, reading can stimulate new thought or generate connections among seemingly disparate thoughts as well as provide insights into ways that other creative people — such as authors — have shown their creativity.

When professional educators — teachers, specialists, and adminstrators — are asked, "When do you read fiction?" they almost all concur in their answers. They respond "at night . . . just before bedtime . . . during the summer and on weekends . . . at the beach . . . while on vacation." Not only do these responses show that professionals find the reading of fiction competitive with their job-related print world, but also they associate the activity with "time off" from job tasks. During "time off" when relaxation occurs, fiction is included as a time-off pleasure. We can see, conversely, how poor reading habits become more disabling for the reading disabled; reading of anything is not included in their recreational, pleasure activities and when it is forced as an unwanted task, the right hemisphere contributes in a negligible way.

THE POWER OF METAPHOR

The right brain has been described as the metaphorical mind while the left brain, the analytic mind. Nebes (1977) found in his work with split-brain patients that a clear mode of right-brain thought was nonverbal metaphor. Using the split-field tachistoscopic technique, two pictures could be flashed to the two different hemispheres without interpretation between the brains. Subjects would select a straw hat rather than an eating utensil as relating to a birthday cake or select a bicycle wheel rather than yarn as being related to a spinning wheel. A metaphorical trait, in each case "roundness," was selected as the basis of similarity. The process of metaphorical thinking requires the visionary "seeing" of a related trait for that perceiver, while the process of analytic thinking requires a literal focus generally relating to naming, describing, or telling the functions of the object perceived.

The strength of the metaphorical image is dependent on the depth of vision of the individual perceiver and the use of the language to describe that vision. Metaphor itself is subsumed within the thinking of synthesis, but it is the clarity of metaphor that gives rise to much creative thinking, great literature, and art. The power of metaphor is in the connection and relationships made between traits. The relationships established between the traits allows us to think about the traits and the things of which the traits are composed in new and unique ways. Poetry is often used as the teaching vehicle of metaphor because poetry as an art form deals with traits in an economical way and is dependent upon clear, crisp word choice.

Unfortunately, the thinking of metaphor and ways to develop the use of figurative language are not often taught in school. The thinking of metaphor often occurs during periods of incubation and illumination described earlier in this chapter. Students would need conditions and time to engage in such reverie. At the present time, the teaching of figurative language generally comes "at" students and not "from" them. Students are given exercises in which they have to locate and to analyze similes, metaphors, and images of personification but they are not shown how to generate these in their own thinking or writing. By not synthesizing these from within, students are curtailed in a vital, vivid way to achieve thought. The remaining part of this section will discuss in greater detail how teachers can develop on the visions and power of metaphorical thinking.

One concrete step in developing vivid pictures is to make the student aware of his own senses and the strength of appealing to the senses of others. Both writer and reader have shared many common life experiences through the senses of sight, sound, smell, taste, and touch. When the writer strives to make the sense experience even more alive with the picturesque use of language, the reader feels the experience in a unique, intense way. One way to do this is to display real objects, pictures, photos, or slides either simply or in pairs side by side. The stimulus here is a visual one and by asking students to focus on particular aspects of the object, visual, sensual, and visionary impressions can form. For instance sunlight glistening through icicles formed on a sailboat's mast lines can generate many colorful phrases and sentences from students.

Another aspect of writing style to develop is the distinction in function between denotative and connotative meanings of words. The denotative word is exact and strictly delimits meaning. It is the word used in its literal sense. Denotative words are quite essential to expository and informative writing in which the essential quality is factual accuracy. The connotative word, on the other hand, transcends the literal. The writer's word choice is both appropriate in its syntactical and semantic context, but the word's meaning conjures up overtones of feelings and imagination. In connotative usage of a word, the writer senses the aura of possibilities that the word suggests. He/she plays upon the associations aroused through the word's identification with sound, historical meaning, and the images released in making a concrete identity. Sensory language and connotative flavors add vistas to the imagination.

The abstract can be made more concrete when figurative language is used to bring about sharp associations among aspects of reality. While a number of figures of speech have been identified, the use of three — similes, metaphors, and personification have great utility for students. Through such figures, abstract and uncommon ideas are clarified to bridge the gap between uncertainty and the known. Since the abstract word has no visual or tactile qualities, it does not readily appeal to the senses or to the imagination. By using the three figures, the writer highlights the quality of comparison as one aspect of experience is described in terms of another. This highlighting arouses concrete associations of likeness. The writer deliberately attempts to juxtapose two unlike qualities, experiences, or objects by distinctly illuminating one compelling characteristic that is shared by both. In this vivid highlighting of one attribute of sameness, the reader senses an imaginative and emotional impact. In fact, the apt writer tries to startle, to jar the reader to see things in a novel way.

A simile is a figure of direct comparison. The little words "like," "as," or "than" precede the concrete image to which attention is directed. For instance in the line, "His words cut like steel through the blackened night," the reader experiences a vivid picture of strength and deliberation. Someone's speech is compared to the qualities of steel through the use of the word "cut." Furthermore, the connotative use of "blackened" contrasted with the cutting of steel (the mental association, of course, could be a sword) lends further strength to the forcefulness of someone's words. The creative aspect of the simile is the achievement of freshness while remaining appropriate to the quality being compared. In the literal sense, there is no truth in the comparison. In the figurative sense, the comparison becomes meaningful because of the effectiveness of the compared elements.

A metaphor is an implied comparison; one object or thing is said to be another without the use of the special words required for the simile. In a sense, metaphors could be considered stronger than similes because the objects, persons, or qualities compared are said to be the same. The writer strives to give added vision to idea by creating the fresh vivid metaphor. The intense search for the one similiar characteristic between two seemingly disparate bodies can sharpen the difference of each. Metaphors can also lead to fresh insight into everyday events. The metaphorical treatment of a common topic, scene, or idea provides a deeper, richer view of the commonly lived experience. As similarities of features are noted, difference between the two things being compared stand out. What is essentially created is a powerful image of central focus silhouetted by sharp contours and shadows.

One figure of speech appropriately used by students could be personification. This is when an object or animal is described as having human qualities. A nonliving thing is made to appear lifelike so that the reader can interpret human qualities. Arousing associations to human experiences closes the gap in understanding the thing described. The reader feels more when the nonliving thing possesses a human characteristic, in figures such as, "the chair pleaded under his weight" or "the sun caressed the fertile earth."

In the following sequence, watch how one teacher, Miss Allison Reardon, provoked fifth grade students to use both thinking modes of analysis and synthesis in the development of metaphor. The teacher first placed the sentence, "Mary's hair looked like strands of gold," on the chalkboard. Students were asked to find what two things were being compared in the sentence. After the students selected hair and gold, the teacher underlined the word "like." She then repeated the procedure with two additional sentences, "The train slithered like a snake" and "The wind howled like an army of ghosts." Next the word "as" was introduced and used in more sentences to replace the word "like." Students then analyzed the sentence, "Tom was as busy as a bee" and "The ice was as smooth as glass." Always the teacher focused on the two things being compared and on the trait the author was trying to emphasize. For instance, in the train sentence, the trait comparison was of curviness; in the wind sentence, the trait was of forcefulness; in the ice sentence, it was of smoothness. The teacher to this point did not even need to use the word "simile" since naming the figure wasn't as important as cultivating the thought process. The students had been mainly involved in analysis-finding the two things of comparison — and a bit of synthesis — searching of the connection, the trait of sameness.

Then the teacher moved the students quite simply into the visionary world of metaphor as students synthesized their own figures of speech. She placed two columns of words on the board as follows:

A	B
water	leather
steak	bell
voice	crystal
muscles	steel

She again asked students to select a word from column A that would match up with a common characteristic or trait of a word in column B. With repeated guidance, students were asked to think what the two words had in common. Soon students produced their own similes such as, "The water was as clear as crystal," "The steak was as tough as leather," "His muscles were as strong as steel."

Additional ways to develop the thinking inherent in uses of figurative language are provided by Mrs. Donna Carini, a graduate student in Reading and a second grade teacher. Mrs. Carini's strategies were formulated after students read a selection entitled "Mr. Picklepaw's Popcorn" (Durr, LaPere, & Niehaus, 1971). First she showed students the figures of speech that were present in the selection itself, such as "There were sunflowers as big as your daddy's head. . . There were pink and blue flowers running wild all over. . . The next morning the sun popped up like a kernel of corn."

Then she prepared a number of activities to help the second graders master the use and thinking of simile in particular. These activities follow:

1. From some of the similes present in the story, the following questions were asked:
   a) "Why did the author compare _____ to _____?"
   b) "Is _____ the same as _____?"
   c) "Sometimes words paint pictures. What pictures came to your mind while reading the sentence _____?"
2. The younsters were asked to hunt for the remaining similes in the story. As they were located, they were written on the board. The pictures painted in their minds through the use of each simile were discussed. Finally, the words "like" and "as" were circled.

3. The younsters were asked to pantomime similes as they were read to them.

4. Each child was given a worksheet containing a list of similes from the story. While one child pantomimed the simile in front of the room, the rest of the class tried to identify that simile from the worksheet. Then the acting child read the correct simile aloud.

5. The children were taught to make their own similes by changing the similes from the story. This was done as either an oral or written activity. For example, the simile "There were sunflowers as big as your daddy's head" was changed to: "There were sunflowers as big as **hoola hoops**."

6. Popcorn was made with the class. At appropriate times throughout the activity, children made up similes using their senses.

   For example:

   The kernels look like _____.

   The kernels are as hard as _____.

   The cooking popcorn smells like _____.

   The popcorn feels as light as _____.

   The popcorn tastes as buttery as _____.

7. The children made their own similes for each of the many colorful pictures in the story, "Mr. Picklepaw's Popcorn."

Other follow-up suggestions by Mrs. Carini for development of simile understanding are:

8. A simile book can be started by each child. As a new simile is read to the class each day or several times a week, they can write and illustrate it in their simile book.

9. Two adjectives and a noun can be presented. Children are told to make a simile using these words plus any others they want to add. This can be an oral or written activity. The following are some examples:

adjectives		noun	possible simile
snow	white	beard	Santa's beard was white as snow.
coal	black	boots	His boots were black like coal.
cherry	red	nose	Rudolph's nose is red as a cherry.

10. A picture may be displayed. Children can brainstorm words that literally describe the picture. The words can be listed on the board. The class can then be asked to compare similes that capture the flavor of the picture's meaning.

11. Pictures may be displayed that capture the following emotions: sadness, joy, anger, frustration, nervousness, fright. Children can attempt similes for each picture.

12. Children may make books entitled, "Similes About Me." For each page, children are to make up a simile about themselves and illustrate it. They can begin with similes describing their physical appearance move on to similes describing their family, home, likes, and dislikes. These similes

also could be used for a guessing game. Children could be asked to write their similes on a piece of paper with their names hidden on the back. The papers could be put in a box. One paper could be chosen each day, and the simile read to the class. The children can try to guess who was the author of that day's chosen simile.

13. The topics of similes can be integrated with other subject areas. For example, if the class is learning about animals in Science, they can be asked to capture the various traits of certain animals with similes.

14. A more abstract picture such as a cloud form can be displayed. Children can choose three things that the picture reminds them of (other than what it really is). They may then make up a simile comparing the real identity of the picture to its look alike identity.
For example:
The cloud is as fluffy as cotton.
The cloud looked like a face.
The cloud is as round as a flower.

15. A mystery object can be placed in a bag. The object should be something appealing to the sense of touch such as something soft, rough, or sticky. Children can insert a hand into the bag to feel the object while their eyes are closed. Similes can be composed based on that sense experience. Other activities could be planned around isolation of the senses of smell, taste, movement, and hearing.

16. Similes can be composed from the forms made by a string painting. This is a painting made by dipping string in paint and laying it on or folding it on paper. The children write similes about what the abstraction looks like.

17. Finally, to extend the use of the senses, a situation picture such as children running on the beach can be displayed. The class would complete the following simile to describe their feelings and reactions to the picture:
The waves sound like _____.
The sand feels like _____.
The sky looks like _____.
The air smells like _____.
The water tastes like _____.

Besides helping thought to be more vivid and visionary, practice in composing similes and metaphors lays the foundation for the understanding and production of analogies. According to Pearson and Johnson (1978), analogies are powerful logical and linguistic organizers and deserve to be taught as a comprehension strategy as early as kindergarten. They tell of a wonderful strategy that could be included as a culminating visual/verbal strategy in the list of simile activities above. In one classroom they visited, they witnessed the unending construction of a giant cardboard ice cream cone. Students pile on a cardboard figure of a new scoop of ice cream everytime they logically complete the message written in the base of the cone. For instance if the cone says "A _____ is like a _____ only smaller," a pile can be added to the existing scoops if the relationship fits the meaning of the analogy. All types of displays can appear on the ice cream cone base such as, "A _____ is like a _____ only colder," or "A _____ is like a _____ only tastier," etc.

This chapter has examined the rich world of the imagination. We have noted that composing and comprehending find strength from within. Parents and young people, however, are often duped today into thinking that over-indulgence in rapidly-changing video games will stimulate the imagination from without. Rossel (1983), a psychologist from Burlington, Vermont, writes in **Psychology Today** that video games are made in such a way that they limit imagination and restrict the options that the child has during play. He writes, "Parents may buy these toys out of an ill-formed hope that they will expand the child's imagination and enjoyment of play. This is a misguided notion because in reality both parent and young person have failed to see that imagination is in the play, not in the toy, and both are being seduced into a process of searching for a new, more imaginative toy."

Educators have noted, instead, that creative, imaginative thinking is a very part of young children's life styles and this thinking can be cultivated as children mature through the grades. Stimulating the visions of imagery and teaching the crystalization of metaphor are two powerful ways to assist the thinking of synthesis. Synthesis, also the energy of creativity, can find natural outlets during composing and "the best way for the receiver to learn to comprehend is to compose" (Moffett and Wagner, 1983, p. 10).

CHAPTER NINE

INTERFACING THE VERBAL AND NONVERBAL DURING READING AND WRITING

THIS CHAPTER represents a culmination of the energy of this book. Not only does it contain the final grouping of strategies of the third section, but it also completes and fulfills the goal of the book. That fulfillment was to show how all the facets of the various literacies could be interfaced in particular, creative ways to achieve the thinking of synthesis in holistic, meaningful learning. The practitioner will find this chapter most useful and will often turn to the various strategies to implement in the classroom.

Presented in this chapter are also many strategies that are near and dear to the author. Through the years, these have been taught in graduate reading classes, have been field tested by the author, teacher colleagues and graduate students, and some have been researched. The author is also well aware that many other techniques and strategies interfacing visual literacy with the verbal literacies could have found their way into this chapter. However, the reader can note that a number of such strategies have been sprinkled about in earlier chapters. These were used to illustrate particular points raised in the text regarding the efficacy of using visual literacy representational modes to achieve written literacy growth.

Chapter Two showed how the arts provided the sensory store of written messages and how computer programming advanced the thinking of synthesis. Chapter Three raised the value of movement and kinesthetic activity in the transmission of messages. Chapter Seven discussed the importance of direct experience in learning and demonstrating how a few models worked to bring experience to the classroom in aiding conceptual and vocabulary development. In Chapter Seven, as well, we noted the analogous relationship between pictures and reading comprehension and why pictures are powerful as analogues of experience. Finally in Chapter Eight, we saw how imagery, metaphor, and synthesis combine to reveal the very core of composing and comprehending. An essential theme of all previous chapters was the intricate relationship among the primary visual literacy modes of viewing and doing, imagery, and creativity.

Chapter Nine will continue presenting some strategies that harmonize these basic relationships but will then advance rapidly beyond. The goal of Chapter Nine is to present visual literacy strategies that have arisen out of modern technology and to fuse more metaphorical, configurational ways to interface with traditional written literacy mode. While the visionary power of right-hemisphere thought was covered in depth in Chapter Eight, we must also realize that imagery and new visions arise out of the fabric of the material covered in this chapter.

MOVEMENT AND EARLY DECODING

Movement is a useful tool in helping young or disabled children to read. Moreover, one dissertation using parameters of learning style showed that when 40 seventh graders revealed a strong preference for either mobility or passivity and were tested for word recognition in an environment in which they preferred, they had stronger word recognition in the preferred environment. The study indicated that mobility-preferred students performed significantly better in the active environment than in the passive environment, and passive-preferred students performed significantly better in the passive environment than in the active one (Della Valle, 1983).

The reader may also recall that in Chapter Three the sign and action categories of nonverbal forms of communication were covered in some depth. The power of these categories was found to be in the way they transmitted information rapidly through analogic representation. We noted the way that gestures, manual signs, body movements, and facial expressions are used to communicate meaning. The importance of "show and tell" activities for young learners was emphasized, especially how the showing aspect can evolve into meaningful, holistic language arts activities. The next four programs and activity suggestions show how action and movement can help youngsters learn written language parts to assist them in the understanding and production of more global aspects of written language.

Pantomiming Phonics

Action language can be used to help early readers learn their phonic elements. The teacher can have children pantomime the action associated with a phonic element. For instance, one graduate student, Miss Jean Brashear, was working with her second grade class on the sound of "ow" as in "snow." She printed a number of short statements on cards such as "someone mowing the lawn, someone rowing a boat, a pitcher throwing a ball, children having a pillow fight." A child was asked to come to the front of the room and select a card from the pile. The child silently read the card and pantomimed the action in front of the class. Of course, the class had to guess the meaning of the action fulfilled by a word that had the "ow" sound. Once the statement was guessed, the child wrote it on the chalkboard so that the class got reading feedback to associate with the nonverbal communication.

Symbols That Move You

A very interesting, decoding-type strategy was conducted by a Special Education Teacher, Mrs. Suzanne Green. She used movement for five-and-six-year-old, nonverbal, emotionally handicapped children some of whom exhibited autistic-like behaviours. Children learned about 20 or so symbols which represented types of movements. For instance, **hop-in-place** was represented by ↑↓ (one foot up, one foot down) and **stamp one foot** was represented by ! (the symbol portrays the impact of stamping). Teachers can try to develop other symbols whose very configuration suggests a type of movement.

The symbols and associated actions are presented one by one to the children. Soon, however, motion phases can be created which children will decode with their bodies. The sequence of presentation of the movement cards are first read by the youngster (decoded) and then acted out (encoded). To build both memory and sequence understanding, also necessary for the decoding of words, the teacher groups several movement symbols. After a movement phase is completed with use of two or more symbols, a youngster can be asked to repeat the movement without looking at the symbol cards. The child can be asked, "What came first, second, . . . last?"

Finally the teacher uses features of the symbol configurations to teach the grapho-motor skills necessary for writing. Youngsters may be first asked to reproduce the movement symbols they have been reading all along. Then prior to the actual writing of real words they can be asked to focus on some of the basic strokes of manuscript writing such as the line and the circle. Children can reproduce the strokes with their bodies, toothpicks, strings, fingers, or paint brushes before they turn to paper and pencil.

Blissymbols: A Visual Language

A visual symbol system created by Charles Bliss to serve as a nonverbal Esperanto or international symbol system has received instead world-wide acceptability for use with non-speaking, physically-handicapped people, often those confined to wheelchairs. The system called Blissymbolics (Helfman, 1981) also serves as a substitute or auxiliary language system for many youngsters and adults who are mentally retarded, autistic, or aphasic. Because the symbols are ideographic, pictorial, and holistic, they can be used to aid the development of language and reading of children who have perceptual disabilities or children who have difficulty mastering digital, syllabic language systems.

The design of each symbol generally conveys a direct relationship to its meaning. According to Helfman (1981), from the approximate 100 basic symbol elements initiated by Charles Bliss, thousands of meanings can be generated. The Blissymbolic Communication Institute in Toronto, Canada, working with Mr. Bliss through the 1970s, has increased the standard form to over 1400 symbols. From these standard symbol forms, symbol elements can be combined and recombined with other elements to form new meaning. A total communication system results among the language impaired students and their teachers through the simple, direct way the pictorial, ideographic symbols convey meaning. The visual simplicity of the symbols also makes them quickly and easily learned by low functioning youngsters. However, the capability residing in the symbols allows them to form new concepts and to represent a range of meanings beyond the concreteness of pictures. This capability opens up a whole communication potential.

The symbols consist of pictographs, such as: ⊙ eye; Å girl; Ⱦ adult; ⊢◁ bed and ideographs such as: ♡↑ joy; ♡↓ sadness; •⏐ before, in front of; ⏐• behind, after. Grammatical rules are also applied to the basic pictographs and ideographs. For instance, from the basic symbol ⊥ representing a human being, pronouns meaning I or me ($\perp_1$), you ($\perp_2$), or we ($\overset{x}{\perp}_1$) can be formed.

Blissymbolics also parallels the learning of traditional reading accomplished through the alphabetic system in that it requires a left to right orientation, requires manipulation of syntax, requires visual perceptual functioning, and requires the ability to integrate and process a number of symbols to communicate thought. As the immersion into Blissymbols proceeds, children are conditioned to perform the same kinds of cognitive and perceptual tasks that are necessary for the learning of written English.

According to graduate student Mrs. G. Sabina Parks, who used the Bliss method with cerebral palsied children whose abilities to speak and use sign language were severely impaired and whose intelligence was lower than that which could be accurately diagnosed by traditional IQ measures, movement is built into early stages of learning the symbols. She points out that it is necessary that the child's kinesthetic and visual perceptive senses be conditioned to receive the Blissymbols as stimuli. Perceptual integration and differentiation can be exercised daily as a means for the visual stimuli reception. This can be done by the tracing of large circles, triangles, squares, dots and lines with and on whatever materials can be suited to youngsters physical limitations. The tracing is effective even if it requires the teacher's complete physical assistance. Manipulating three dimensional shapes which represent the form of the standard symbols can provide visual/tactile imput to accommodate differentiation. Moving such shapes in rhythmic exercises, up-down, left-right, will also help to intergrate experiences of laterality and directionality.

After the visual/kinesthetic/tactile introduction to the symbols, the basic symbol shapes, printed for instance on large oaktag cards, can be substituted for the three dimensional, concrete shapes. The rhythmic exercises can be repeated with use of the oaktag cards. This first use of printed Blissymbols may also require the accompanying use of pictures. The picture helps to form a mental image of the concept while the symbol is seen in its associative meaning role. Mini-stories prepared by the teacher can accompany each introduction to a symbol set. These mini-stories will assist the youngsters' imaginative capabilities.

Individual words in the form of the symbols themselves, sentences, and stripes can be recorded in personal language-experience books. These self-generated books will also become an important transitional tool in the teaching of the reading of English from the Blissymbols. Translations of individual Blissymbolic stories can become reading matter for other children in the class or classes of the future.

Eight sets of Blissymbol Workbooks are available in print and may be ordered from the Blissymbolics Communication Institute, 350 Rumsey Road, Toronto, Ontario, Canada M4G 1R8. The eight sets of workbooks, comprised of approximately 40 individual books, focus on the eight themes of the individual, school, people, love, season, animals, outdoors, and holidays. The authors suggest that each book may be made more meaningful to the child by the addition of appropriate pictures and names relative to the child's home experiences.

In the entire series of workbooks, the child will be introduced to the standard Blissymbols. The symbols help children understand and remember words and concepts found on each page. Children can color, paste, trace and print the symbols as well as add pictures or words as aids to stimulating independent reading. Much repetition of basic sight words and sentence structures occurs. Such repetition assists the preschool children, beginning readers, and reading disabled children to enjoy reading the workbooks independently. In the back of each book is a review of the symbols and words used. The review is similar to a mini-dictionary which is helpful for children when they want to spell words for their own stories.

The authors suggest that while the workbooks are designed to be used over the course of a year, it is not necessary to have the complete set. The books are on different levels of symbol usage, language, and reading, requiring different degrees of interaction from parents and teachers who are helping the Blissymbolic learning youngsters.

A microcomputer software program, compatible for the Apple system, is also available for Blissymbol language users. The program called Talking Blissapple (Vanderheiden and Kelso, 1982) is available on two disks for approximately $35.

A Kinesthetic Reading Program

An actual kinesthetic reading program has been designed for use with normal children in grades Kindergarten through two and with mildly handicapped children at the primary and intermediate levels. The Kinesthetic Reading Program (de Grandpre, 1983) takes a unique instructional approach and uses large-motor kinesthetic movement as its primary vehicle for learning 34 reading skills. The 34 skills can be generally classified as word recognition and word attack skills and are similar to most skills taught in reading readiness and basal reading programs.

The program's rationale is to assist those children who learn most efficiently by means of large-motor movement. Secondly, the program's method promotes large muscle coordination with the learning of academic skills. This is done by placing large alphabet and phoneme mats on the classroom floor and having children step or hop to perform word, letter, and sound blending operations. For instance, one skill is the learning of difficult-to-spell sight words. Children see the word, recall the letters in sequence, and then hop about the mat finding the letters to spell out the word. Children use their whole bodies three times in such sequences to learn the word automatically.

For information and ordering of the Kinesthetic Reading Program, the reader can write to Mrs. Betty Poitras, PSUC Bookstore, State University of New York, Plattsburgh, NY 12901.

ACTION THROUGH CAMERA CONSTRUCTION

The merits of composing through the selective eye of the camera were discussed in Chapter Seven when we noted how visual composing sets the stage for written literacy production. Use of the camera in the environment involves action and movement as well. It becomes, therefore, a suitable tool for many learners who show a preference for an action oriented, kinesthetic style of learning. Teachers could incorporate even more "hands on" learning with the camera besides picture taking and story-boarding the developed photos. Students can build a simple camera! For a very nominal cost, the Kodak Company publishes a delightful customer service booklet on "How to Make and Use a Pinhole Camera" (1979). The pamphlet discusses and illustrates in step-by-step fashion how a camera can be constructed with the use of common household materials. Such an activity will provide youngsters with a basic knowledge of photography while providing an inexpensive and interesting way to take pictures. Don't forget, as well, the pride youngsters will have when they display the pictures they have shot from their own pinhole cameras.

Two types of pinhole cameras can be constructed — the cartridge pinhole camera and the box or can pinhole camera. The pinhole camera is defined as "a small, lighttight can or box with a black interior and a tiny hole in the center of one end" (1979, p. 2). It can be designed for use with regular film or to accept a size 126 film cartridge. With the cartridge pinhole camera, the film can be loaded and unloaded in daylight, at least 12 pictures can be made, and a local photo dealer can process the film. With the can or box pinhole camera, the student must cut the film, load and unload the camera in a darkroom, reload the camera after each exposure, and learn how to process the film.

Kodak has additional pamphlets for sale which can be purchased at local photography shops or ordered from the company. If the teacher wanted to help students learn more about good picture-taking, they could order the 192-page Kodak handbook, "How to Make Good Pictures" (AW-1). To help students process film and photo paper, the following two publications would be helpful:

Basic Developing, Printing, Enlarging in Black-and-White (AJ-2), about $3.00;

Basic Developing, Printing, Enlarging in Color (AE-13), about $3.75

All Kodak publications may be ordered directly from the Eastern Kodak Company, Department 454, Rochester, NY 14650.

If, however, the teacher is a camera-buff and wishes his/her students to learn both the concepts and vocabulary of the photography world, a lesson can procede according to the Cone of Experience Model discussed in Chapter Seven. One fifth-grade teacher had her class learn the vocabulary words of "film, shutter, lens, focus, exposure, fixer, stop bath, developing, and chemicals" when they learned how to manipulate a 35 MM camera and to develop its exposed film. One interesting way she had them recall the new vocabulary was when the youngsters had to label the parts in a camera diagram and tell the functional use of each part.

PHOTOGRAPHY AND INSTANT FEEDBACK

The revolution in instant photography such as that exemplified in Kodak's Kodamatic 940 Instant Camera or Polaroid's One Step provides teachers with a means to work with disabled youngsters having short attention spans and traditional verbal learning difficulties. For younger children, instant photography can provide a vehicle for immediate learning success. When youngsters provide their own oral or written accounts to explain the meaning of their photography, they are joining verbal literacy skills with visual composing skills.

There are exciting educational offerings from the two leading instant camera companies. One such offering in the use of instant photography is that of Polariod's Education Project which has assisted 8,000 schools since 1978. The Polaroid Corporation along with a small group of educators collaborated in a project to test the effectiveness of the use of instant photography in the classroom to enhance language learning. The project initially offers each newly interested teacher or school a **Curriculum Guidebook** ordered from the Polaroid Education Project, 549 Technology Square, Cambridge, MA 02139. The guidebook contains well over a hundred ways in which photography was used by former teachers to create interesting and meaningful learning exercises. These experiences are further indexed by subject and grade level. The guidebook serves as a resource guide to prospective teachers and students who wish to use the Polaroid instant cameras in more creative ways. Then upon proof of purchase of 20 packs of Polaroid SX-70 or Time-Zero film, two Polaroid instant cameras are given to the school for teacher and student use.

Kodak offers schools a free Creative Instant Photo Kit which includes a new Kodamatic 940 Instant Camera, one Photo-Story Discovery Set package, and a Visual Learning Materials folders. To receive one free kit, the school or teacher needs to purchase 10 packs of Kodamatic Instant Color Film or Kodamatic Trimprint Instant Color Film, and send the original receipt of purchase along with a note on school stationery to: Creative Instant Photo Kit, Education Market Services, Dept. 053, Eastman Kodak Co., Rochester, NY 14650.

Teachers can use the kit to begin or expand an existing photography program with learners at almost any age or educational level. The shape of the Kodamatic 940 Instant Camera and the shutter release location encourage a firm grasp and smooth operation to minimize camera movement - even for novice photographers.

A Camera Curriculum Project

The Kodak Company is also a sponsor of a national curriculum project called Cameras in the Curriculum. In August 1982 the National Education Association and the Eastman Kodak Company announced a joint NEA/Kodak program which attempted to promote the inclusion of photography as an integral aspect of classroom instruction at all grade levels. The 1982-83 program administered by the National Foundation for the Improvement of Education (NFIE), was made possible by a quarter-million grant from the Kodak Company. The first "Cameras in the Curriculum: A Challenge to Teacher Creativity" program established a national teachers' competition to select and widely disseminate the best teacher-developed programs which use photography as an integral part of the curriculum, K-12. The initial volume of the first 119 teacher projects that won awards has become a popular resource tool for those wishing to enter the competition at a later date (Nixon, 1982-1983). Those wishing to order this first volume of **Cameras in the Curriculum** can send a check or money order for $5.95 payable to the National Educational Association at the NEA Professional Library, P.O. Box 507, West Haven, CT 06516. The book code is A701-00328.

Those wishing to enter the curriculum competition can write to "Cameras in the Curriculum," 1201 16th Street NW, Washington, DC 20036. The competition for each year generally closes about mid-December or so. Those eligible to apply are teachers or teams of teachers at all instructional levels from kindergarten through higher education and in all subject area domains. The project emphasizes that teachers need not be camera experts to apply. If the teacher is willing to follow the simple entry procedures for submitting a proposal, he/she could win $200, $500, $1000, or even $1500. In previous years, 150 awards of $200 each and 7 national awards ranging from $500 to $1500 were made each year.

To emphasize the role that activity and creativity play in use of photography as a viable learning activity, the program rules announce the following to applicants: Teachers need to explain ways in which students are to be creatively and actively involved in the camera activities. Students' roles should be active, in other words, they should be more than passive observers of photographic activities.

PHOTOGRAPHY AS THERAPY

Another relatively new photography movement has begun in the past several years. This movement, called Phototherapy, examines the therapeutic value of still and video photography in helping human relationships. A recent book has been published (**Photography in Mental Health**, Fryrear and Krauss, 1983), Phototherapy Centers have been established, conferences have taken place, and a journal is available. Interested readers may contact Ms. Judy Weiss, Director Psychologist, 1107 Homer — 3rd Floor, Vancouver, B.C., Canada V6B 2Y1 for information regarding workshops, membership in the International Phototherapy Association, or for information regarding the **Phototherapy Journal**.

Phototherapy is a way of helping people to aid their self awareness and communication skills. Professionals working in the helping professions have found that by incorporating Phototherapy techniques in their counseling work, their clients' understandings, communication skills, and mental attitudes have improved. This has been found to be most true for those people for whom the verbal mode has been limited or guarded.

Within the concept of Phototherapy, the client may be either picture taker or picture viewer. When clients take pictures, respond to pictures they have selected to talk about, or explore how they wish to be photographed, they provide rich information about themselves. The counselor understands that picture reactions provide valuable information about the client. Each response to a photo is individually unique, shaped by personality, past experience, and family traditions. While Phototherapy makes use of private information gained while shooting, talking about, and examining pictures, educators can make use of some of the very same techniques in their work with reluctant and recalcitrant students.

HOLISTIC PICTURE POWER

In Chapter Seven, the rationale was advanced for using pictures as an active way to promote written literacy growth. We saw that there are levels of meaning communicated through picture arrangements, that an implicit or interpretive grammar exists among sequences of pictures, and that high levels of thought are stimulated through visual composing. This section will show how single pictures and drawings can be used to expand thinking and language power. This will be followed by another section which will outline how combinations of pictures, photos or slides can be used to achieve even higher levels of understanding regarding the structure of discourse.

Pictures and photos have been traditionally used by teachers of all grade levels to heighten students' perceptions and learnings. Teachers of primary children have used pictures to sharpen young children's awareness of similarities and differences that exist among life situations. They have also used pictures to increase youngsters' understanding and speaking vocabularies. Reading and bilingual teachers have used pictures to increase the vocabulary and word proficiency of students. English teachers have used photos to increase student's visual awareness and to spark imaginative written compositions (Sohn 1969, 1970 and Leavitt and Sohn, 1969). Grade level and content area teachers have used photos and film depicting historical events and scientific processes to enrich students' knowledge and conceptual development. In all of these examples, visuals bring the concrete world to the classroom. Teachers know that when they couple a visual mode of presentation with associated verbal explanation, they provide a powerful means for expanded thinking.

Furthermore we saw the value when children are taught as visual composers to create their photo essays or stories. Collins (1980) described how children with learning and language disorders formed photo essays through drawing, pantomime, and picture-taking phases. Debes and Williams (1974) described one program for Spanish speaking children in which they composed their own visual compositions after they reviewed vocabulary words concerning the activity they planned to photograph. In another instance, the combination of shooting pictures, acting out preset roles, and verbalizing about the visual experience helped second language learners make solid progress in reading (Debes and Williams, 1974). In one visual literacy project described earlier, migrant youngsters who were given the opportunity to become visually literate by planning and photographing their own stories sharpened their self-concepts, deepened their environmental awareness, and discovered new parallels in verbal language — in its phonology, morphology, and syntax (Fransecky, 1969).

Rubbings

Rubbings are a nice way to integrate holistic picture power and literacy stimulation with a strong affective component. The effect of the rubbing is a bit beyond the real. Because the literal has been transcended, the interpretive and imaginative can blossom. Mr. Manny Rodriguez, a Reading Through the Arts Teacher at Intermediate School 138, Bronx, New York, uses rubbings with low achieving, inner-city youngsters as a vehicle of self esteem. Mr. Rodriguez, who over the years has enriched my own views of the varied ways that the graphic and visual arts can stimulate the written word, uses "rubbings" with these youngsters who he says lack belief in the power of their own imagination to create written stories.

Students cut out objects and figures from pictures found in newspapers and magazines and place these under a piece of art paper. Just like the technique of rubbing a crayon or a pencil over a piece of paper covering a coin, the rubbing produces pictures where the general outline of characters and objects can be noted. An exact replica with all details is not produced. When the pictures producing the rubbings are positioned in certain ways, imaginative effects are produced. For instance, one student wrote about the spirit invading a house and her picture showed a sequence of rubbings of one figure leaving the ground and entering the walls of the house.

Another seventh grader reading at third grade level wrote the following short paragraph based on her rubbing:

> One day when the sun was rising a girl when to the park to jog. And the flowers was blossem and the bird was singing and it was a beautiful day.

Her picture showed the outline of a figure ostensibly gliding over the green grass surrounded by yellow and green flowers and trees. A rubbing of birds over the figure's head also gave the illusion of movement.

Interaction occurred now between teacher and writer. Mr. Rodriguez noted the quality of the first-draft composition and the student's feeling exibited in the rubbing. He met with the seventh grader and helped her group ideas and edit her mechanical errors while the essence of her intended meaning remained faithful:

> One day when the sun was rising, a girl went to the park to jog. The flowers were just blossoming, birds were singing, and the air was fresh with a hint of morning dew. It was such a beautiful day of her life.

Logos: Environmental Signposts

Familiar, commercial logos can be used to initiate a beginning reading program for very young children (Wepner, 1983) or for severely, disabled readers (Perry, 1984). Youngsters have the experiential background to react to familiar logos especially those of the fast-food eating places. Both color and logo configuration contribute a nonverbal effect to which verbal language can be immediately and probably and pleasurably associated. The logo can be displayed in a rebus-like-way while basic sight words and children's actual names complete the idea statement.

Wepner (1983) provides the following list of suggestions in using commercial logos to build a beginning reading program:

1. During the time of family travels of shopping trips, develop a visual interest and sight recognition of logos.
2. Reinforce childrens' recall by pointing to logos in the environment

or identifying them in printed advertisements. Ask, "What does this say?"

3. Begin to collect logos by removing them from advertisements, store flyers, food and beverage products. Involve children in this highly important recognition and meaning activity so that children learn that each sign has a different meaning.

4. Begin to make a separate logo-reading book for each child. The teacher or parent can initially write short sentences for each child, using a rebus-like context. For instance, a sentence might read, "Peter loves Duncan Donuts." Instead of the words "Duncan Donuts" the logo would be in that position. Perry (1984) attached the logos to oak tag cards. Then she used the cards to provide a context for the words she wanted remedial third graders to learn. For instance, she would create sentences for students, such as "Tracy went to MacDonald's" or "Ronnie got three blue hats at TG & Y." Of course, in place of the logo words were the logo singposts themselves.

5. Both Wepner (1983) and Perry (1984) indicate that as children accumulated more and more words and stories, they experienced a strong sense of accomplishment in the ability to read.

Let's investigate other ways that combinations and sequences of pictures increase students' conceptual and language development beyond single picture power.

BUILDING COMPLEX SENTENCES
WITH PICTURES

A combination of two or more pictures can be used along with a nonverbal, model sentence configuration and visually displayed function words to develop usage of more complex English sentence patterns. The pictures suggest the idea content to be expressed in the new sentence; the visual configuration illustrates the standard English pattern the sentence will follow; and the function words indicate what words are necessary to make the pattern work. As students synthesize and compose new sentences using this technique, they learn to comprehend meaning found in more complex writings.

Before actually implementing the student writing phase, the teacher should introduce each new sentence model separately, making students aware of the appropriate function words and other language cues that express the meaning relationship in that sentence type. The function words are essentially relative pronouns and coordinating conjunctions while the other language cues are punctuation and verbal phrase endings, such as -ing, -ed, -en. In another source, the author has identified 14 syntactic arrangements which lend themselves to more complex sentence development and which can be expressed in the visual/verbal arrangements (Sinatra, 1983a). Four of the sentence models are used to develop coordinate instruction and 10 sentence patterns are used to develop subordinate level ideas and relationships. Figure 37 shows the 14 syntactic arrangements by name of construction, by function or relationship expressed through the construction, and by the function words and visual cues that allow the construction to be formed.

In coordinate construction, the common types of relationships of addition, contrast, choice, and result or consequence are expressed. The coordinate ideas are joined by the singular use of a coordinate conjunction which helps dictate the type of relationship that will be formed. For example, use of one of the coordinating conjunctions "but, however, still, yet, nevertheless" syntactically establishes equality between the clauses to the left and right of the conjunction. However, the author's intent was to show that the meaning contained in the clause after conjunction contrasted, contradicted, or was different than the idea expressed in the first clause.

Subordinate construction occurs when an idea of secondary importance is added to the main thought of a sentence expressed as an independent clause. Adverb, adjective, and noun clause constructions, the appositive, and the verbal relationships of participle, gerund, and infinitive are examples of subordinate relationships. Each of these 10 constructions found on Figure 37 is signaled by particular function words and grammatical cues.

Several examples will suffice to show how the sentence development idea could be profitably explored with students of differing language (Sinatra and Spiridakis, 1981) and ability levels (Sinatra, 1983a). The teacher must be fully aware that he or she is not teaching the names of the structures of formal grammar but allowing students to discover how grammar works to compose new and more complex sentences. Students using this strategy are using the thinking of synthesis rather than analysis.

1. The first step is to present a visual pattern of the sentence on the chalkboard or on enlarged poster paper so that the group can see the

Coordinate and Subordinate Constructions		
Name of Construction	Function or Relationship	Phrase or Clause Connectors and Cues
1. Coordinate Clause	Adding on to previous idea	and, also, besides, likewise, furthermore, moreover, then
2. Coordinate Clause	Contrasting with previous idea	but, however, still, yet, though, nevertheless
3. Coordinate Clause	Establishing choice or alternate possibility	or, nor, otherwise, either, or, neither, nor
4. Coordinate Clause	Stating result or consequence of previous idea	thus, hence, therefore, accordingly, consequently, so that (plus use of semicolon)
5. Subordinate Adverb Clause	Showing a time or sequence relationship	after, as, before, since, until, when, while, during
6. Subordinate Adverb Clause	Expressing cause or reason relationship about the idea in main clause	because, whereas, as, since
7. Subordinate Adverb Clause	Showing purpose or result relationship about the idea expressed in main clause	that, so that, in order that
8. Subordinate Adverb Clause	Expressing a condition about the idea of the main clause	although, though, while, provided that, unless, if
9. Subordinate Adjective Clause	Refers to, describes or modifies a noun or pronoun previously mentioned	relative pronoun - who, which, that, whom, whose; where and when
10. Subordinate Noun Clause	Functions as a subject, object or predicate nominative of larger sentence	indefinite relative pronoun - who, that, which, what, whoever, whatever
11. Subordinate Verbal Phrase-Participle	Used to describe or modify a noun or pronoun previously mentioned	Introduced by present or past participle form of the verb-...ing, ...ed, ...en
12. Subordinate Verbal Phrase-Gerund	Used in a noun role as subject, object, or predicate nominative of larger sentence	introduced by present participle form of the verb + ...ing
13. Subordinate Verbal Phrase-Infinitive	Used in a noun role generally as subject or object but may also be used as adverb or adjective modifier	introduced by the preposition "to"
14. Subordinate Appositive Phrase	Used as a noun to explain or identify a noun or pronoun set alongside	Set off by commas if two or more words

Figure 37. Fourteen syntactic constructions which can be developed through visual/verbal sentence strategy. From Richard Sinatra: Sentence development: A nonverbal approach. *Academic Therapy, 19,* Sept. 1983. Courtesy of Academic Therapy Pub Co., 20 Commercial Blvd., Novato, CA.

form of the sentence. The form will show the placement of the clauses or phrases, the position of the function words and participle endings (the bound morphemes), and the punctuation needed. Model sentences can be read aloud while the teacher points to appropriate parts on the visual pattern. In this way, students receive both verbal and nonverbal modeling. The adverb clause construction is interesting because two major patterns are usable in standard English. Using the visual/verbal technique to illustrate subordinate clause relationship number six on Figure 37, the teacher would show the following two patterns on the chalkboard:

because
whereas

_____   _____

as
since

or

Because
Whereas
As
Since _____, _____

2. Secondly, two pictures can be used to stimulate verbal content. The teacher should select pictures that will tend to satisfy the construct of the sentence that students will be forming. Generally, the author has found it best if students write a short sentence or fragment about each picture alone. For instance, for the two pictures below, students might write for the picture on the left, "The girl and dog are looking into the pool." and for the picture on the right, "The dog is walking into the little girl's pool."

Figure 38. Use of two pictures to develop adverb clause usage.

3. Now comes the culminating aspect of the sentence synthesizing for each picture into one sentence that follows the visual pattern displayed on the chalkboard. Students now will not adapt their wordings expressed in individual sentences to fit the construct of the pattern. Notice, however, they make the transformation of words and syntactic structures on their own. The visual patterns, the pictures, the display of the function words have pointed to the direction of the transform, but each individual student must manipulate words and structure in his or her own mind to produce a syntactically and semantically correct sentence. The following types of sentences may then be produced:

Because the dog has seen something in the pool, he/she walked in to get it.

Since the dog is fetching his toy bone, he/she treaded into the little girl's pool.

or

The little girl is dismayed because the dog is about to collapse in her pool.

The little girl is ready to cry for help as the dog stepped on her foot.

A teaching sequence using a more difficult construction with seventh and eighth grade students can serve as the second example. The author's intent was to help students compose the participle or verbal phrase construction, number 11 found in Figure 37. The students saw pictures about a little dog running happily along a beach shaking off water apparently after he was hit by a wave. Except in sentence number 5 listed below, the participle construction was correct in each sentence composed by the other six students:

1. Playing on the beach and with the waves, the dog has a fun time.
2. Drenched by the surf, the dog ran home.
3. Running on the sand, the dog gose in the water (spelling error).
4. The dog, approaching the water, ran away from the crashing wave.
5. Trotting along in the water, escaped the following waves (subject omitted).
6. Walking along the beach, a dog lowers his head and leaps into the waves.
7. The dog, testing the water grajully (spelling error), was tempted to go in.

4. The final step in the visual/verbal, discovery approach to sentence development is for students to write their newly constructed sentences on the chalkboard. They will marvel at the number of different sentences that are generated from the same pattern. This sharing and language interaction is important for continuous mental growth. Both the visual pattern and the intonation of each sentence as it is read aloud will remain in the students' memory to help them form new sentences which fit the pattern. In this discovery approach to complex and novel sentence construction, students contribute their own thought processes and language to make the connections to new meaning.

VISUAL COMPOSITIONS: NONVERBAL ARRANGEMENTS TO TEACH THE STRUCTURE OF DISCOURSE

The impact of using photography to influence students' thinking, composing, and comprehending processes was first revealed to the author back in the early 1970s. As reading specialist for a particular high school, the author was asked to assist another teacher with a rather recalcitrant and malcontent group of students. These students met the entire day with the one teacher; they had been excluded from regular school attendance because their "misdeeds" were felt to be so severe that they had to be separated from the mainstream.

After several false starts, the author came to the technique of using picture sequences in the form of 35 MM slides to motivate these students to discuss a theme and possibly write about it. Well, the technique took hold. They actually began to look forward to the afternoon visits when they would see projected on the Community Center wall, a sequence of slides that told a particular story. However, the group just didn't sit back to passively enjoy story after story.

The time period between each projected story began to get longer and longer. Soon we were roughly covering one slide presentation a week. That was just great for me as composer for I was the one who had to stay one vision ahead of the group and have each new slide composition ready as they finished the one before. What happened in between each slide story projection? Simply, the students began to write . . . and rewrite . . . and write well. Most startling was the discovery that many of these youths were quite literate. One could see a quality, and a level of language in their compositions that could stand up in any English class.

In Chapter Seven, one such example of a highly literate written composition produced from this group was provided. On the other hand, other students were barely literate. An example was revealed by 17 year-old Lydia's beginning composition also found in Chapter Seven. We did. find that the visual presentation drew out the students' thoughts so that all during the week, we could work on their literacy skills.

How to Prepare Visual Compositions

Through the years the author has found that the slide arrangements — now referred to as visual compositions — could be constructed in four major ways. Teachers could intentionally photograph their own visual compositions or they could arrange and rearrange any combination of slides in their possession to form a holistic, visual essay. Secondly the teacher, in conjunction with students, could plan for the use of the camera during traditional class outings. This planning involves the photographing of events and sense that lend themselves to a common theme. The activity itself entails discussion, preplanning, and visualization: all essential ingredients of composing. For instance, one graduate teacher took her sixth-grade class of English-as-a-Second Language students on the traditional outing to the city zoo. To help students record impressions as they took each picture, the following configuration was used. Students listed the picture number, were encouraged to draw a sketch or picture to recall the photographed event or scene, and wrote comments and impressions that would help them during composition writing. Two to four such configurations can be arranged on a page for children to record the visual/verbal essay.

When the 72 exposures (2 rolls of film) were returned from printing, the teacher and students arranged seven different visual compositions. They story boarded simple compositions in a narrative format which photographically recorded the events of the day, and more complicated ones, which would require students to write about specific animals in their environments and to tell an adaptive feature of each animal which enabled it to survive well in its environment. So, in the latter photo essay, a camel was not shown behind a cage but was seen in a desert-like plain.

Take a look at some paragraphs from one such composition written by a sixth grader — an oriental youngster who scored at the 4.6 level of reading during standardized achievement testing. While Margaret's composition ran some full three pages, only the introductory, first,

```
┌─────────────────────────────────────────────────────┐
│                                                       │
│    Picture #              ┌──────────────────────┐   │
│                           │     Sketch-a-shot:     │   │
│                           │                        │   │
│                           │  ‚                     │   │
│                           │                        │   │
│                           │                        │   │
│                           │                        │   │
│                           └──────────────────────┘   │
│                                                       │
│    Notes:_____    │
│                                                       │
│    _____        │
│                                                       │
│    _____            │
│                                                       │
│                                                       │
└─────────────────────────────────────────────────────┘
```

Figure 39. Recording visual/verbal impressions.

third, and concluding paragraphs are printed to serve as an example of
the technique:

Special Features of Zoo Animals

by Margaret

Each animal that I observed at the zoo had very special features all their
own. These special features are part of what enables the creatures to live in
their own environment. When animals are brought to a zoo — the zoo ar-
ranges to have them live in similar conditions to that of their natural habitats.

A seal is a mammal. It lives in the sea or ocean. A seal's body is shaped
like a torpedo. It spends most of its time in water and are excellent swim-
mers. When a female gives birth, she does it on land. The seal uses its brown
fins for swimming. Most of the seals eat fish and squid. Their body has a
very thick fur to keep them warm in cold areas.

An elephant is the largest animal that lives on land. It has a tremendous
body that is gray, with 4 gigantic legs, 2 leaf-like ears and a trunk that looks
like a hose. An elephant uses its trunk to carry food and water to its mouth.
It can even give itself a shower by shooting a stream of water through its
trunk. It weighs about a few tons. It lives in warm places. Elephants eat
grass, leaves, small branches and bark. The zoo provides them with conditions the same as their natural habitat.

These and many more creatures I observed at the zoo on one of our
school field trips.

The third way visual essays can be prepared is again by students in
which they cut out single pictures and picture sequences from news-

papers, brochures, magazines, and old books. Youngsters' own photographs might also be made to fit with certain visual themes concocted from a number of sources. The final, and probably most intellectually rewarding way that visual compositions can be prepared, is when they are photographed by individual students as they compose through the viewfinder. This notion, as well as the levels of thinking achieved through visual composing, was covered in detail in Chapter Seven.

How Visual Compositions Aid Thinking Processes

A most important concept for the teacher to realize is that the visual composition involves more than a single picture. It is an arrangement, a collection of photographs, slides, or pictures that suggests a unified theme. The meaning of the theme is not explicitly told to students. Each student constructs the meaning by making his/her own experiential, conceptual, and language connections. The figure, showing how verbal and nonverbal relational devices interact in Chapter Seven, illustrates the mental processing involved by each student as he/she views each visual composition and is asked to express its meaning through the oral or written language modes. Note that connections between visual parts are inferred while the connections used in language are made explicit.

Essentially the visual composition provides a nonverbal, holistic way of conceptualizing a theme and a way of eliciting and organizing a written composition. The advantage of using "silent" sequences of pictures, rather than film with accompanying dialogue, is that students don't imitate a language source but compose their own logically produced written accounts that serve to report, record, generalize, and speculate.

While the visual arrangements are most often used with more "difficult" populations to spark language expression, they also serve to make the good writer even better. For instance 16 year-old Wesley in a developmental reading and writing class saw a slide composition of life on a sheep farm in California. The first five or six slides illustrated the peace and contentment of sheep life as they played and grazed on verdant fields during a sunny day. Then, two slides focused on a dead lamb near a rain puddle as the drops continued to splash. The sequence ended with a lone sheep peering out into the distance as darkness approached. Of course, it was the author's intent to figuratively use the lone sheep as the dead lamb's mother. However, also in the last slide was a solitary pine tree unnoticed during the taking of the shot. It was the tree that energized Wesley's thoughts as he began his concluding paragraph with, "A

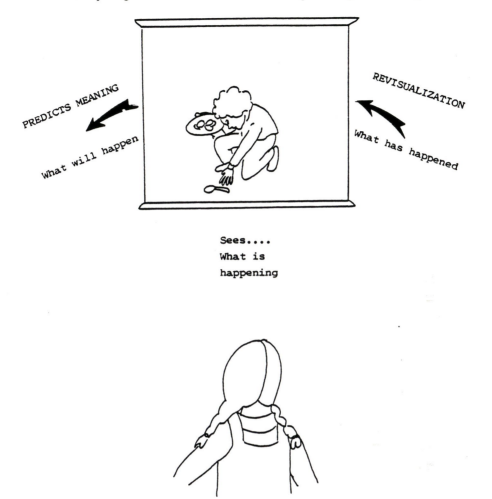

Figure 40. The mental processing of viewer as composer.

lone dead pine tree in the background symbolizes their existence. . . ."
Another student after seeing a 13 slide sequence of the traditional events
in a bull fight did not describe the events in a sequential way as do most.
He began his essay, "The brevity of life is portrayed by a bullfight. . . ."
and continued to develop that theme while weaving in traditional aspects of the spectacle.

The use of the visual composition strategy is powerful for the reluctant and language-deficient student because the known, the concrete, is
used to influence and shape written language development. Because
photographs or slides are replicas of real life situations, they offer concrete glimpses of life that students can match with their own verbal ac-

counts. Murray (1978) had indicated that picture viewing is just one of many previsionary strategies that serve to incite and limit a topic. Note in the following figure how the viewer must revisualize what has already happened in the visual story, tie that meaning with what is currently being viewed on the screen, and predict what will happen next. All of this mental processing serves to stimulate language.

It is at a basic level of visual compostion usage that two types of students benefit most. The first type is the one who has been categorized as language deficient and who has difficulty conceptualizing or imagining what to write about. When the visual presentation has been translated into a verbal one, the language-disabled student demonstrates that a language facility **does** exist. The second type of student who benefits from the use of the visual mode of presentation is the one who has a processing strength for the nonverbal mode of communication. These types of learners were discussed at length in Chapter Six.

However, the real impact of the visual composition strategy is that it can more than motivate and stimulate language. Otherwise, single pictures would do just as well. Through organized visual arrangements students can learn how to write in different organizational styles and can learn to transfer this knowledge to the reading experience. The three levels of literacy achieved with use of each visual composition is illustrated in the following figures. The second purpose indicates that be-

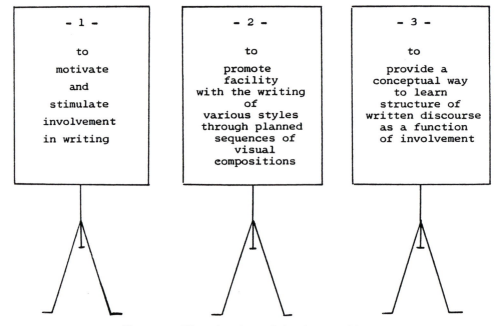

Figure 41. Three functions of visual compositions.

Relationship of Visual Compositions
to
Written Style and Organization

Visual Composition Arrangements	Writing Style Achieved
	Narrative and Sequential Ordering of Events
Show events in a sequence or steps involved in a process. All sports events, contests, adventures, and process-oriented activities show action occurring in sequence.	Narrative and process-oriented construction develops in which the unifying element is time-order or sequence. The writer focuses on sequential telling of events. During initial writing activities, it is helpful to provide students with transition words and phrases that carry the direction of thought forward.
	Description
Present a descriptive scene in which each picture contributes a little more detail to how the scene is organized. Live and inanimate objects could be arranged along horizontal, vertical or distance planes.	The writer describes the scene and arranges features in relation to each other. Connectives that relate spatial orientation will help students coordinate the positioning of characters, objects, and details within scenes.
	Comparison/Contrast
Show how likenesses and differences exist amongst people, events, and surroundings. Styles of dress, eating habits, housing conditions are easy to compare and contrast in visual arrangements.	Students write about similarities and differences they see occurring in the picture presentation and learn the comparison/contrast style of organization. Presenting coordinating conjunctions which signal contrast will aid students in the development of that style.
	Enumeration or Development by Example
Show a picture that presents a group or class and then a number of	Students will name the group to which the separate items belong and then develop each separate

Figure 42. Relationship of visual compositions to written style and organization. From R. Sinatra: How visual compositions aid visual and verbal literacies. In R.A. Braden and A.D. Walker (Eds.), *Seeing Ourselves: Visualization in a Social Context.* Blacksburg, VA.: Virginia Polytechnic Institute, 1983. Courtesy of R.A. Braden and A.D. Walker. 1/29/85.

Figure 42. (continued)

pictures which illustrate examples of that class. For instance, show the group pose of an athletic team and then each member of that team at his/her position.

item in ensuing sentences.

Imply that something happened as a result of something else or that a problem exists. Focus on the central idea and include enough pictures to develop that idea. For instance, by showing a developing storm or hurricane and then the damage resulting from that storm, a cause and effect relationship is visually portrayed. A visual problem can also be suggested with a number of pictures to show how that problem was resolved.

Exposition

A number of expository patterns may be developed here, i.e., cause and effect, problem/solution, and development by main idea with supporting details. Sequential arrangement may be featured in the writing style while development of the theme occurs.

Focus on characters who appear to be involved in a controversy or highlight on character who seems to be persuading another to act a certain way.

Argumentation

The student uses the style of argumentation or persuasion in developing the composition. Specific reasons may be noted in the details. A dialogue may be written between characters outlining the points of the argument or controversy.

Combination of Styles

Combine visual arrangements to achieve a more detailed visual story. For instance, the sequence of an event can be shown while additional pictures can highlight the surroundings or locale in which one part of the event occurred.

Several writing styles may be achieved. Narrative-descriptive writing is rather easy to achieve. Students tell the particular story in sequential fashion while stopping to describe places or scenes in which the action occurred.

cause visual compositions are arranged in particular ways, students can be led to write in a style that was exemplified by a particular visual composition arrangement. They can then read each others' selections projected via an overhead to see how each modeled the particular style.

Finally as suggested by the third purpose, they can be asked to read selections by "published" writers that are organized in the same way they wrote.

Organizational arrangements that are not too difficult to visually compose and which will tend to elicit various styles are the narrative, descriptive, comparative and contrastive, persuasive, and cause and effect patterns. Figure 42 illustrates a number of visual composition arrangements and particular writing styles achieved.

How Writers Compose Using Visual Compositions

Is there a grade or ability level distinction in the ability to write a particular organizational style based on a visual composition arrangement? Look at the four pictures displayed in the following arrangement. They came from a longer visual composition of about 15 slides which were mostly shot in January 1973 when an ice storm crystalized most of the East. Of course the photographs were taken after the storm had arrived and left its damaging effects of torn tree limbs, downed wires, and blockaded streets. In order to compose a cause and effect type pattern, which by the way is a highly used writing style in the areas of Social Studies and Science, the author had to wait for the announcement of another storm front. As the front approached, the author was ready with camera to shoot the darkened clouds as they occluded the sun. Now there was visual evidence to suggest a cause.

Look at the four compositions produced by four different students on differing days as they composed within their classrooms. The reader can see that without any language prompting about **what** and **how** to write, the compositions were written in very much the same way by the third grader, the sixth grader, the Special Education adolescent, and the College Freshman. Audrey, Eric, Albert, and Angela all share the same basic organization. They began with the arrival of the storm (the cause) and discussed the damage that followed in the wake of the storm (the effect). While the level of language and point-of-view differs among writers there is a consistency of composing development. Even 15 year-old Albert with his meager language proficiency was able to achieve a rather literal account.

"Storm" by Audrey — 3rd Grader

This story is about a storm. In the morning the sky was light blue. Then the sky started to get some clouds. It started to snow and it turned into a

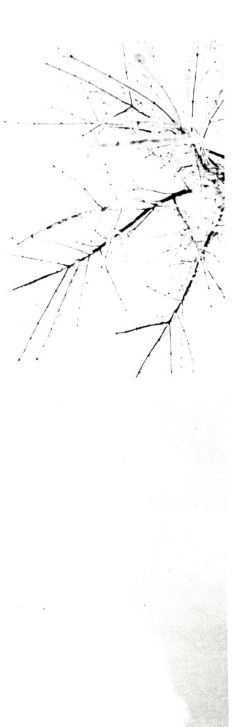

Figure 43. Four slides selected from larger visual composition.

snow blizzard. Then the snow turned into ice. The trees had ice on their branches. The trees started to fall on the street because the storm and half of the trees were split in half. . . One big tree fell on the bush. The sky kept on getting darker and darker. The trees started to fall on the houses. . . Ice was on the streets. . . Their (sic) was a man and lady in a car. They came to a sign that said Dead End.

"The Damage of the Storm" by Eric — 6th Grader

At first, the day was calm, peaceful and faily cool outside. . . These large clouds started to block out the sun. The clouds filled the sky with a white blanket until they turned grey. . . The storm started to get tough and the winds came.

The storm raged for five days and finally came to a stop. The people got out and started to shovel and some walked to a store. As people came back from there (sic) walks, they told about trees (that) were cracked in half and frozen. . . A man came out to saw off the branches of a falled tree for fire wood.

"After the Storm" by Albert — Special Education Adolescent

A storm can ruin property and cause damage. A storm is forming the sky. Then the storm hits the town. The storm blows trees over. One tree fell across the street. Then some kids looked at the fallen trees. One tree fell on a man's fence. The storm left alot of damage.

Composition by Angela — College Freshman

The sky was very deceiving today. The gray clouds started to invade the elaborate blue one. . . I awoke the next morning glancing out my window. My favorite oak tree lay helplessly in the street. Ice cycles (sic) were formed everywhere. The storm had hit and recklessly destroyed everything. Trees were battered and scattered around. The force of the wind split several trees in half. At the end of the gate was a sign, a dead end zone. I was trapped, no one to talk to. . . It was a horrible sight, but yet a pretty ending. A man stood in front of my house taking pictures. It was beautiful and ornate scenery. A storm that has torn us apart, but built a new world, a world of art.

Steps in Arranging Visual Compositions

Now that the teacher can see what is possible from student writers, how does the teacher set up the strategy for classroom use? Secondly, while the focus has been on writing, don't forget that you can use the same technique to improve oral discourse.

In fact, in one study conducted in a Special Education Adolescent facility, a group of mental retardates (IQ's in the 50s) significantly improved in their ability to tell oral narratives (Sinatra and Venezia, in review). Because their writing was so illegible, teachers first transcribed the stories that the students told and then had them read back by the students.

The next figure indicates that six levels of literacy development are achieved through the use of each slide arrangement. The first and last levels indicate that teacher-directed strategies result in whole class involvement. Strategies such as reading student papers aloud, projecting them for whole-class viewing and editing, and developing new vocabulary would occur after individual student involvement. The middle bands show the processing and composing modes achieved by each individual writer. The processing modes may overlap through various reading and writing interactions within the six stages, but the structure of the figure suggests that each literacy level is strengthened through participation in a lower one.

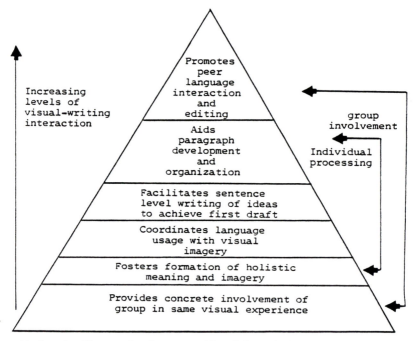

Figure 44. Levels of literacy development achieved through classroom use of visual compositions.

Generally, at least two showings of each visual composition are necessary to accomplish the first draft of the written composition. During the first visual presentation, the teacher should not interject his/her comments about what to look for and what to say. To allow students to discover their own facility for using language, teachers merely need to show each slide for just a few seconds. The teacher can urge those students who request information about certain slides to wait for the end and to put their own ideas together.

By the end of the first showing, students will have seen a unified theme. The teacher could now prompt by saying, "What whole meaning did you sense or feel after seeing that slide arrangement?" Rather than have individual students blurt out their answers, teachers can have students write one sentence that best captures the meaning of that slide theme. This sentence may become the main idea or thesis sentence for the forthcoming composition.

Now the visual composition can be projected a second time, but at a slower pace. Generally, the rate of changing slides will be dictated by actual writing involvement. The author usually found it best to wait until almost all his students were looking up from their papers, waiting to see the next slide. During this second viewing, students will be asked to write individual sentences based on each slide or combination of slides. What usually occurs is that they write one sentence per slide and then combine several sentences into one during the next stage of the writing process. The highly important visual/verbal strategy to impart to students is the notion that as each picture contributed a thread of meaning to the visual composition, so each sentence should relate to the central idea expressed in each student's thematic sentence.

By the end of the second showing, each student will have a page of related sentences. Some may well have a good first draft. Teachers can prepare a dittoed worksheet, if they like, to help students record these sentences, but regular sheets of lined paper will suffice. Students can now direct their energies toward the final goal of the visual composition activity — the written composition. Paragraphing may or may not be a feature here, dependent upon the length and arrangement of the slide story. If it was a simple narrative such as the recording of the phases of an event, then the composition could be in the form of one paragraph. However, whatever the length, when the student starts to arrange his/her sentences during the first draft he or she will be continually supplied by visualization of the whole, visualization of particular shots within the whole, and by a sense of organizational structure.

Undoubtedly as many students work through the first and subsequent drafts, they will generate mechanical and grammar-related mistakes. This, of course, is natural and understandable. Because each student has had the same previsionary experience to think through the pictorial mode, language has been prompted as a function of meaning. The student has not looked at the printed language nor copied other sources to achieve his/her composition. The student, relying on his or her own inner strength to compose, has found that the desire to communicate has preceded the knowledge of correctness.

As the final drafts are turned in, the teacher can use the services of the whole group to assist in the revision and editing processes. Students can help each other at the idea level, the vocabulary level, the syntactic level, and the mechanical level. Many spelling errors, in particular, may be prevelant because students have been stimulated to use words to fit a particular visual meaning. The editing and correcting process may, in actuality, be a lot easier for both student and teacher since each has a clear, concrete referent in mind. Finally, the teacher can involve the group in the formal discussion of the type of discourse they were led to compose. Notice that the teaching about discourse follows student involvement in its very organization and structure. This strategy of teaching form and function of written discourse has in essence meshed the structure of the subject with the structure of the students (Moffett, 1983).

Strengths of the Visual Approach

The strength of the visual composition approach is that it provides a holistic procedure for language discovery. Language has predominated in our many classrooms, but it is almost always the language of reporting and not the language of discovery nor of achieving connections. The visual composition technique provides a mechanism for language involvement, allowing each student to become involved in the process of composing before product is analyzed. Furthermore, involvement in the process becomes the means to learn the internal structure of discourse; in other words, how themes are put together. The power of the slide story medium is that it reaches the most stubborn eyes, can motivate the most reluctant writer, and can enrich the language capabilities of even the low functioning youngsters.

The point of using such a technique as the visual compositions is that as the previsionary experience, the teacher can help all levels of students to improve in verbal and organizational proficiency once they have demonstrated their own composing potential.

DESIGN AND CONFIGURATION AS METAPHOR

Nonverbal designs and configurations are other ways to represent experience. But in this case, they are not exact replicas of the original as was the case for photographs or literal drawings. Designs and configurations are types of nonlinguistic metaphors since comparisons to real life experience are implied. In such metaphorical representations, a model or a "blueprint" suggests a unified meaning in which the connections among the parts have to be read correctly to understand the relationships implied. This is the world of maps, graphs, diagrams, timelines, flowcharts, frames, and networks. All of these convey meaning implied through nonverbal configuration.

Metaphorical representations compact a great deal of information into a single configuration. For instance, when one says that they are going to use the "tip of the iceberg" metaphor to explain a point or concept, the listener knows that while an observable quality exists above the waterline, a host of non-observable and possibly more important qualities exist below the waterline. Because of their wholeness and compactness of form, a configurational metaphor can serve to represent a great deal of verbal information. This fact is often overlooked by teachers of written literacy.

Unlike pictures, the designing and "reading" of configurational metaphors often have to be intentionally taught to students. For instance, when asked to represent the number of boys and girls in the third grade classes at one school through the use of a bar graph, youngsters have to be shown how to logically arrange the verbal, mathematical, and graphical relationships that will compactly display the whole meaning. But this type of conceptualization could profitably begin in kindergarten. Once youngsters have been provided a direct experience and have formed the mental schemata related to that experience, they can be asked to represent it in a metaphorical way. For instance, after young children have taken their traditional walk through the school building, their route can be represented in a two-dimensional map complete with labels and scaled size. Likewise after 4th graders have surveyed the grade for food preferences, students can be shown how to arrange the hierarchical order of preferences through pie, bar, or line graphs. Or older students could be shown how to diagram relationships they perceive in written texts in order to understand the relationships in more meaningful ways. This concept will be developed in full in the next section.

By teaching students such uses of nonverbal metaphors through construction of graphic arrangements, teachers will help them conceptualize ideas and relationships, help them to relate new vocabulary to these linked relationships, and can dramatically help them with logically organized writing. A key feature in helping students to write in more logical fashion is to originate lessons in which the construction of nonverbal designs precedes the assignment of the written composition. When students compose the nonverbal relationships needed to complete the diagram, graph, or chart prior to writing, they have established the connections among the topics they will write about. A fallacy in the use of graphic aids in junior and senior high schools is that the graphical displays and arrangements are often used to embellish text and students are not shown nor encouraged how to "read" these compact units prior to textual reading.

The Literacy of Graphs

Graphs provide a compact way to visualize meaningful relationships between a concept and its related parts. Furthermore, teaching the ability to graph, teaches the ability to think and to solve problems in very holistic, concrete ways. A graph may be thought of as a two-dimensional nonverbal representation of a direct experience or of a concept. Through graphing, thinkers can record events, describe relationships, and project ideas without the use of a great deal of verbal language. However, once the graph relationships are thought through and visually and often mathematically expressed through such design features as lines, bars, circles, and space, it often takes a great deal of verbal information to express the meaning of the graph to another. Thus, there is a "decoding" aspect to understanding the meaning expressed through graphs, and there is an "encoding" aspect of composing and expressing relationships through graphs. Both reading and producing graphs can be and should be taught quite early in the curriculum and taught within a number of content disciplines. Because graphs can be used to express the content of various disciplines, they provide another way to learn and express information.

Two simple ways to use the power of graphing in the curriculum are to have a graphical guide to follow and to have a lesson plan format that will develop the idea relationships of each type graph in the guide. An excellent guide that focuses on a range of graphs suitable for various relationships is Edward Fry's Taxonomy of Graphs (1981).

Illustration of the Taxonomy of Graphs

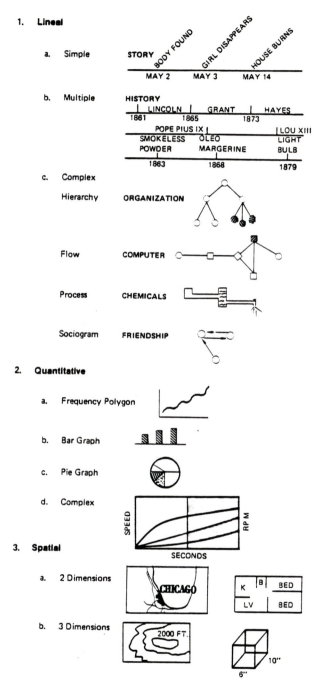

Figure 45. Fry's taxonomy of graphs. From Edward Fry: Graphical literacy. **Journal of Reading**, Feb., 1981. Courtesy of International Reading Association, 800 Barksdale Road, P.O. Box 8139, Newark, Delaware 19174.

Figure 45. (continued)

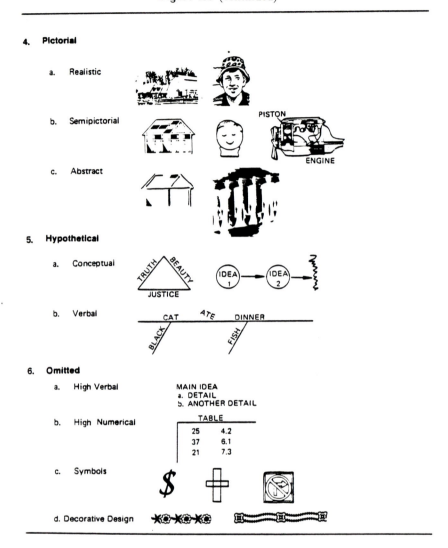

4. **Pictorial**

    a.   Realistic

    b.   Semipictorial

    c.   Abstract

5. **Hypothetical**

    a.   Conceptual

    b.   Verbal

6. **Omitted**

    a.   High Verbal

    b.   High Numerical

    c.   Symbols

    d. Decorative Design

Next, the teacher can use the following steps in developing a graphical lesson suitable as a thinking, reading, or writing strategy:

1. First the teacher must focus on the type of thinking relationships in which children are to be involved or on the type of problems the graph will help portray. Because particular graphs portray particular relationships, the type of graph selected will assist students to visualize new and varied information the best possible way. For instance, a lineal "time line" is most often used to show events in sequence, a line graph or frequency polygon often expresses a growth or decline over time, a bar graph is often used to express comparison and contrast of

products, concepts, and beliefs, while a pie graph is often used to express mathematical parts of a whole. If during science, the teacher wished students to visualize the percent of the various gases in the atmosphere, a pie graph would aptly portray that relationship. The same graph could be used during Social Studies to help students see the distribution of products exported by a country. On the other hand, a counselor could help youngsters work through a Sociogram as a way for youngsters to express their feelings for one another.

2. The next stop would be for the teacher to decide where to place the graphing concept in a particular sequence through the levels of literacy. Recall the stages of literacy presented during Chapters One and Two and the Three Levels of Coding presented by Moffett and Wagner (1983) in Chapter Seven. Where the graphing concept would be used would be dependent upon learners' conceptual understanding of a particular topic and their language facility to express that topic. So, for instance, if primary children had little understanding of two-dimensional maps, the teacher would best bring them to the primary level of visual literacy first. The children should walk through and physically see the particular environment they will be asked to represent with a map. An intermediary stage from concrete experience to abstract two-dimensional map representation would be the construction of a three-dimensional map, much like a scaled-down architectural display.

Older children, who are more familiar with graphs and can think through the literacy level of reading, can be asked to graph relationships that they read about in their various school texts. In this use of the graphing concept, reading has served as the source of information followed by projection to the nonverbal level of visual literacy as representational thought. The teacher could complete the literacy cycle by having children orally express how their graph represented the ideas of the reading selection or by having children do it in writing.

In **Thinking Networks for Reading and Writing** (Sinatra et al., 1985) learners interact with the microcomputer as they help construct organizational types of graphic designs during reading comprehension processing. More will be said about the interactive effect of the graphing, reading, writing approach near the end of this chapter.

3. With the type of graph construction and the entry level of literacy selected, the teacher can allow the graphing concept to flow naturally through oral and written language experiences. Because graphs compact a great deal of information into one configuration, they can be used as vehicles to strengthen verbal understanding and expression. Too often, graphs are treated as a unit of isolated instruction and not taught as a means of conceptualizing idea in all areas of content instruction.

Let's take a look at various aspects of literacy lessons using graphs to note how integrative effects can be achieved. In example 1 by graduate student, Susan Silver, youngsters had already practiced reading the composition of the atmosphere from a pie graph. The graph visually displayed, with size, color, and percentages, the amount of the various gases in the atmosphere. In the exercise below, students had to apply the correct meanings of words expressing quantative relationships in a cloze exercise. But note students had to refer to the pie graph to answer correctly.

Nitrogen is a very important gas. It is found in the (1) ____ amount in the atmosphere. Argon, carbon dioxide, helium, xenon, and some other gases make up only 1% of the atmosphere. They are found in the (2) ____ amount. Oxygen makes up 20% (3) ____ of the atmosphere than do the "other gases" all together. It is still found 57% (4) ____ nitrogen. All of these gases are important in making up the (5) ____ atmosphere.

Answer Key: 1) greatest, 2) least, 3) more, 4) less than, 5) total

Mrs. Marlene Rutsky developed the concept of the bar graph for second graders in a very nice progression from concrete experience, to oral language, to mathematical quantification, to graph. The concrete stimulus was each child's birthday. However, because there were 30 children in the class, 30 different birthday celebrations were considered to be too much. The class decided they would have one party per month to honor all the children who had birthdays that month. The July and August birthday children would be included with the June celebrants. Other content words developed with the children during the oral exchange were "celebrate, total, tally, share, graph" while the highly important function words, "most, least, none, highest, lowest, more, less" were developed as well.

Then at the chalkboard a tally or a counting was made of all the birthdays which occurred each month. The tally chart, with the three following headings, is shown for just the first five months:

Month	Tally of Birthdays	Number of Birthdays
September	11	2
October	1111	4
November	1	1
December	111	3
January	V	5
	etc.	

It was quite easy and natural, then, for children to transfer the number concepts to the bar graph concept illustrated in the following figure.

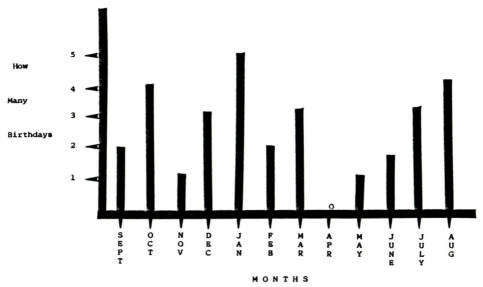

Figure 46. Bar graph developed from use of tally procedure.

Many reading and writing activities were generated after the bar graph construction. Children, for instance, had to read and respond to questions which asked about concepts of "most, least, move," etc. as well as give more literal answers to questions concerning numbers of birthdays per month. Of course, the graph was also a perfect vehicle for a language experience chart as well.

Mrs. Janet Steiner also used the bar graph with fifth graders. However, this time the initial stimulus was a number of written reports taken from health education textbooks and medical articles found in newspapers and magazines. From the number of materials children read, the following bar graph was constructed which singularly represented a major concept important in the children's lives. That concept generalization was — More Cigarettes — More Likelihood of Lung Cancer. Note the following questions posed by Mrs. Steiner which prompted children to inferentially interpret the information from the graph:

a) What do you expect might happen if a smoker increases the number of cigarettes smoked daily?

b) What do you expect might possibly happen to a smoker's health if the number of cigarettes smoked decreased?

c) When looking at the graph, what is the main idea in reducing the death rate? Keep in mind that the smoker may not be able to give up smoking completely.

d) If the number of packs smoked is increased from one to two, how many more smokers will be expected to lose their lives?

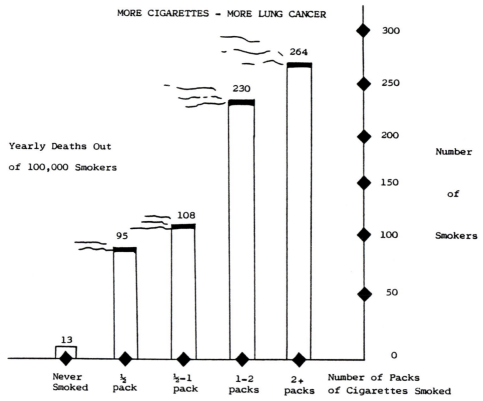

Figure 47. Bar graph developed to help students visualize important generalization on smoking.

e) If there are a number of deaths happening from lung cancer where the person did not smoke, what are some other possibilities for the cause of this disease?

Distinctive Design

Diagramming and flowcharting are two design methods that allow the composer to be more distinctive in communicating ideas than through the use of most graphs. Maps and graphs are bound by somewhat rigid design features and conventions. For instance, the circle graph can only show relative parts or percentages of a whole while the bar graph is bound by two vectors. The diagrams and flowcharts, however, are not bound by any particular style, they take shape to conform to the message shaped by the individual thinker. Teaching youngsters how to diagram and flowchart, then, can provide them with very powerful tools for solving problems and perceiving relationships. What Fry includes in the complex lineal and hypothetical categories on his

Taxonomy of Graphs would encompass this type of freer design.

Such designs based on expressing concepts to solving problems become heuristics. A heuristic is a problem-solving device that can be applied to the solution of many problems irrespective of the nature of the one problem that is being confronted at the moment. Polya (1975), the mathematician, identified certain heuristics worth learning because they are independent of individual problems and can be applied to the solution of many problems. He noted that one powerful type of heuristic is to represent problems through the use of graphs or diagrams.

Hardin (1983) has identified four design traits of diagrams. The first trait, linearity, has to do with the overall flow or straightness of the diagrammatic path. The second, order, considers the symmetry of the overall design. For instance, is it balanced or symmetrical around a central axis? If not, why not? Was there a reason for the lack of symmetry that the composer as designer wished to convey? The third trait, continuity, considers the clarity of the connections between the idea stages of the diagram. The final trait, geometry of forms, investigates the use of recognizable geometric forms to represent stages of information. If nongeometric shapes were used to explain an idea concept, did the designer intentionally use that shape and not a more conventional one to transmit the idea? Was there a particular configuration that nonverbally conveyed the idea the designer wished to communicate? For instance, in computer flowchart language the reader is probably aware that particular symbols are used to convey particular relationships. Use of the circle generally means a program start or finish, a diamond means that a decision or branching operation is to be made, while the rectangle holds the operations expressed in the program. In studies conducted with university students, Hardin concluded that the "design structure of nonverbal diagrams does communicate information about the range of explicitness of diagrammatic messages" (1983, p. 145).

Teachers can help students conceptualize abstract concepts through the use of diagramming or flowcharting. Furthermore, when the student uses the design as a heuristic during the composing process, he/she leaves behind a graphic trail of thought. Teachers could initially model the process for diagramming. This could be done visually on the chalkboard based on information contained in a flow of events. The teacher could show how he/she used certain design traits for particular communicative reasons. For instance, in the second design in the following figure, the teacher can point out that symmetry was changed to give

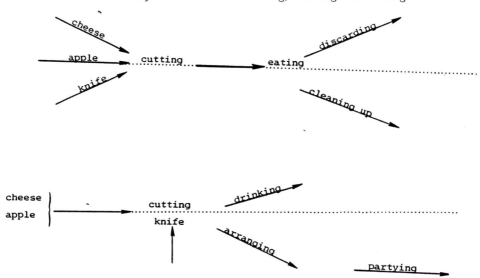

Figure 48. Use of two distinctive diagrams to portray thought.

greater meaning to the knife, on one hand, and to give greater emphasis
to the arrangement of the cheese and apple slices before the party.

Next a rather simple situation could be read to children much like the
ones contained in the above figure. Once a paragraph like "Making a
Sandwich" is read, students can be asked to diagram or flowchart it.
Youngsters could be made aware that shapes — often called nodes —
house particular bits of information. Most of the words in the first diagrammatic sequence above could have been placed in rectangular
nodes. The word "eating" may have been placed in a diamond shape because a branching decision occurred as a result of that stage in the sequence. In the second sequence, the "cheese" and "apple" words may
have been placed in the same rectangular node since they shared equal
weight while the word "cutting" might have been best represented by the
diamond shape.

Children should be also made aware of the usefulness of nongeometric shapes to portray or convey particular meanings and the
power of the connecting links. Arrows, dotted paths, lines, equal signs,
and the like can be arranged singularly or in groups to convey particular
relationships and ranges of meaning. For instance, use of the three lines
in the "cutting" to "arranging" relationship indicated in the figure above
suggest three times the greater frequency than having the cheese and apple slices for lunch.

Now children seated or standing by their desks can arrange cut-out cardboard nodes on a piece of poster paper. They can refer to the reading selection if necessary. Once each child has arranged his/her nodes to individual satisfaction, he/she can be asked to paste the nodes in place and to draw the connectors between and among the nodes. Once the connectors in the form of lines, dots, arrows, bars and the like are in place, a meaningful relationship has been visually constructed.

An important thinking activity could now follow. To complete the verbal/nonverbal cycle, youngsters could be asked to write a paragraph or composition based on the completed designs. Children, now acting as verbal composers, will need to rethink the entire meaning relationships and use verbal relational connectors such as those arranged in Figure 42 in lieu of visual connectors. The arrows, lines, and dots have implied direction of thought but during writing, the youngster will find it necessary to make these explicit. Such a strategy will help each youngster conceptualize his/her heuristic use of design. If errors in design have occurred, for instance in symmetry or continuity, the youngster may discover it during the time of verbal composing.

While use of the graphing strategy discussed earlier generally leads to convergent thought process, use of diagramming and flowcharting has more divergent outcomes. Distinctiveness of such design accents distinctiveness of thought.

Symbolizing Paragraphs

Particular symbols and design features can help students with the comprehension and composing of paragraphs. One singular strategy which has a high utility value in all of the content areas is the use of paragraph construction codes. The codes are holistic symbols which identify the paragraph's construction relative to its main idea identity. Figure 49 shows that five symbols are used.

Students will enjoy having the figure of the five codes placed on their desks as they read through selected paragraphs the teacher has distributed. As the student thinks through the meaning of each paragraph, he/she draws the symbol appropriate for the main idea identity of that paragraph. No words are necessary. Once the symbol is drawn, the student visualizes the construction of that paragraph and knows its main idea identity.

When the main idea is listed first, the inverted triangle symbol is used. The central idea is initially stated and all supporting details, ideas, or events are linked to it. An author uses the main idea last when he/she

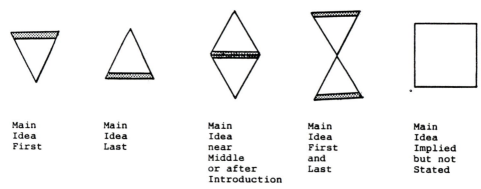

Main	Main	Main	Main	Main
Idea	Idea	Idea	Idea	Idea
First	Last	near	First	Implied
		Middle	and	but not
		or after	Last	Stated
		Introduction		

Figure 49. Codes used for paragraph structures.

wants to build curiosity or suspense. The reader realizes the reasons listed had an ultimate purpose — found last. As a writing strategy, the teacher could emphasize the sentence last purpose as the "clincher" sentence. The third symbol is used when the main idea sentence is explicit but it is not found in the first sentence location. Many times authors use one or two sentences as transition statements from the ideas of the previous paragraphs. They then state the main idea of the next paragraph a bit along in its development. The thinking through of this symbol use takes deliberate thought.

The hourglass symbol is used for a classic-type paragraph construction, that of stating the main idea in the first and last sentences. The wording in the first sentence may not be exactly the same as in the last sentence, but enough of the wording will be used to show that the author is repeating or restating his/her idea. The author may be wishing to close the paragraph with a summary statement. The author may feel that his/her idea is so important that the re-emphasis is necessary. Look at the wording of these two sentences found in a paragraph in a book about reading. The first sentence reads, "Speed reading is not suggested when studying most science chapters." Six rather long sentences followed elucidating the author's ideas. Then the author concluded the paragraph with, "In other words use your own judgement when attacking reading materials with speed, but don't look upon science in general as speed-reading material." Notice how the author re-stated his/her premise of the first sentence in order to insure that the reader understands that science reading is not the place to practice speed.

The square symbol, used to identify paragraphs with no stated main idea sentence, may be held off from students until they have practiced using the other four symbols with some degree of success. They will be lulled into thinking that all paragraphs have stated main ideas. By giving students sample paragraphs with no stated main idea last in your teaching sequence, you will be helping them in two ways. First, they will already know where main idea sentences can be located, why they are used, and what they mean. Secondly, after analyzing paragraphs with no stated main idea, the teacher can turn the analysis activity into a synthesizing one, by asking students to compose the main idea sentence themselves. The teacher may want to do this first as a whole class venture.

One of my favorite paragraphs to practice with graduate students involves the use of a paragraph about animals with unusual tongues written at a third grade level of readability. Upon first analysis of the paragraph, many students think the third sentence which states that "Many reptiles have unusual tongues" is the main idea sentence. However, near the end of the paragraph the anteater is introduced in the string of animal examples. Someone finally realizes that the anteater is not a reptile; setting the state for an implied main idea construction.

The square symbol is useful for the implied construction because students can find enough room in the square to write their own main idea sentence. Or the sentence may be composed in the margin while a bar is drawn across the square to reveal placement of that main idea as either first, middle, or last.

PARAGRAPH SKELETONS

The use of paragraph skeletons presents another strategy that uses both design and conceptual features to aid students in reading and writing growth. The technique makes use of skeletal paragraphs in which either content or transitional words are absent. Furthermore, both Nichols (1980) and Fowler (1982) have shown that such slotted arrangements can help students understand and write different types of discourse.

The author has found that teachers use the skeleton strategy in two major ways. First they help students understand how different kinds of paragraph patterns, such as narrative, comparative/contrast, description, and cause/effect are constructed. Teachers must first focus on the types of paragraph patterns and discourse relationship they want students to understand. Examples of these might be relationships of addition, sequencing, spatial relationships, comparison/contrast, and rank-ordering of ideas. The discourse relationship is a key feature in the understanding of the particular paragraph pattern. Then teachers construct model paragraphs in which most of the content wording is "left in " while most or all of the transitions, connecting relationships are "clozed out." Let's look at a few examples of these skeletal paragraphs in which the focus is on the transition relationships within the paragraph pattern.

In example 1, graduate student James Cunningham, wanted high school remedial students to apply correct spatial words in a paragraph of description. While they looked at a picture, they filled in the following paragraph with spatial words randomized from the answer key below:

Example 1 — Use of Spatial Connectors

In the 1) _____ of the street was a traffic light that was "spaced out" and flying 2) _____ the "unfriendly" skies. To the 3) _____, of the traffic light was a flying saucer with a space monster inside. 4) _____, the flying saucer was "Igor the Eagle" who was very upset because the "Mad Bomber" had just flown right 5) _____ his head. The "Mad Bomber" was 6) _____ the traffic light and heading 7) _____ "Wanda the Witch." Wanda was right 8) _____ the "Mad Bomber," so she tried to turn her broom and fly over his head. Although the strangers in the night were 9) _____ each other, by some miracle they didn't collide 10) _____ one another.

Answer Key: (1) middle, (2) around, (3) right, (4) below, (5) over, (6) under, (7) toward, (8) in front of, (9) next to (10) into

In example 2, graduate student, Miss Karen Richmond, wanted younger children to learn the connector words used in comparison/contrast writing by having them complete the skeleton paragraph below on Children and Television.

Example 2 — Use of Comparison/Contrast Connectors

Children and Television

Children should be allowed to watch television 1) _____ the amount should be limited. 2) _____ there is a great deal of garbage on television today, there are 3) _____ some fine programs. 4) _____ than allowing their children to watch anything, parents should analyze the programs that are available. 5) _____ this is time consuming, at least the children will be watching the 6) _____ shows on television. 7) _____, it would be 8) _____ for the children to read books or play with puzzles. Such activities can also be entertaining 9) _____ the children. Parents will be happier 10) _____ well.

Answer Key:
1. but 2. although 3. also 4. rather 5. while 6. best 7. Nevertheless 8. better 9. for 10. as

Ms. Ada Suarez set up the skeletal paragraph exercise by giving youngsters a choice of words. Her focus was on the relationship of addition in example 3.

Example 3 — Relationship of Addition

Johnny Smith 1) _____ (and, or) his mother lived in the outskirts of the city. With them 2) _____ (also, then) lived Mindy, their German Shepherd dog. 3) _____ (Besides, However) playing with his dog, Johnny had a lot of friends. 4) _____ (Nevertheless, Furthermore) Johnny's family was large and many times he had a lot of his cousins at home to play with. 5) _____ (Moreover, Otherwise) Johnny was an easy going, friendly boy and made friends easily. 6) _____ (Thus, Another) good thing was that he 7) _____ (also, besides had a lot of toys 8) _____ (too, both). 9) _____ (Both, But) Johnny 10) _____ (and,t(and, too) his mother had a very happy life.

Answer Key: (1) and, (2) also, (3) besides, (4) furthermore, (5) moreover, (6) another, (7) also, (8) too, (9) both, (10) and

The second way teachers use the skeletal paragraph idea to help students learn to write paragraphs of different types. In this construction, the major meaning bearing words are omitted while the transitional elements are "left in." Let's look at a few examples of these and the types of paragraph patterns they help develop. In example 4, graduate student, Ms. Mary Dawber, had students complete the following skeleton paragraph after they finished reading the **Red Badge of Courage**. The skeleton briefly recaptures the essence of the story. Note how students must sequence some of the major events while portraying some of the traits of the main character.

Example 4 — Character Analysis and Time Order

Stephen Crane is one of our great American novalists. In this story of the _____, he has _____ a tale of _____ that _____ both the _____ and the _____. It is a moving story of _____ who _____ that _____. Henry _____ with a _____ and in his first _____, he _____ when _____ that the _____. Disgusted with his _____, he helps the _____ as _____ and is _____ in the _____ by the _____. To his surprise, he _____ back in _____, a _____ in the eyes of _____.

In example 5, Mrs. Michelle Martin implemented students' use of spatial relationships differently than the way it was done in example 1. Now the connector words relating to spatial relationships are "left in" while the content is "clozed out." During this exercise, students were allowed to refer to a United States map in their Social Studies book as they applied the correct spatial relationships to connect regions of the country.

Example 5 — Paragraph of Description

_____ is divided into _____; _____. _____, _____ and _____.
_____ is between _____ and _____. _____ is northwest of _____.
_____ is in the middle of _____. _____ is on the opposite side of
_____ from _____. _____ is next to _____ and _____ is next to
the _____.

The construction in example 5 again looks at the comparison/contrast relationship. The teacher used this as both a review of the chapters on mammals and reptiles and as a way of showing fifth graders how comparison/contrast is constructed. The answer key was provided to students at the end of the activity.

Example 6 — Comparison/Contrast Paragraph

1) _____ are different from 2) _____ in several ways. First of all 3)
_____ are 4) _____ while 5) _____ are 6) _____. Secondly, 7)
_____ whereas 8) _____. In addition, 9) _____ while 10) _____.
Therefore, it is very obvious that 11) _____.

Answer Key:
1) Mammals 2) Reptiles 3) Mammals 4) Warm-blooded 5) Reptiles 6) Cold-blooded 7) Mammals bare young 8) Reptiles lay eggs 9) Mammals nurse their young 10) Reptiles abandon their young 11) Mammals differ from reptiles

Example 7 shows a clever way to help students visualize and organize the steps necessary in sequential writing. The teacher had students read a selection about building a house and exhorted the students to be sure their sequential plan was in the correct order or the house would fall apart. After students completed the exercise, they were asked to draw or flowchart the steps of the plan.

Example 7 — Sequential Order on Process Paragraph

build the frame	clear the land
construct the roof	lay out the foundation
erect the walls	dig for the foundation
construct the floor	begin the interior

To build a house, the first thing you must do is _____. Then _____.
The next thing to do is _____. Once this is complete _____. The fifth
step involves _____. Next _____. The final step in constructing the exterior of the house involves _____. Now you can _____.

CONTINUING CONNECTIONS

Other visual configurations are quite useful in helping students visualize relationships in reading and writing. These strategies will encourage students at all grade levels to use connector and function words in meaningful relationships.

Greek Crosses

The first strategy makes use of a Greek Cross configuration based on a technique suggested by Brooks (1970). He placed names of concrete objects into the five squares made from a Greek Cross. The teacher can easily make the Cross figure on a ditto master by drawing two long rectangular bars that intersect each other. This will make a figure with four equal arms with a square in the middle.

The object of using the square is to assist youngsters in constructing sentences based on spatial relationships. For instance if the word "girl" was placed in the middle square, and the words "bird" and "dog" were placed in the arms above and to the right of the girl square, students would say or write "The girl is below the bird and to the left of the dog." By changing the placement of the words, other sentences would be formed, indicating a correct understanding of the diverse meanings of words of position. Partial lists of these words may be found in the earlier figure in this chapter, showing the connector words used in compound/complex sentence construction and in the exercises just listed in the "Paragraph Skeleton" section.

For young children, second language students, and special education youngsters, a floor model of the Greek Cross could be constructed in the classroom or gym floor. One youngster would be asked to stand in the central square while objects or other children are placed in some or all of the four arms. Then the child in the middle could be asked questions regarding relative position such as "Who is in front of you?" Who or what is to the right of you?" etc. Once students understand the meanings of the spatial words, the cross configuration can be transferred to a ditto sheet. Now youngsters can be asked to write the spatial words in the various arms as one object is portrayed in the middle while others are in the remaining arms. Finally, if five different objects are shown in the five squares, the teacher could write a short selection about the relationship of the five objects to each other. The spatial words could be omitted, as was illustrated in the previous section, "Paragraph Skeleton." Using the cloze technique, students can apply the meaning of the function words by completing the paragraph.

Picture Board Displays

Another easy-to-construct strategy that helps youngsters use spatial connectors is to use a storyboard display. On a piece of cardboard or poster paper, the teacher or students would paste pictures or drawings related to a common theme. Such themes could be photographs of all the children in the classroom, kitchen utensils, or barnyard animals. In the photograph display the teacher could draw a schematic of the classroom with the teacher's desk in its locale and all of the children's desks in their relative position. Dependent on how the classroom is organized, the desks would appear in rows or in clusters. The photos of the children and teacher are then glued right on the desk position. Many questions can be asked to encourage children to use the correct words of relative position. For instance, any child in any desk position can be asked, "Tell the position of the other children around you."

Reading activities can easily be integrated with use of the spatial words. For example, after a number of pictures of kitchen utensils have been glued on a storyboard in rows and columns, the teacher can print written situations and instructions on large index cards. While youngsters look at the utensil display, the teacher can hold up cards such as, "_____, _____, and _____ are in the middle row," "_____, _____, _____ are in the last column," or "What is the position of the frying pan to the dish drain?"

Comic Strip Sequencing

Cartoon and comic strip panels found in the daily and Sunday newspapers are generally based on the movement of sequence. Furthermore, the situations depicted are so common that most viewers can respond to the picture-panel sequence without the necessity of verbal reinforcement. Mr. Ronald Vanchieri came up with a clever reading strategy for poorly motivated reading disabled junior high students. Saving editions of comic strips that appeared over several weeks time, Mr. Vanchieri would select about 10 or 14 frames which implied a complete story. The frames contained minimal dialogue. They were then displayed vertically on the left side of a piece of copy paper. Generally, three to five such frames can be pasted one below the other.

For each frame, the teacher types a sentence on the right-hand side of the paper. The sentence relates the action that is occurring in the picture frame but also makes use of function words, generally a coordinating or a subordinating conjunction. A blank is typed where the connector should go. Students are sometimes provided with a list of such connectors with the meaning relationships provided for each connector as well.

After the teacher copies the comic strip page for each student, students are asked to write in the appropriate transitional, function words in the space provided. Then students visually "read" the sequence, verbally read the typed sentences, read the function words from the function word list, and write in the correct word choice. Mr. Vanchieri completed one such sequence with the Blondie cartoon strip. The first cartoon frame showed Dagwood in the bathtub with the word "ring" splashed across the frame. The typed sentence to the right of the frame read," _____ Dagwood was taking a bath, the doorbell rang." The next frame showed Dagwood descending the stairs with a towel wrapped about him. The typed sentence to the right read, "Wrapping a towel around himself, he _____ went downstairs." So the story continued with 12 more such visual/verbal situations.

A variation of this idea would be to coordinate it with the Paragraph Skeleton strategy presented earlier. Appropriate connectors could be "left in" while the student supplies the content words for the unfolding story.

Signaling Idea Direction

Graduate student, Ms. Beth Schecter, made use of the traffic sign shape to help display appropriate direction-of-thought function words. The next figure shows that four types of relationships are expressed by these direction-of-thought words.

The "straight ahead" words are used by a teacher or writer when the direction of thought is forward. The "detour" words are used when the direction of thought will be reversed or switched to an opposite idea. The "slow-down" words are used to provide the listener or reader with some examples or illustrations to make the point clear. The "thought ending" words are used when the idea sequence is about to end or to be summarized. They may wish to use this figure so that youngsters may have examples of the transition words when they do many of the activities listed in this chapter, particularly the visual/verbal activity coming text.

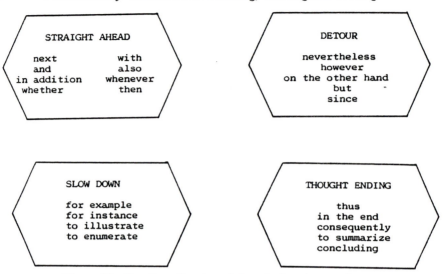

Figure 50. Signaling direction-of-thought function words.

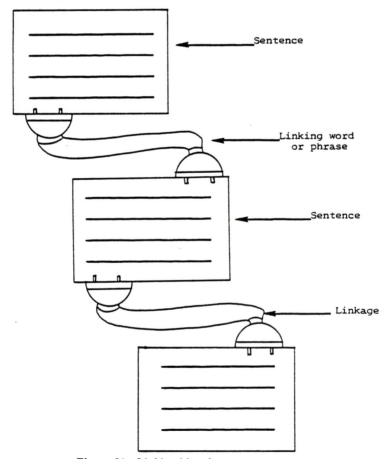

Figure 51. Linking ideas between sentences.

Linking Ideas

The author has found a high degree of success with the use of Figure 51. In the rectangular frames, the student writes a sentence. The ideas for the sentence can be generated from individual slides of a Visual Composition or from frames from a comic strip. Within the power cord connecting two sentence frames, the student writes a connecting word as a transition phrase. Students visually see how ideas are connected. Generally, on a regular page, five sentence frames interlaced with four connecting words, can be constructed.

NETWORKING TO IMPROVE THINKING LINKS

The readers may recall that in Chapter Two the topic of schema theory was advanced. Theorists created nonverbal images such as the building block metaphor, the template idea, and pictures in the head to explain how schema theory works to hierarchically and associatively relate concepts and relationships.

The topic of this section is to extend that discussion by presenting a nonverbal, practical way to implement schema theory in the classroom. This will be accomplished through the use of the semantic networking strategy. Semantic networks, also called semantic maps or semantic webs, are graphic arrangements displaying the major ideas and relationships that exist for a printed text or soon-to-be written account. The network consists of "nodes" which can be drawn in circles, rectangles, squares, or diamonds containing key words or phrases and connecting links in the form of lines and arrows drawn between the nodes. Fredrickson (1975) described semantic networks as graphs consisting of semantic "tokens" or "concepts" connected by relational links. Hardin (1983) likened the nodes to "entities" in efforts to differentiate the visuospatial quality of the semantic information from the network links or connections. Braden (1983) suggested that the visual display of information within such an outline transcends the more traditional, linear arrangement of text. He adds that the graphic can be used to enrich and organize verbal material in a way that some outlines will be linear in configuration, others will be hierarchical, and others may have a loose application of subtopics.

Using the networking strategy becomes highly practical because it can be adapted to almost any text and can be done with individual students, groups of students or with the whole class. When the teacher constructs the informal network on the chalkboard or overhead prior to reading or writing, students see how the ideas they will read or write about mesh with the previous knowledge they have about the topic. De Beaugrande notes the advantage of such a conceptual use, "a network for an entire text can be modeled . . . a main advantage is that an ideal pattern of concepts and relations is obtained against which the patterns of readers' reports of the content can be matched" (1981, p. 290). Davidson (1982) favors the whole-class use of the mapping activity because it actively requires students to interpret their pre-existing knowledge and experience while helping them recall and retain text information.

A second appeal of the networking procedure is the nonverbal, holistic way it conceptualizes a content. The network of nodes and connecting lines visually displays the relationship of the whole to the parts and the parts to the whole. The informational network becomes a spatial configuration which substitutes for the more traditional outline arranged linearly and vertically on a page. However, a major thinking tool of the networking strategy is in the arrangement of the overall map organization. That is, the relationships expressed through the overall configurations and connective links are more important than how the nodes themselves are graphically portrayed.

Various practitioners have reported success with the mapping technique. Pearson and Johnson (1978) proposed that semantic maps can be developed with students to build and extend vocabulary comprehension and to expand their intuitive notions about the similarities and differences among concepts. Freedman and Reynolds (1980) showed teachers how to construct maps from basal reader stories to help students predict story events while Cleland (1981) showed teachers how to generate three types of semantic webs — the episodic web, the inductive web, and the emotions web — to help remedial second grade readers organize relationships among story characters and events.

The author has found that the networking strategy can be used in three global contexts — to increase vocabulary and conceptual understandings, to aid reading comprehension, and to advance writing development. Each use will be developed in turn.

Increasing Vocabulary and Conceptual Development Through Networks

In using the networking technique to aid vocabulary and conceptual development there are a number of steps that require students to make key conceptual contributions to the process. The steps of teacher/student interaction are listed in the following logical sequence:

1. The teacher focuses on a key word central to a selection to be read or central to overall conceptual development, such as the words "fossil," "behavior," or "weather."

2. That key word could now be written on the chalkboard and circled or boxed-in, ready to serve as the central node for a developing network.

3. The teacher now asks the class group to contribute as many words they know of that are related to the key word. Students can individually think of these words and write them down in any order on a sheet of paper, or the teacher can jot them down on the chalkboard in random order as they are offered by students. This "brainstorming" step is important because students bring what they know, their pre-existing knowledge schema, to the topic. Secondly, they will undoubtedly contribute some vocabulary words that are designated as new reading words in the forthcoming reading selection.

4. Once all the words have been solicited from the class or group, the teacher should now ask students the key mental strategy to group the words that go together. This requires that students rewrite the words in associative lists, and it is probably best done as an individual strategy. In this way, each student has the opportunity to look for similarities and differences among word meanings, a task which requires active mental participating. Students are grouping qualities, attributes, and examples of word meanings; in a sense connecting relationships that are related to a more global meaning.

5. After the individual word groupings are completed, the teacher can now have the word groups displayed on the chalkboard. An interesting event usually occurs here. A word may appear on two or more different lists, each contributed by individual youngsters. For instance, if the key concept word was "fossil," one youngster may have included the word "print" in a grouping with such words as "remains," "impression," or "mold," while a second youngster may have included the word "print" in a grouping with "draw," "trace," or "carve." The first youngster considered the word in a context of an imprint left in the earth while the second focused on the way that fossils may have been constructed by early humans as they left remains behind. Both conceptions are correct, and the teacher is now helping students to expand their meaning concepts by establishing new mental connections.

6. With all the word groupings displayed on the board, a rectangular box could now be drawn above each such list. Another concept strategy now occurs. The teacher should ask each student individually to think of a category label for each word grouping. At this point, each group of words could begin to be copied into a more permanent-type notebook as the student writes the classifying word or word phrase above the group. For instance, if the key concept in Step 1 was "weather" and students grouped together such words as "barometer," "thermometer," and "weather vane," the classifying heading could be "Instruments for Measuring Weather." After the individual attempts at the category labeling, students and teacher should agree on the final label as it is listed in the empty box on the chalkboard. This label should then be copied

above the lists in the individual notebooks.

7. If other new vocabulary words are to be found in the forthcoming reading selection but were not elicited from students during the brainstorming and grouping phases, the teacher could write these new words in the appropriate lists at this time. For instance, if a new word is "thermocouple," it would be listed under the grouping "Instruments for Measuring the Weather."

8. Now the teacher is ready to construct the network on the board. With the key word acting as the central node, the teacher would draw in as many nodes as there were category or classifying labels. Lines would connect the drawn-in nodes to the central node. Then boxes or circles would be drawn around each classifying node to house all the vocabulary words that were listed in each separate word grouping. Lines would connect these smaller nodes to the larger classifying node. By drawing the key node in the center, the effect is one of a radiating hub with the lines acting as spokes to connect all the parts to the whole. Students now visually see the range of their knowledge, and as they read these words singularly and in phrases in the nodes, they can connect the meanings in a conceptual hierarchy. If a particular word is forgotten, a student may be prompted to remember by its associate group or by the classifying label. The completed holistic effect would look something like this:

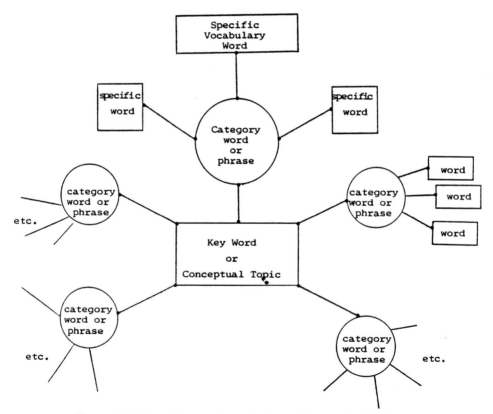

Figure 52. Networking to aid vocabulary and conceptual development.

Using Networks to Aid Reading Comprehension

The networking strategy can be used before, during, or after reading of a textual selection. The teacher's purpose would dictate when and to what degree to use the mapping strategy. For instance, if a new concept area was to be covered with students, the teacher may wish to begin a partial construction of the map on the chalkboard with key conceptual nodes filled in. In this way, the map would serve as a graphic advanced organizer. As students read an assigned selection, the prior networking of ideas would help them process the text more efficiently. Ausubel (1968) had indicated that advance organizers increase learning and aid recall because they help clarify and organize the learner's cognitive structure prior to the learning task.

Students would complete the remaining nodes after silent reading. This use of the strategy allows students to see the entire range of the content as well as the major areas that will be covered in the text. In the partial map that follows, students will understand that in the unit to be read called "Bedouins of the Sahara," the Bedouins refer to a group of people who are conceptually related to the larger topic Nomads or wandering people of the world. Furthermore, students see that they will learn of what the Bedouins eat, how they clothe themselves, and how their homes are constructed.

The teacher could fill-in some of the detail nodes under the three subcategories or could leave out the words "food, clothing, homes" and have students conceptually figure out these category headings.

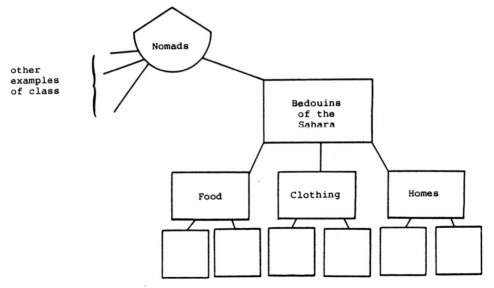

Figure 53. Partial classification map constructed for "Bedouins of the Desert."

A teacher colleague, Dr. Josephine Stahl-Gemake of St. John's University, actively involves students in text and map participation as she constructs the map in conjunction with silent reading. Generally, focusing on a selection of conflict involving several key characters, she has students read an assigned number of pages, then transfers their knowledge onto the map projections. For instance, after reading the beginning pages of a tale of conflict, she asks students about the character traits of the characters involved. Focusing on each character in turn with his or her name included in a central node, the traits are webbed to the character. Then, she asks students to verify from the text why they selected a certain word to designate a character trait. Students must then find explicit and implicit text clues which verify a particular personality trait. Because of the personality traits of each character, she then asks students to predict what will happen next in the tale before the next group of pages are assigned. At other times, elements of conflict could become the central focus with particular incidents serving as the attached nodes. Finally, the mapping strategy can be effectively used after silent reading. Students can collectively modify, amend, or correct a pre-reading map to verify and extend their knowledge (Pearson and Spiro, 1982). More importantly, the map format and the selection content can serve as previsionary stimuli for writing activities that follow.

To help students understand how text is organized, various graphic outlines of map formats can be developed with students after silent reading. The type of map format selected by the teacher will be dictated by the type of discourse organization read by the students. The author, with a number of colleagues, has experimented with at least four such graphic outlines as indicated in Figure 54.

For narrative-type organization in which incidents follow in order, the map format can be used. Dependent upon the number of key incidents, nodes are constructed in the form of large arrows with the apex of the arrow pointed to the right. Details or related events to each key incident are arranged almost in a time line fashion down below the key-incident node. This web is called the episodic web after a suggestion by Stein and Glenn (1977) for schema of story organization. Stein and Glenn proposed that a story grammar is composed of settings and one or a series of episodes. Story grammar is within the schema of youngsters for it is based on the unfolding of time sequences in a logical, chronological order. In the episodic web, the nodes show information relating to unfolding story episodes while the network links in the form of arrows bind information that occurs in each episode. For instance, in the partial map printed below for the selection" Around the World with the Graf

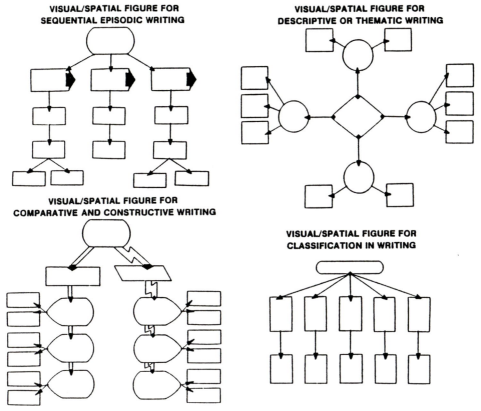

Figure 54. Four visual/spatial figures which portray four writing styles.

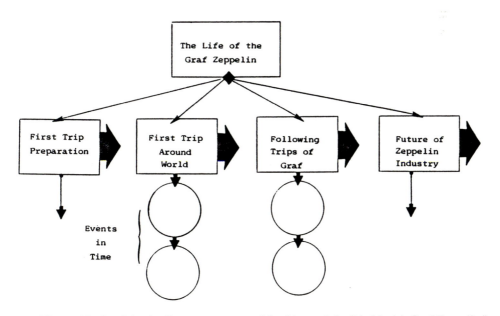

Figure 55. Partial episodic map constructed for "Around the World with Graf Zeppelin."

Zeppelin" (Reader's Digest, **Reading Skill Builders**, Silver Edition), the reader can see that four major episodes will be covered in the selection.

A second type map, the thematic or descriptive map, relates selections, elements and details about persons, places, or things in a display around the central node. Narrative or unfolding action is missing in this map framework. Instead, it displays associative connections among components of a topic. The earlier map structure created for vocabulary development is the graphic outline used to capture this type of written organization. A thematic network created for a level four Reader's Digest Skill Builder, "Fossils Underfoot" is shown in the following figure.

Thematic map for "Fossils Underfoot"

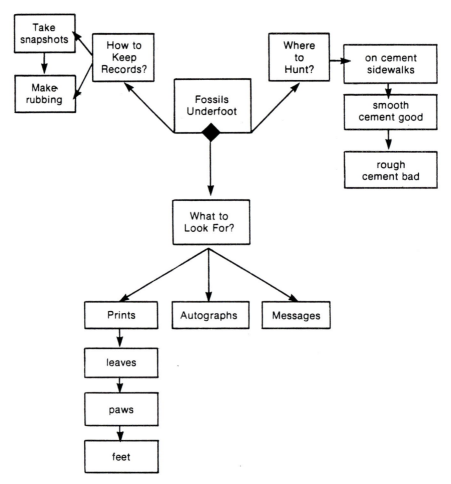

Figure 56. Thematic map for "Fossils Underfoot." From R. Sinatra, J. Stahl-Gemake, and D. Berg: Improving reading comprehension of disabled readers through semantic mapping. *The Reading Teacher, 38*, Oct. 1984, p. 26. Courtesy of International Reading Association (2/14/85).

The thematic map highlights the important features of the hobby of fossil hunting: places to hunt, clues to look for, and how to keep records. New vocabulary words are found in detail nodes supporting the hobby's particular subthemes.

For instance, in a selection dealing with the many faces of winter, the effect of winter on trees, seeds, and animals could be displayed in nodes radiating out from the center. New conceptual words such as "insulates" and "hibernate" would be found in detail nodes that support the category of animals. Notice that by placing the thematic node in the center, as shown in the figure, associated relationships are portrayed as stemming from the main concept.

A third type of network, the classification map, is based on a model presented by Pearson and Johnson (1978) and is especially suited for development with expository discourse. This configurational network shows the relationship that exists among concepts by displaying how class, examples, and properties or attributes are related. The earlier figure, showing the organization of the reading on Bedouins, follows this format. The class, Bedouins of the Sahara, attributes of how the Bedouins live, and examples of the attributes are arranged in a pyramidal design in this framework. Incidentally, the larger class is "Nomads" while the node "Bedouins of the Sahara" now becomes an example of the larger class.

Networks for cause/effect and comparison/contrast text organization have been developed as well, the latter being displayed in Figure 54.

Using Networks to Develop Writing Skills

A very important strategy which shows the relationship of reading comprehension to that of the organization skills needed for writing is to show students how to develop compositions after map construction of a reading selection. In this case the reading selection serves as the stimulus for map organization and writing. Students are asked to reconstruct a selection just read according to one of the network graphic outlines. The reconstruction process allows for two major thought processes to occur. First, students are encouraged to remember the information presented in the textual selection in a hierarchical way and, most importantly, they are asked to arrange that information in a map format that best captures the selection organization.

Initially, students can be given the appropriate map format by the teacher after they have a particular type of discourse organization, such as narrative, theme, or classification. However, a bit later in the training, students can be asked to select the map format that they think best suits the selection organization. After selection, students are given a skeleton map format, meaning a dittoed sheet containing one of the configurations previously presented. They each, in turn, fill in the information in the empty node slots. Once the information is arranged, they are then asked to reconstruct the selection in writing according to their map format. The pay-off activity comes at a later date, when students are given a skeleton map format and asked to write their **own** composition based on the way they organized information on their map.

Using the mapping procedure to improve writing and discourse understanding, a number of things are noted. First, students at all grade levels improve in the quality and quantity of their writing. Secondly, they learn how to organize their thoughts. Finally, with continued practice and teacher guidance, students begin to draw their own nodes and connective links on the skeleton maps provided. In other words, they are adding and organizing more information that will find its way in a soon-to-be-written composition. Note in the following Figure, Sean's partial map based on a selection he read about "Scuba Diving."

The reader can see that 6th grade Sean "busted out" of the provided map nodes and connective links, and added information in ways that he

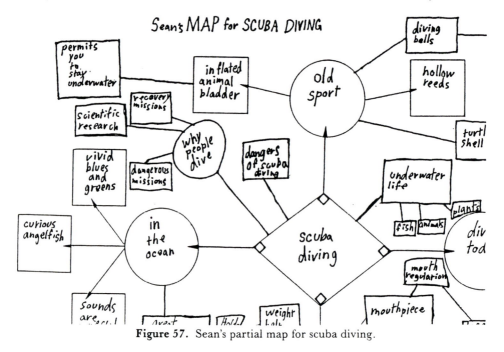

Figure 57. Sean's partial map for scuba diving.

saw related best to key ideas. For instance, the key idea "why people dive" was not covered nor contained in any other node arrangement. Therefore, Sean added that idea and the associative details related to it. All the ideas, information and connective links came from Sean himself and provided the organizational plan for his forthcoming composition.

A key feature of the networking procedure is that the naming of the content — the information contained in the nodes — is secondary in importance to the map conceptualization or map organization. This means that when students select a particular map format, they will arrange their information in connective and hierarchial ways dictated by the map format. While the filled-in nodes contain the potential information for a forthcoming composition, the network links or connectors bind the graphic display into a distinct conceptual organization.

Researching the Effects of Networking

At St. John's University, Jamaica, New York, four separate research studies have been conducted to date to investigate the effects of networking and graphic outlines on reading comprehension and writing. Sinatra, Berg, and Dunn (1985) wished to determine the effects of using the networking technique upon reading comprehension for a small group of learning disabled youngsters. The graphic outline was constructed for each child prior to silent reading of five different selections. This strategy was matched with five different reading selections in which a more traditional, verbal and discussion approach was used prior to silent reading. Reading comprehension was compared between the two approaches. In 11 of 15 trials, reading comprehension was stronger when the mapping procedure was used to graphically outline the story before reading.

In a second study (Sinatra, Stahl-Gemake, and Berg: 1984), 27 disabled readers ranging in grade level from third to eighth were assigned to 27 graduate teacher interns. During a five week period, the interns covered 10 reading selections at appropriate reading levels with each remedial student. For five reading selections, the teacher presented the vocabulary and concepts through networking by using one of the three graphic outlines presented earlier.

Results comparing the mapping procedure with a verbal-oriented readiness approach showed that in 19 of the 27 cases, the total comprehension score based on the five selections was greater when the mapping procedure was used. In two cases, the comprehension score was the same for both approaches and in six cases, comprehension was stronger under the verbal approach. For all 27 students in the five week period, the mean number of comprehension questions correct under the semantic map approach was 37.9 while for the verbal approach the mean number of questions correct was 35.9. The mean difference of 2.0 in favor of the mapping approach was significant at the .05 level ($t = 2.41$, $df = 25$).

A third study was conducted over one college semester with three sections of freshmen enrolled in special classes to increase reading and writing proficiency (Sinatra, 1984). All 53 freshmen, 18 males and 35 females, were assigned to the special class during their first college semester upon administrative review of their high school records and verbal SAT scores. Their average reading score in Reading Comprehension assessed during the first week of the course was a grade equivalent of 10.62 ($s = 2.4$). A composition written on the same topical theme was also collected from all students during the first week in efforts to determine their processing level in writing prior to the introduction of the networking technique. Their average composition score was 71.32 percent ($s = 7.3$) based on the average of three raters using a holistic rating scale ranging from 0 to 100 percent. Their writing ability was not that advanced since a student needed only 65 percent mastery in writing to graduate from high school in New York State.

During the initial weeks of the course, students were introduced to four different types of network outlines: the narrative design, the thematic design, the classificatory design, and the comparative/contrastive design. The procedure followed in this study was that over a period of weeks; students read four assigned selections that were written in four different styles. After silent reading, students were asked to reconstruct the content of the selection using an appropriate blank or "skeleton" network outline provided by the instructor. In the reconstruction process, students filled in the nodes with information they remembered about the content selection. During the next scheduled class period, students wrote their own version of the previously read selection by using their own map as a guide.

In a subsequent class period, students were provided with an additional skeleton map format. The task was now to write their own composition using the map outline and structure as a guide for composition development. Four additional compositions were therefore produced by each student. All four structured and four creative compositions were evaluated holistically by the three independent raters.

Analysis of variance indicated that no significant affects existed among types of writing and that none of the four structured compositions nor any of the four creative compositions were written significantly better than the pre-study writing sample. However, results of a t-test comparing the pretest and post-test scores of the Comprehensive battery of the Nelson-Denny Reading Test revealed a significant effect for reading comprehension (t = 4.82, df = 52, p < .001) with a mean grade level difference of 1.58 between pre and posttesting for the 53 freshmen. This means that as a result of one procedure only, the semantic mapping technique, college freshmen increased approximately a year and a half in reading comprehension in one semester.

In all three studies, reading comprehension improved as a result of the mapping strategy used before or after silent reading of a selection. In the freshman study, however, the large gain in reading comprehension occurred when the mapping strategy was individually applied after silent reading. After each freshman silently read a selection, each conceptualized and restructured the organization of the content in an organizational, nonverbal "blueprint." This thinking through of previously read content and rearranging the content conceptually in nodes and linking relationships aids the reading comprehension process.

Wishing to assess the effects of networking upon the writing process a bit further, a fourth study was initiated with 39 reading disabled students. Students were at a mean age of 11.2 (s = 1.8), at a mean grade level of 5.4 (s = 1.7), had a silent reading performance of 3.5 (s = 1.2), and a spelling level of 4.8 (s = 1.7). Their average writing score on a scale ranging from 0 to 100 percent was 58 percent (s = 9.4) according to average scores assigned by three judges who rated their compositions.

During the course of the three week study, the students wrote six compositions. Three compositions were written from ideas on a topic that were arranged in lists in front of each student. Three compositions were written from ideas that were arranged in three of the network outlines — the narrative, the thematic, the classificatory network designs.

When the two writing treatments were compared with the group's original score of 58 percent competency in writing, there was a significant effect noted for the network procedure (t = 2.02, df = .38, p = < .05) but not for the list procedure. The improvement for writing in the three week period for the network procedure was 2.03 points compared to .92 points for the listing procedure. The results from this last study show that writing can improve over short periods of time when the graphic outline is used to help organize thoughts prior to writing.

Networking on the Microcomputer

The semantic networking strategy reaches its culmination in a micro-computer software program called **Thinking Networks for Reading and Writing** (Sinatra et al, 1985). Thinking Networks also completes the literacy cycle illustrated earlier in Figure 7 by integrating written literacy, computer literacy, and graphic representations of visual literacy in one program. Five distinct Thinking Network formats are used. The key feature of each is the separate configurational design or network that the student helps construct during the reading comprehension phase. Each network design models a particular style of written discourse. For each design, the student is initially involved in constructing the network, then uses the completed design to restructure the original reading selection, and finally composes via word processor an original composition based on the design format.

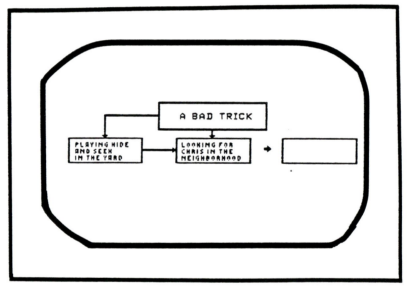

Figure 58. Screen of microcomputer software program interfacing nonverbal networking with reading comprehension and writing.

Figure 58 shows one of the many screens for selection "N-6" which means narrative discourse at the 6th grade level of reading. After filling-in the title node, "A Bad Trick," the student is asked to correctly name the three most important episodes or events in the story selection. As each of these are selected, they are linked to the main idea node and to one another. Note that the cursor arrow is prompting the student for the answer to the third grade episode node. The details or sequenced events that are related to each episode node are arranged in smaller sized boxes below. The size of the node boxes corresponds to their idea value. The main idea rectangle is the largest node while the detail nodes are somewhat smaller than the major episode nodes.

CONCLUSION

This final chapter has presented a number of ways that educators can use specific visual literacy strategies to develop thinking, reading, and writing competency through the grades. The visual literacy strategies were grouped into general category areas to help teachers focus on the specific steps needed to achieve visual/verbal connections. While applications of direct experience, analogy and metaphor were discussed in earlier chapters, these uses merge with many of the strategies presented in this chapter to foster the thinking of synthesis. Hopefully the goal of the latter third of the book as well as the scope of the book itself will assist educators in the fields of visual, verbal, and computer literacies to help students think, comprehend, and compose to their fullest potentials.

REFERENCES

Adams, M.J. and Collins, A.: A schema-theoretic view of reading. In Freedle, R.
(Ed.): *New Directions in Discourse Processing.* Norwood, NJ, Ablex Pub. Co., 1979.

Alexander, P.: The other gifted. *Reading Improvement, 19*:25-30, 1982.

Allen, W.: Intellectual abilities and instructional media designs. *Audio-Visual Communication Review, 23*:139-170, Summer 1975.

Anastasiow, Nicholas: Cognition and language: Some observations. In Laffey, J,
and Shuy, R. (Eds.): *Language Differences: Do They Interfere?* Newark, Delaware, International Reading Association, 1973.

Anderson, Richard: *Schema-directed processes in language comprehension.* Technical report
No. 50, Urbana, IL. Center for the Study of Reading, University of Illinois,
1977. (ERIC Document Reproduction Service No. Ed 142 977).

Arnheim, Rudolph: *Art and Visual Perception: A Psychology of the Creative Eye.* Berkley,
University of California Press, 1954

Asbell, B.: Writers' workshop at age 5. *The New York Times Magazine*, 55-63; 69-72,
Feb. 1984.

Ashton-Warner, Sylvia: *Teacher.* New York, Bantom Books, 1963.

Athey, Irene: Syntax, semantics, and reading. In Guthrie, John, (Ed.): *Cognition,
Curriculum, and Comprehension.* Newark, Delaware, International Reading Association, 1977.

Ausburn, L.J. and Ausburn, F.B.: Visual literacy: Background, theory, and practice. *Programmed Learning and Educational Technology, 15*:291-297, 1978.

Ausubel, D.P.: *Educational Psychology — A Cognitive Review.* New York, Holt, Rinehart,
and Winston, 1968.

Bakan, P.: Hypnotizability, laterality of eye movements and functional brain asymmetry. *Perceptual and Motor Skills, 28*:927-932, 1969.

Balajthy, E.: Computer simulations and reading. *The Reading Teacher, 37*:590-593,
1984.

Bannatyne, Alexander: *Language, Reading, and Learning Disabilities.* Springfield, IL,
Charles C Thomas, 1971.

Bartlett, F.C. *Remembering.* Cambridge, England, The Cambridge University Press,
1932.

Becker, Samuel: Visual stimuli and the construction of meaning. In Bikkar, R. and
Coffman, W. (Eds.): *Visual Learning, Thinking, and Communication.* New York, Academic Press, 1978.

Berry, Mildred: *Language Disorders of Children: The Bases and Diagnoses.* New York, Appleton-Century-Croft, 1969.

Bettelheim, Bruno and Zelan, Karen: Why children don't like to read. *Families*, 56-60, March 1982.

Bloom, L.P. and Braden, R.A.: Creative visualization with microcomputers. In Walker, A.D., Braden, R.A., and Dunker, L.H. (Eds.): *Enhancing Human Potential: Readings from the 15th Conference of the International Visual Literacy Association.* Blacksburg, VA, Virginia Polytechnic Institute, 1984.

Bogen, Joseph: Some educational implications of hemispheric specilization. In Wittrock, W. (Ed.): *The Human Brain.* Englewood Cliffs, NJ, Prentice Hall, 1977.

Bork, Alfred: *Computerworld,*: 4, 1981.

Bower, Gordon: Mental imagery and associative learning. In Gregg, L. (Ed.): *Cognition in Learning and Memory,* New York, Wiley, 1972.

Braden, R.: Visualizing the verbal and verbalizing the visual. In Braden, R.A., and Walker, A.D. (Eds.): *Seeing Ourselves: Visualization in a Social Context.* Blacksburg, VA, Polytechnic Institute and State University, 1983.

Braden, R., and Horton, J.: Identifying theoretical foundations of visual literacy. *Journal of Visual/Verbal Languaging.* 2:73, 1982.

Brooks, L.: An extension of the conflict between visualization and reading. *Quarterly Journal of Experimental Psychology,* 22:91-96, 1970.

Bugelski, B.R.: Imagery and Verbal behavior. *Journal of Mental Imagery, 1*:39-52, 1977.

Cameron, Jack: Promoting talk through 35 MM slides. *English Journal, 69*:14-19, Sept. 1980.

Chall, Jeanne and Mirsky, Alan: The implications for education. In Chall, J. and Mirsky, A. (Eds.): *Education and the Brain.* Chicago, IL, University of Chicago Press, 1978.

Clark, R.W.: *Einstein: The Life and Times.* New York, The World Publishing Co., 1971.

Claxton, C., and Ralston, Y.: *Learning Styles: Their Impact on Teaching and Administration,* Washington, D.C., American Association of Higher Education, Research Report N0. 10, 1978.

Cleland, C.: Highlighting issues in children's literature through semantic webbing. *The Reading Teacher, 34*:642-646, 1981.

Cochran, L.: Defining visual literacy. *AECT Research and Theory Division Newsletter, 5*:3-4, 1976. (Also in ERIC 136 822).

Cohen, B., Berent, S., and Silverman, A.: Field-dependence and lateralization of function in the human brain. *Archives General Psychiatry, 28*:165-167, 1973.

Cohen, Rosalie: Conceptual styles, culture conflict, and nonverbal tests of intelligence. *American Anthropologist, 71*:828-856, 1969.

Coleman, S., and Zenhausern, R.: Processing speed, laterality patterns, and memory encoding as a function of hemispheric dominance. *Bulletin of the Psychonomic Society, 14*:357-360, 1979.

Collins, Carmen: Creating a photo essay. *Language Arts, 57*:268-273, 1980.

Condon, W. and Sander, L.: Neonate movement is synchronized with adult speech: Interactional participation and language acquisition. *Science, 183*:99-101, 1974.

Cordoni, B., O'Donnell, J., Ramaniah, N., Kutz, J., and Rosenheim, M.: Wechsler adult intelligence score patterns for learning disabled young adults. *Journal of Learning Disabilities, 14*:404-407, 1981.

Cromer, J., and Thompson, N.: The electronic sensory languages: A return to Lascaux. *English Journal, 69*:89-92, 1980.

Cureton, George: Using a Black learning style. *The Reading Teacher, 13*:751-756, 1978.

Dake, Dennis: *An education strategy for the right hemisphere of the brain.* Paper presented at the 9th Annual Meeting of the International Visual Literacy Association, Iowa City, Iowa, 1977. (ERIC Document Reproduction Service No. ED 154 432).

Dale, Edgar: *Audio-visual Methods in Teaching,* 3rd ed. New York, Holt, Rinehart, and Winston, 1969.

Das, J., Kirby, J. and Jarman, R.: Simultaneous and successive synthesis: An alternative needed for cognitive abilities. *Psychological Bulletin, 82*:87-103, 1975.

Das, J., Kirby, J. and Jarman, R.: *Simultaneous and Successive Cognitive Processes.* New York, Academic Press, 1979.

Davidson, Jane: The group mapping activity for instruction in reading and thinking. *Journal of Reading, 26*:52-56, 1982.

Dawkins, J.: *Syntax and Readability.* Newark, Delaware, International Reading Associaiton, 1975.

DeBeaugrande, R.: Design criteria for process models of reading. *Reading Research Quarterly, 16*:261-315, 1981.

Debes, John: The loom of visual literacy. *Audiovisual Instruction, 14*:25-27, 1969.

Debes, John: Jack in the pulpit. *Visual Literacy Newsletter, 10*:2, 1981.

Debes, John and Williams, Clarence: The power of visuals. *Instructor, 84*:31-38, 1974.

Debes, John and Williams, Clarence: *Visual Literacy, Languaging, and Learning: Provocative Paper Series #1.* Washington, D.C., Gallaudet College, 1978.

de Grandpre, Byrne: *Kinesthetic Reading Program.* Plattsburgh, NY, SUNY-Plattsburgh Printing Center, 1983.

Della Valle, Joan: *An experimental investigation of the relationship(s) between preference for mobility and the word-pair recognition scores of seventh-grade students to provide supervisory and administrative guidelines for the organization of effective instructional environments.* Unpublished doctoral dissertation, St. John's University, Queens, NY, 1983.

Doktor, R., and Bloom, D.: Selective lateralization of cognitive style related to occupation as determined by EEG alpha asymmetry.. *Psychophysiology, 14*:385-387, 1977.

Doughty, P., Pearce, J., and Thorton, G.: *Exploring language.* London, Edward Arnold Publisher, 1972.

Duchastel, P.: Illustrating instructional texts. *Educational Technology, 18*:(11), 36-39, 1978.

Duckworth, Eleanor: Language and thought. In Schwebel, M., and Raph, J. (Eds.): *Piaget in the Classroom.* New York, Basic Books, 1973a.

Duckworth, Eleanor: Piaget takes a teacher's look. *Learning,* 22-25, October 1973b.

Dunn, R.: Teaching students through their individual learning styles: A research report. In Keefe, J. (Ed.): *Student Learning Styles and Brain Behavior.* Reston, VA, National Association of Secondary School Principals, 1982.

Dunn, R.: Learning style and its relation to exceptionality at both ends of the spectrum. *Exceptional Children, 49*:496-506, 1983.

Dunn, Rita and Dunn, Kenneth: *Educator's Self-teaching Guide to Individualizing Instructional Programs*. New York, Parker Pub., 1975.

Dunn, R., Dunn, K., and Price, G.: Identifying individual learning styles. In Kiernan, O. (Ed.): *Student Learning Styles: Diagnosing and Prescribing Programs*. Reston, VA, National Association of Secondary School Principals, 1979.

Dunn, R., Dunn, K., and Price, G.: *Learning Style Inventory*. Lawrence, Kansas, Price Systems, Inc., 1978, 1981, and 1985 (in revision).

Durr, W., La Pere, J., and Niehaus, B.: Mr. Picklepaw's Popcorn. In *Rewards, Level 7*. Boston, MA, Houghton Mifflin Co., 1971.

Eastman Kodak Company: *How to make and use a pinhole camera*. Kodak Publication No. AA-5, Rochester, NY, Consumer Market Division, 1979.

Eckhardt, Ned: The learning potential. *Media and Methods, 13*:48-53, January 1977.

Eckhoff, B.: How reading affects children's writing. *Language Arts, 60*:607-616, 1983.

Edwards, Betty: *Drawing on the Right Side of the Brain*. Los Angeles, CA, J.P. Tarcher, 1979.

Ehrlichman, Howard and Wienberger, Authur: Lateral eye movements and hemispheric asymmetry: A critical review, *Psychological Bulletin, 85*:1080-1101, 1978.

Eisner, Elliot: Mind as cultural achievement. *Educational Leadership, 38*:466-471, 1981.

Ekwall, Eldon: *Diagnosis and Remediation of the Disabled Reader*. Boston, Allyn and Bacon, 1977.

Elkind, David: We can teach reading better. *Today's Education, 64*:34-38, 1975.

Emmett, A.: American education: The dead end of the 80's. *Personal Computing, 7*:96-105, 1983.

Epstein, Herman: Phrenoblysis: Special brain and mind growth periods. 1. Human brain and skull development. *Development Psychobiology, 7*:207-216, 1974.

Epstein, Herman: Growth spurts during brain development: Implications for educational policy and practice. In J. Chall and A. Minsky (Eds.), *Education and the Brain*, Chicago, University of Chicago Press, 1978.

Fadley, Jack and Hosler, Virgina: *Understanding the Alpha Child at Home and in School*. Springfield, IL, Charles C Thomas, 1979.

Fagan, Edward: Brain hemispheres: Panacea 2001? *The Clearing House, 52*:407-410, 1979.

Fillion, Bryant: Visual literacy. *Clearing House, 47*:308-311, 1973.

Fisher, D.: *Visual language processing as it relates to instructional practice in beginning reading*. Paper presented at the 23rd International Reading Association Conference, Houston, Texas, 1978.

Fork, D., and Jonassen, D.: Research in visual literacy: Where to begin. *AECT Research and Theory Division Newsletter, 5*:12-14, 1976. (Also in ERIC 136 822).

Foster, Harold: *The new literacy: The language of film and television*. Urbana, IL, National Council of Teachers of English, 1979.

Fowler, G.L.: Developing comprehension skills in primary students through the use of story frames. *The Reading Teacher, 35*:176-179, 1982.

Franklin, Margery: Non-verbal representation in young children: A cognitive perspective. *Young Children, 29*:33-52, 1973.

Fransecky, R.: Visual literacy and teaching the disadvantaged. *Audiovisual Instruction, 14*:31, 116-118, October 1969.

Fransecky, Roger and Debes, John: *Visual Literacy: A Way to Learn — A Way to Teach.* Washington, D.C., Association for Educational Communication and Technology, 1972.

Fransecky, R. and Ferguson, R.: New ways of seeing: The Milford Visual Communication Project. *Audiovisual Instruction,* three part series, *18*: April, May 56-65, June/July 47-49, 1973.

Fredrickson, Carl: Effects on context-induced process operations on semantic information acquired from discourse. *Cognitive Psychology, 7*:139-166, 1975.

Freedman, G., and Reynolds, G.: Enriching basal reading lessons with semantic webbing. *The Reading Teacher, 38*:677-684, 1980.

Fromkin, V., Krashen, S., Curtiss, S., Rigler, D., and Rigler, M.: The development of language in Genie: A case of language acquisition beyond the "critical period." *Brain and Language, 1*:81-107, 1974.

Frostig, M., and Maslow, P.: Neuropsychological contributions to education. *Journal of Learning Disabilities, 12*:538-552, October 1979.

Fry, Edward: Graphic literacy. *Journal of Reading, 26*:383-390. 1981.

Fryrear, J.L. and Krauss, D.A.: *Photography in Mental Health*, Springfield, IL, Charles C Thomas, 1983.

Furth, Hans: *Piaget and Knowledge.* Englewood Cliffs, NJ, Prentice-Hall, 1969.

Furth, Hans: *Piaget for Teachers.* New York, Prentice-Hall, 1970.

Galin, David: Educating both halves of the brain. *Childhood Education, 53*:17-20, October 1976.

Galin, David: EEG studies of lateralization of verbal processes. In Ludlow, C., and Doran-Quine, M. (Eds.). *The Neurological Bases of Language Disorders in Children: Methods and Directions for Research.* Bethesda, Maryland, USDHEW, NINCDS Monograph No. 22, 1979.

Galin, D. and Ornstein, R.: Lateral specialization of cognitive mode: An EEG study, *Psychophysiology, 9*:412-418, 1972.

Galin, D. and Ornstein, R.: Individual differences in cognitive style: I. Reflective eye movements. *Neuropsychologia, 12*:367-376, 1974.

Gallagher, J.: *Teaching the Gifted Child*, 2nd ed. Boston, MA, Allyn and Bacon, 1975.

Galvin, G.: Uses and abuses of the WISC-R with the learning disabled, *Journal of Learning Disabilities, 14*:326-329, 1981.

Gawronski, J.D. and West, C.E. Computer literacy. *Association for Supervision and Curriculum Development Curriculum Update*, October 1982.

Gazzaniga, M.: The split brain in man. *Scientific American, 217*:24-29, 1967.

Gazzaniga, M.: Brain-corpus callosum. *Journal of Learning, 8*:35-36, November 1975.

Gazzaniga, M.S., Bogen, J.E., and Sperry, R.W.: Dyspraxia following division of the cerebral commissures. *Journal of Nervous and Mental Disease, 16*:606-612, 1967.

Gazzaniga, M.S., LeDoux, J.E., and Wilson, D.H.: Language praxis and the right hemisphere: Clues to some mechanics of consciousness. *Neurology, 27*:1144-1147, 1977.

Gazzaniga, M.S., and LeDoux, J.: *The Integrated Mind.* New York, Plenium Press, 1978.

Geschwind, Norman: Language and the brain. *Scientific American, 226*:76-83, April 1972.

Geschwind, Norman: Specialization of the human brain. *Scientific American, 241*:180-199, September 1979.

Geyer, J.J. and Kolers, P.A.: Reading as information processing. In Voigt, M. (Ed.): Advances in Librarianship, New York, Academic Press, 1974.

Gibson, E. and Levin, H.: *The Psychology of Reading.* Cambridge, MA, MIT Press, 1975.

Gibson, J.J.: *The Senses Considered as Perceptual Systems.* Boston, Houghton Mifflin, 1966.

Gilbert, Luther: Speed of processing visual stimuli and its relation to reading. In Singer, H. and Ruddell, R.: (Eds.): *Theoretical Models and Processes of Reading,* 2nd ed. Newark, Delaware, International Reading Association, 1976.

Glassner, Benjamin: Preliminary report: Hemispheric relationships in composing, *Journal of Education, 162*:74-95, 1980.

Goodenough, D.R., and Witkin, H.A.: *Origins of the Field-independent and Field-dependent Cognitive Styles.* Princeton, NJ, Educational Testing Service (ETS rb-77-9), 1977.

Goodman, Kenneth: The know-more and the know-nothing movement in reading: A personal response. *Language Arts, 56*:657-663, 1979.

Goodman, Kenneth and Goodman, Yetta: *Reading of American children whose language is a stable rural dialect of English or a language other than English: Final Report.* Arlington, VA, 1978. (ERIC Document Service No. ED 173 754).

Goodman, Yetta and Goodman Kenneth: Twenty questions about teaching language. *Educational Leadership, 38*:442-473, 1981.

Gowan, J.C.: Incubation, imagery, and creativity. *Journal of Mental Imagery, 2*:23-32, 1978.

Gowan, J.C.: The production of creativity through right hemisphere imagery. *The Journal of Creative Behavior, 13*:39-51, 1979.

Gowan, J.C., Khatena, J., and Torrance, E.P.: *Educating the Ablest: On the Education of Gifted Children.* Itasca, IL, Peacock Pub., 1979.

Graves, Donald: Let children show us how to help them write. *Visible Language, 13*:16-28, 1979.

Graves, Donald: Research update: How do writers develop? *Language Arts, 59*:173-179, 1982.

Green, Ann: *The "how" of film and composition.* Paper presented at the Annual Meeting of the Conference on College Composition and Communication, Denver, Colorado, 1978. (ERIC Document Reproduction Service NO. ED 168 030).

Greenlow, M.J.: Visual literacy and reading instruction: From books to media and back to books. *Language Arts, 56*:786-790, 1976.

Griggs, S., and Price, G.: A comparison between the learning styles of gifted versus average suburban junior high school students. *Roeper Review, 3*:7-9, 1980.

Griggs, S.A., and Price, G.E.: Learning styles of gifted versus average junior high school students. *Phi Delta Kappa, 61*:361, 1980.

Grumet, M.: The line is drawn. *Educational Leadership. 40*:28-38, 1983.

Guilford, J.P.: *The Nature of Human Intelligence.* New York, McGraw-Hill Book Co., 1967.

Guilford, J.P.: Intellect and the gifted. In Gowan, J., Khatena, J., and Torrance, E. (Eds.): *Educating the Ablest*. Itasca, IL, Peacock Pub., 1979.

Gur, R.E.: Conjugate lateral eye movements as an index of hemispheric activation. *Journal of Personality and Social Psychology, 31*:751-757, 1975.

Gur, R.E., Gur, R.C., and Harris, L.J.: Cerebral activation, as measured by subject lateral eye movements, is influenced by experimenter location. *Neuropsychologia, 13*:35-44, 1975.

Guyer, B.L., and Friedman, M.P.: Hemispheric processing and cognitive styles in learning-disabled and normal children. *Child Development, 46*:658-668, 1975.

Haber, Ralph: How we remember what we see. *Scientific American, 222*:104-112, 1970.

Hacker, C.J.: From schema theory to classroom practice. *Language Arts, 57*:866-871, 1980.

Hairston, M.T., and Cooper, M.F.: *Visual Imagery: A Means for Improving Self-Concept, 1973 Evaluation*. ERIC Document Reproduction Services, 1973, (ED 093297).

Haley-James, Shirley: Twentieth-century perspectives on writing in grades one through eight. In Haley-James, Shirley (Ed.): *Perspectives in Writing in Grades 1-8*. Urbana, IL, National Council of Teachers of English, 1981.

Hardin, P.: Investigating visual communication in diagrams. In Braden, R. and Walker, A. (Eds.): *Seeing Ourselves: Visualization in Social Context*. Blacksburg, VA, Virginia Polytechnic Institute, 1983.

Harris, L.J.: Neurophysiological factors in the development of spatial skills. In Eliot, J. and Salkind, N.J. (Eds.): *Children's Spatial Development*. Springfield, IL, Charles C Thomas, 1975.

Helfman, E.S.: *Blissymbolics: Speaking Without Speech*. New York, Elsevier/Nelson Books, 1981.

Hellige, Joseph: Cerebral hemisphere symmetry: Methods, issues, and implications. *Educational Communication and Technology Journal, 28*:83-98, Summer 1980.

Hennis, R.S.: Needed: Research in the visual language. *English Journal, 70*:79-82, 1982.

Henry, George: *Teaching Reading as Concept Development: Emphasis on Affective Thinking*. Newark, Delaware, International Reading Association, 1974.

Hewes, Gordon: Visual learning, thinking, and communication in human biosocial evaluation. In Randhawa, B., and Coffman, W. (Eds.): *Visual Learning, Thinking, and Communication*. New York, Academic Press, 1978.

Hill, Joseph et al.: *Personalized Educational Programs Utilizing Cognitive Style Mapping*, Bloomfield Hills, Michigan, Oakland Community College, 1971.

Hochberg, J.: Components of literacy: Speculation and exploratory research. In Levin, H. and Williams, J.P. (Eds.): *Basic Studies in Reading*. NY, Basic Books, 1970.

Hoffman, C. and Kagan, S.: Lateral eye movements and field-dependence-independence. *Perceptual and Motor Skills, 45*:767-778, 1977.

Horton, J.: A need for a theory of visual literacy. *Reading Improvement, 19*:257-267, 1982.

Howie, S. and Sinatra, R.: *Verbal and nonverbal factors in content area reading instruction*. Paper presented at the Sixth Regional Reading conference of the Rocky Mountain Region International Reading Association. Billings, Montana, October 1982.

Ihde, D.: *Experimental Phenomenology: An Introduction.* New York, Paragon Books, 1977.

James, William: *Principles of Psychology.* New York, Holt, 1890.

Judson, Horace: *The Techniques of Reading,* 3rd ed. New York, Harcourt, Brace, and Jovanovich, 1972.

Kagan, J.: *Matching Familiar Figures Test.* Cambridge, MA, Harvard University Press, 1965.

Kaufman, Alan: Cerebral specialization and intelligence testing. *Journal of Research and Development in Education, 12*:96-107, 1979.

Kaufman, Alan: The WISC-R and learning disabilities assessment: State of the art, *Journal of Learning Disabilities, 14*:520-526, 1981.

Kaufman, A. and Nadeen, L.: *Kaufman Assessment Battery for Children, K-ABC.* Circle Pines, Minnisota., American Guidance Service, 1983.

Keefe, J. Assessing student learning styles: An overview. In Keefe, J. (Ed.): *Student Learning Styles and Brain Behavior.* Reston, Va, National Secondary School Principles, 1982.

Kellog, Ralph: Listening. In Pose Lamb (Ed.): *Guiding Children's Language Learning.* Dubuque, Iowa, William C Brown, 1972.

Khatena, J.: Creative imagination through imagery. Some recent research. *Humanitas, 1*:227-242, 1978.

Khatena, J.: Advances in research in creative imagination imagery. In Gowan, J.C., Khatena, J., Torrance, E.P.:(Eds.): *Educating the Ablest: On the Education of Gifted Children.* Itasca, IL, Peacock Pub., 1979.

Kinsbourne, M.: Eye and head turning indicates cerebral lateralization. *Science, 176*:539-541, 1972.

Kirby, Patricia: *Cognitive Style, Learning and Transfer Skill Acquision.* Information series No. 195. Columbus, Ohio, National Center for Research in Vocational Education, 1978.

Kleinfeld, J.S.: Intellectual strengths in culturally different groups: An Eskimo illustration. *Review of Educational Research, 43*:341-359, 1973.

Kodak Education Market Services: *First graders from inner city lead 14 classes in reading skills.* Kodak Pamphlet No. VR-5, Rochester, Kodak Education Market Services, 1976.

Kolb, D.: *Learning Style Inventory, Teacher Manual.* Boston, McBer and Co., 1976.

Kolb, David: Learning styles and disciplinary differences. In Chickering, Arthur, and Associates (Eds.): *The Modern American College.* San Francisco, CA, Jossey-Bass, 1981.

Kraft, R.H., Mitchell, D.R., Languis, M.L., and Wheatley, G.H.: Hemispheric asymmetries during six-to-eight-year olds performance of Piagetian conservation and reading tasks. *Neuropsychologia, 18*:637-643, 1980.

Kundu, M.R.: Visual literacy: Teaching nonverbal communication through television, *Educational Technology, 16*:31-33, 1976.

Lamberski, Richard: Introduction. In *AECT Research and Theory Division Newsletter, 5*: November 1976. (Also in ERIC 136 822).

Lassen, N., Ingvar, D., and Skinhoj, E.: Brain function and blood flow. *Scientific American, 239*:62-71, October 1978.

Lawson, L.: Opthalmological factors in learning disabilities. In Myklebust, H. (Ed.): *Progress in Learning Disabilities*, Volume 1. New York, Grune and Stratton, 1968.

Leavitt, H.D. and Sohn, D.: *Stop, Look, and Write*. New York Bantom Pathfinder Edition, 12th Printing, 1969.

Lesser, Gerald: Cultural differences in learning and thinking styles: In Messick, S. and Associates (Eds.): *Individuality in learning*. San Francisco, Jossey-Bass, 1976.

Levin, Joel: Inducing comprehension in poor readers. *Journal of Educational Psychology*, *65*:19-24, 1973.

Levy, Jerre: Cerebral asymmetries as manifested in split-brain man. In Kinsbourne, M., and Smith, W. (Eds.): *Hemispheric Disconnection and Cerebral Function*. Springfield, IL, Charles C Thomas, 1974.

Levy, Jerre: The mammalian brain and the adaptive advantage of cerebral asymmetry. *Annals of New York Academy of Science, 229*:264-272, 1977.

Levy, J.: Research synthesis on the right and left hemispheres: We think with both sides of the brain. *Educational Leadership, 4*:66-71, 1983.

Levy, J., and Trevarthan, C.: Metacontrol of hemispheric function in human split-brain patients. *Journal of Experimental Psychology: Human Perception and Performance*, *2*:299-312, 1976.

Lewis, Richard: The forest of the mind: Nurturing imagination in children and teacher. *Today's Education, 69*:47-49, 1980.

Lindsay, Peter, and Norman, Donald: *Human information processing: An introduction to Psychology*, 2nd ed., New York, Academic Press, 1977.

Luria, A.R.: *The Working Brain*. New York, Basic Books, 1973.

MacLean, Paul: The brain in relation to empathy and medical education. *Journal of Nervous and Mental Disease, 144*:374-382, 1967.

MacLean, Paul: A mind of three minds: Educating the triune brain. In Chall, J. and Mirsky, A. (Eds.): *Education and the brain*. The 27th Yearbook of the National Society for the Study of Education. Chicago, University of Chicago Press, 1978.

Mann, Andy and Mann, Gwen: *Blissymbol Workbooks*. Toronto, Canada, Blissymbolics Institute, 1981.

Marcel, T., Katz, L., and Smith, M.: Laterality and reading proficiency. *Neuropsychologia, 12*:131-139, 1974.

Marcel, T. and Rajan, P: Lateral specialization for recognition of words and faces in good and poor readers. *Neuropsychologia, 13*:489-497, 1975.

McConkie, G. and Raynor, K.: An online computer technique for studying reading: Identifying the perceptual span. In Singer, H. and Ruddell, R. (Eds.): *Theoretical Models and Processes of Reading*, 2nd ed. Newark, Delaware, International Reading Association, 1976.

Messick, S.: Personality consistancies in cognition and creativity. In Messick, S. and Associates (Eds.): *Individuality in Learning*, San Francisco, Jossey-Bass Pub., 1976.

Metcalf, D.: *An Investigation of Cerebral Lateral Functioning and the EEG:* Final Report. Bethesda, Md., Office of Economic Opportunity, National Institute of Child Health and Human Development, 1975. ED 147 319.

Metz, C.: The perceived and the named. *Studies in Visual Communication,* *6*:56-68, 1980.

Moffett, James: Writing, inner speach, and meditation. *College English, 44*:231-245, March 1982.

Moffet, James: *Teaching the Universe of Discourse.* Boston, Houghton Mifflin, 1983.

Moffett, J. and Wagner, B.J.: *Student-Centered Language Arts and Reading, K-13:* A handbook for teachers. Boston, Houghton Mifflin, 1983.

Monteith, Mary: Schemata: An approach to understanding reading comprehension; an ERIC/RCS review. *Journal of Reading, 22*:368-371, 1979.

Morrow, J.: Media literacy in the 80's. *English Journal, 69*:48-51, 1980.

Murch, Gerald: *Visual and Auditory Perception.* New York, Bobbs-Merrill, 1973.

Murry, Donald: Internal revision: A process of discovery. In Cooper, C. and Odell, L.: (Eds.): *Research on Composing: Points of Departure.* Urbana, IL, National Council of Teachers of English, 1978.

National Assessment of Educational Progress: *Reading Comprehension of American Youth: Do they understand what they read? Results from 1979-1980 national assessment of reading and literature.* Denver, Colorado, National Assessment of Educational Progress, Education Commission of the States, 1982.

Nebes, Robert: Dominance of the minor hemisphere in commissurotomized man for the perception of part-whole relationships. In Kinsbourne, M., and Smith, W. (Eds.): *Hemispheric Disconnection and Cerebral Function.* Springfield, IL, Charles C Thomas, 1974.

Nebes, Robert: Man's so-called minor hemisphere. In Wittrock, M.C., (Ed.): *The Human Brain.* New Jersey, Prentice Hall, 1977.

Nichols, J.N.: Using paragraph frames to help remedial high school students with written assignments. *Journal of Reading, 23*:228-231, 1980.

Nickel, T: The reduced Rod-and-Frame Test as a measure of psychological differentiation. *Educational and Psychological Measurement, 31*:555-559, 1971.

Nixon, S.J.: *Cameras in the Curriculum,* Vol I. West Haven, CT, National Federation Association, 1982-1983.

Norton, R. and Dorman, G.: The gifted child fallacy. *The Elementary School Journal, 82*:249-255.

O'Connor Cody, C.: *Learning styles, including hemispheric dominance: A comparative study of average, gifted, and highly gifted students in grades five through twelve.* Unpublished doctoral dissertation. Temple University, 1983.

Otteson, James: Stylistic and pesonality correlates of lateral eye movement: A factor analytic study. *Perceptual and Motor Skills, 5*:995-110, 1980.

Paivio, Allen: *Imagery and Verbal Processes.* Hillsdale, New Jersey, Lawrence Erlbaum Associates, 1979.

Paivio, Allen: Imagery as a private audiovisual aid. *Instructional Science, 9*:295-309, 1980.

Pearson, P.D.: Some practical applications of a psycholinguistic model of reading. In Samuals, S.J. (Ed.): *What Research Has to Say About Reading Instruction.* Newark, Delaware, International Reading Association, 1978.

Pearson, P.D., and Johnson, D.: *Teaching Reading Comprehension.* New York, Holt, Rinehart, and Winston, 1978.

Pearson, P.D. and Spiro, R.D.: The new buzz word in reading is Schema, *Instructor,* *91*:46-48, 1982.

Perfetti, C.: Language comprehension and fast decoding: Some psycholinguistic prerequisites for skilled reading comprehension. In Guthrie, J. (Ed.): *Cognition, Curriculum, and Comprehension.* Newark, Delaware, International Reading Association, 1977.

Perrone, P. and Pulvino, C.: New directions in the guidance of the gifted and talented. *The Gifted Child Quarterly, 21*:326-340, 1977.

Perry, L.A.: Use of commercial logos to teach basic sight vocabulary. *The Reading Teacher, 88*:122, 1984.

Piaget, Jean: The Origin of Intelligence in Children. New York, Norton, 1963.

Piaget, Jean: *Six Psychological Studies.* New York, Random House, 1967.

Pines, Maya: The civilizing of Genie. *Psychology Today, 15*:28-34, 1981.

Pirozzolo, F. and Rayner, K: Hemispheric specialization in reading and word recognition. *Brain and Language, 4*:248-261, 1977.

Pirozzolo, F. & Rayner, K: Cerebral organization and reading disability. *Neuropsychologia, 17*:485-491, 1979.

Polya, G.: *How to Solve It.* Princeton, NJ, Doubleday, 1957.

Pestman, Neil: *Teaching as a Conserving Activity.* New York, Delacorte Press, 1979.

Postman, Neil: The ascent of humanity: A coherent curriculum. *Educational Leadership, 37*:300-303, 1980.

Postman, Neil: "TV's disastrous impact on children." *U.S. News and World Report, 90*:43-45, 1981.

Price, G.E., Dunn, K., Dunn, R., and Griggs, S.A.: Studies in students' learning styles. *Roeper Review, 4*:38-40, 1981.

Pryluck, C.: *Sources of meaning in motion pictures and television.* Unpublished Ph.D. dissertation, University of Iowa, 1973.

Radlike, F.: *Handbook for Teacher Improvement: Utilizing the Educational Sciences.* Bloomfield Hills, Michigan, Educational Science Asociation, 1973.

Ragan, T. and Huckabay, K.: *Development and implementation of a visual communication course in a university setting.* Paper presented at the Annual Meeting of the International Visual Literacy Association, Rochester, NY, 1978. (ERIC Document Reproduction Service No. ED 198 104).

Ramirez, Manuel III and Castaneda, Alfredo: *Cultural Democracy, Bicognitive Development and Education.* New York, Academic Press, 1974.

Randhawa, B.: Visual literacy: Prospectives for the future. *AECT Research and Theory Division Newsletter, 5*:14-15, 1976. (Also in ERIC 136 822).

Reinert, H.: One picture is worth a thousand words. Not necessarily!, *The Modern Language Journal, 60*:160-168, 1976.

Renzulli, J. and Smith, L.: *Learning Style Inventory.* Manfield, CT, Creative Learning Press Inc., 1978.

Restak, Richard: *The brain: The last frontier.* Garden City, New York, Doubleday, 1979.

Restak, Richard: Newborn knowledge. *Science, 358*-65, 1982a.

Restak, Richard: The brain. *The Wilson Quarterly, 6*:89-115, 1982b.

Richardson, Alan: Verbalizer-visualizer: A cognitive style dimension. *Journal of Mental Imagery, 1*:109-126, 1977.

Robeck, Mildred: *Sensorimotor bases for language*. Paper presented at the 29th International Reading Association Conference in New York City, NY, May 1975.

Rockefeller, David, Jr.: *Coming to Our Senses: The Significance of the Arts in American Education*. New York, McGraw-Hill, 1977.

Ross, E.: The divided self. *The Sciences*, February, 8-12, 1982.

Ross, Samuel, Jr.: Visual literacy — A new concept? *Audiovisual Instruction, 17*:12-15, 1972.

Rossel, Robert: Addictive video games. *Psychology Today, 17*:5, 1983.

Ruby, J., and Chalfen, R.: *The teaching of visual anthropology at Temple*. Paper presented at the Annual Meeting of the American Anthropological Association, New Orleans, 1973. (ERIC Document Reproduction Service No. 098 135).

Ruesch, J., and Kees, W.: *Nonverbal Communication*. Berkley, CA, University of California Press, 1956.

Rugel, R.P.: WISC subtest scores of disabled readers: A review with respect to Bannatyne's recategorization. *Journal of Learning Disabilities, 7*:48-55, 1974.

Rumelhart, David: Schemata: The building blocks of cognition. In John Guthrie (Ed.): *Comprehension and Teaching: Research Review*. Newark, Delaware, International Reading Association, 1981.

Rumelhart, D.E. and Ortony, A.: Representation of knowledge. In Anderson, R.C., Spiro, R.J. and Montague, W.E. (Eds.): *Schooling and the Acquistion of Knowledge*. Hillsdale, NJ, Lawrence Erlbaum Assoc., 1977.

Samuels, S. J.: The age-old controversy between holistic and subskill approaches to beginning reading instruction revisited. In McCullough, C. (Ed.): *Inchworm, Inchworm: Persistant Problems in Reading Education*. Newark, Delaware, International Reading Association, 1980.

Satz, P: Laterality test: An inferential problem. *Cortex, 13*:208-212, 1977.

Schnitker, Max: *The Teacher's Guide to the Brain and Learning*. San Rafael, CA, Academic Therapy Pub., 1972.

Schwartz, S.A., and DiMattei, R.: Mobius Psi-Q Test. *Omni, 4*:132-134, 136, 138, 159-160, 1981.

Schwebel, Milton and Raph, Jane: Before and beyond the three R's. In Schwebel, M., and Raph, J. (Eds.): *Piaget in the Classroom*. New York, Basic Books, 1973.

Shahn, Ben: *The Shape of Content*. New York, Vintage, 1960.

Shuy, Roger: A holistic view of language. *Research in Teaching English, 15*:101-111, 1981a.

Shuy, Roger: The rediscovery of language in education. *Educational Leadership, 38*:435, 1981b.

Sigel, Irving: The development of pictorial comprehension. In Randhawa, B. and Coffman, W. (Eds.): *Visual Learning, Thinking, and Communication*. New York, Academic Press, 1978.

Sinatra, R.: Language experience in title I summer camping programs. *Reading Improvement, 12*:148-156, Fall 1975.

Sinatra, R.: The cloze technique for reading comprehension and vocabulary development. *Reading Improvement, 14*:86-92, Summer 1977.

Sinatra, Richard: Visual literacy: A concrete language for the learning disabled. In Gottlieb, M. and Bradford, L. (Eds.): *Learning Disabilities an Audio Journal of Con-*

tinuing Education, 4, New York, Grune and Stratton, 1980. (Also in ERIC 203 556).

Sinatra, R.: Using visuals to help the second language learner. *Reading Teacher, 34*(5): 539-546, February 1981.

Sinatra, R.: Sentence development: Using a nonverbal approach. *Academic Therapy, 19*:79-88, Spring 1983a.

Sinatra, R.: Helping students to get things done by using visual compositions. *The English Quarterly, 16*:59-62, Summer 1983b.

Sinatra, R.: The parent's role in healthy brain development. *Early Years, 14*:32-37, 1983c.

Sinatra, R.: Use of three writing tasks at an adolescent treatment center. *Perceptual and Motor Skills, 59*:355-358, 1984.

Sinatra, R.C.: Visual/spatial strategies for writing and reading improvement. In Walker, A.D. and Braden, R.A. (Eds.): *Visual Literacy: Enhancing Human Potential.* Blacksburg, VA, Virginia Polytechnical Institute and State University, 1984.

Sinatra, Richard and Taber-Kinsler, Karen: Values strategies in the teaching of reading. *The Elementary School Journal, 77*:159-164, 1976.

Sinatra, R. and Spiradakis, J.: A visual approach to sentence combining for the limited-English proficient student. *Bilingual Resources, 4*:21-24, 1981.

Sinatra, Richard, and Stahl-Gemake, J: *Using the Right Brain in the Language Arts.* Springfield, IL, Charles C Thomas, 1983.

Sinatra, R., Stahl-Gemake, J., and Berg, D.: Improving reading comprehension of disabled readers through semantic mapping. *The Reading Teacher, 38*:22-29, 1984.

Sinatra, R., Berg, D., and Dunn, R.: Semantic mapping improves reading comprehension of learning disabled students. *Teaching Exceptional Children, 17*:310-314, Summer 1985.

Sinatra, R., Geisert, G., DeMeo, V., Tsarnas, E., and Makar, E.: *Thinking Networks for Reading and Writing*: A microcomputer software program. Think Network, Inc., P.O. Box 6124, New York, NY 10128, 1985.

Sinatra, R., and Venezia, J.: A visual approach to improved literacy skills for special education adolescents. *Remedial and Special Education*, in review.

Smith, E.G., Goodman, K., and Meredith, R.: *Language and Thinking in the Elementary School*, New York, Holt, Rinehart, and Winston, 1970.

Smith, Frank: *Understanding Reading.* New York, Holt, Rinehart, and Winston, Inc., 1971.

Smith, Frank: *Understanding Reading: A Psycholinguistic Analysis of Reading and Learning to Read,* 3rd ed. New York, Holt, Rinehart, and Winston, 1982.

Sohn, David: *Pictures for Writing.* New York, Bantam Pathfinder Edition, 1969.

Sohn, David: *Come to Your Senses: A Program in Writing Awareness.* NY, Scholastic Book Services, 1970.

Sperry, Roger: *Mental Unity Following Surgical Disconnection of the Cerebral Hemispheres,* Harvey Lecture Series, Number 62, New York, Academic Press, 1968.

Sperry, Roger: Lateral Specialization of cerebral functions in the surgically separated hemispheres. In McGuigan, F.J., and Schoonever, R.A. (Eds.): *The Psychophysiology of Thinking: Studies of Covert Processes.* New York, Academic Press, 1973.

Sperry, Roger: Some effects of disconnecting the hemipshere. *Science, 217*:1223-1226, 1982.

Sperry, R.W., Gazzaniga, M.S. and Bogen, J.E.: Interhemispheric relationship: The neocortical commissures; Syndromes of hemisphere disconnection. In Vinken, P., Bruyn, G. (Eds.): *Handbook of Clinical Neurology.* Amsterdam, North Holland Publishing Co., vol. 14, 1969.

Squire, J.: Composing and comprehending: Two sides of the same process. *Language Arts, 60*:581-589, 1983.

Stein, N. and Glenn, G.: An analysis of story comprehension in elementary school children. In Freedle, R. (Ed.): *Discourse Processing-Multidisciplinary Perspectives.* Hillsdale, NJ, Ablex Pub. Co., 1978.

Stone, I.: *The Origin: A Biographical novel of Charles Darwin.* New York, Doubleday, 1978.

Stotsky, S.: The role of writing in developmental reading. *Journal of Reading, 25*:330-339, 1982.

Stotsky, S.: Research on reading/writing relationships: A synthesis and suggested directions. *Language Arts, 60*:627-641, 1983.

Sutton, R.: Preparing a required college course: Visual Literacy. *Visual Literacy Newsletter, 11*:1-5, 1982.

Sykes, George: The case for aesthetic literacy. *Educational Leadership, 39*:596-598, 1982.

Symmes, J. and Rapoport, J.: Unexpected reading failure. *American Journal of Orthopsychiatry, 42*:82-91, 1972.

Taylor, E.: *The Fundamental Reading Skill.* Springfield, IL, Charles C Thomas, 1966.

Tierney, R. and Pearson, P.D.: Toward a composing model of reading, *Language Arts, 60*:520-568, 1983.

Tomlinson-Keasey, C., and Kelly, Ronald.: A task analysis of hemispheric functioning. *Neurophychologia, 17*:345-351, 1979.

Torrance, E.P.: Creativity and its educational implications. In Gowan, J., Khatena, J., and Torrance, E. (Eds.): *Educating the Ablest.* Itasca, IL, Peacock, 1979.

Torrance, E.P.: Hemisphericity and creative functioning. *Journal of Research Development in Education, 15*:29-37, 1982.

Torrance, E.P., Reynolds, R.C., Riegal, T., and Ball, O.E.: Your Style of Learning and Thinking, Forms A and B: Preliminary norms, abbreviated technical notes, scoring keys, and selected references. *Gifted Child Quarterly, 21*:563-575, 1977.

Torrance, E.P., Reynolds, R.C., Ball, O.E., and Reigel, T.: *Revised Norms-Technical Manual for your Style of Learning and Thinking,* Form A and Form B. Athens, GA, Georgia Studies of Creative Behavior, 1978.

Torrance, E.P., and Ball, O.E.: Which gifted students apply what they learn in special programs? *G/C/T/, 7*:7, 1979.

Torrance, E.P. and Reynolds, R.C.: *Preliminary Norms-Technical Manual for Your Style of Learning and Thinking,* Form C., Athens, GA, Georgia Studies of Creative Behavior, 1980.

Trosky, O.S., and Wood, C.: Using a writing model to teach reading. *Journal of Reading, 25*:34-40, 1982.

Tversky, D.: Encoding processes in recognition and recall. *Cognitive Psychology, 5*:275-287, 1973.

Vance, H. and Singer, M.: Recategorization of the WISC-R subtest scaled scores for learning disabled children. *Journal of Learning Disabilities, 12*:487-491, 1979.

Vanderheiden, G.C. and Kelso, D.P.: *Talking Blissapple.* A software program for the Apple Computer System. Trace Research and Development Center for the Severely Communicating Handicapped, University of Wisconsin, Madison, WI, 1982.

Vellutino, F., Harding, C. Stazer, J., and Phillips, F.: Differential transfer in poor and normal readers. *Journal of Genetic Psychology, 126*:3-18, 1975a.

Vellutino, F., Smith, H.M. and Karman, M.: Reading disability: Age differences and the perceptual-deficit hypothesis. *Child Development, 46*:487-493, 1975b.

Vygotsky, L.: A prehistory of written language. In Scribner, S., et al. (Eds.): *Mind in Society: The Development of Higher Psychological Processes.* Cambridge, MA, Harvard University Press, 1978.

Wallas, G.: *The Art of Thought*, Watts, 1926.

Walter, W.G.: *The Living Brain.* London, Duckworth, 1953.

Watt, D.: Informal learning: Software that teaches and entertains. *Popular Computing*, March, 60-64, 1983.

Wechsler. David: Manual: *Wechsler Intelligence Scale for Children.* New York, Psychological Corporation, 1949.

Wechsler, David: Manual: *Wechsler Adult Intelligence Scale.* New York, Psychological Corporation, 1955.

Wechsler, David: Manual: *Wechsler Intelligence Scale for Children-Revised.* New York, Psychological Corporation, 1974.

Wepner, Shelly: Logos: Signs of the times help beginning readers. *Early Years, 13*:36-59, 1983.

White, M.A.: Synthesis of research in electronic learning. *Educational Leadership, 40*:13-15, 1983.

Whitsitt, Robert: An approach to the definition of visual literacy. *AECT Research and Theory Division Newsletter, 5*:9-80, 1976. (Also in ERIC 136 822).

Wiles, J. and Bondi, J.: The middle school/junior high gifted. *Roeper Review, 3*:4-7, 1980.

Wilson, D.H., Reeves, A., and Gazzaniga, M.S., et al.: Cerebral commisurotomy for the control of intractable seizures. *Neurology, 27*:708-715, 1977.

Wilson, D.H., Reeves, A., and Gazziniga, M.S.: "Central" commisurotomy for intractable generalized epilepsy: Series two. *Neurology, 32*:687-697, 1982.

Winterowd, W.R.: A teacher's guide to the real basics. *Language Arts, 54*:625-630, 1977.

Witelson, Sandra: Abnormal right hemisphere specialization of developmental dyslexia. In Knights, R. and Bakker, D. (Eds.), *The Neuropsychology of Learning Disorders: Theoretical Approaches.* Baltimore, University Park Press, 1976.

Witelson, Sandra: Neural and cognitive correlates of developmental dyslexia: Age and sex differences. In Shagass, C., Gershon, S., and Friedhoff, A. (Eds.), *Psychopathology and Brain Dysfunctions*, New York, Raven, 1977.

Witkin, H.A., Moore, C.A., Goodenough, D.R. and Cox, P.W.: Field-dependent and field-independent cognitive styles and their educational implications. *Review of Educational Research, 47*:1-64, 1977.

Wittrock, Merlin: Education and the cognitive process of the brain. In Chall, Jeanne and Mirsky, Allan (Eds.): *Education and the Brain*. Chicago, University of Chicago Press, 61-102, 1978.

Wittrock, M.C.: Writing and the teaching of reading. *Language Arts, 60*:600-606, 1983.

Yokovlev, P., and Lecours, A.R.: The myelogenetic cycles of regional development of the brain. In Minkowski, A. (Ed.): *Regional Development of the Brain in Early Life: Symposium*. Oxford, Blackwell, 1967.

Yarmey, A.D. and Bowen, N.: The role of imagery learning in educable retarded and normal children. *Journal of Experimental Child Psychology, 14*:303-312, 1972.

Zaidel, Eran: The split brain and half brains as models of congenital language disability. In Ludlow, C., and Doran-Quine, M. (Eds.), *The Neurological Bases of Language Disorders in Children: Methods and Direction for Research*. Bethesda, MD, USDHEW, NINCDS Monograph, No. 22, 55-89, 1979.

Zelnicker, T. and Jeffrey, W.: Reflective and impulsive children: Strategies of information processing underlying differences in problem solving. *Monographs of the Society for Research in Child Development, 41*:1-52, 1976.

APPENDICES

APPENDICES

APPENDIX A

VISUAL LITERACY CURRICULUM AND RESOURCE GUIDES

Publication Name	Author/Editor	Source	Short Synopsis
Cameras in the Curriculum Volume 1, 1982-1983	Sonja J. Nixon, Project Director	National Education Assoc., Publications Order Dept., Academic Building, Saw Mill Road, West Haven, CT 06516	Presents summaries of 130 winners of the first Cameras in the Curriculum competition. Reports are arranged according to subject focus and grade level with accent on program implementation.
Catalog of Educational Materials	Agency Catalog	Agency for Instructional Television, Box, A, Bloomington, IN 47402	Illustrated Catalog, over 100 pages, describing program summaries for more than 2000 individual programs such as for social studies, science, music, math, etc., No cost.
Communications and Social Skills Through Use by Pupils of Audiovisual Media: A Report of the Schools Council Project	Carol Lorac and Michael Weiss	Maxwell House Fairview Park, Elmsford, NY 10523	Introduces methods of teaching and learning that allow students to communicate more effectively . . . Secondly, develops higher levels of interpersonal skills along with more thorough subject learning . . . about $11.50, soft cover.

287

Publication Name	Author/Editor	Source	Short Synopsis
Computer Literacy: Elementary Grade and Intermediate and Secondary Grades	Board of Education of the City of New York	Division of Curriculum and Teaching, 110 Livingston St., New York, NY	In two separate curriculum guides are presented ways to use the logic of computer programming for young and older children . . . about $8.00 each.
Curriculum Guidebook	Polaroid Camera Company	Polaroid Education Project, 549 Technology Square Cambridge, MA 02139	A resource and idea guide which contains over 100 photograph-based learning experiences indexed by subject and grade level . . . can work out arrangement for free use of cameras for students.
Curriculums in Visual Literacy, 1982	Dennis Dake, ed.	Iowa State Univ. Research Foundation 315 Beardshear Hall Iowa State Univ. Ames, Iowa 50011	Presents curriculum content of 19 exemplary programs in visual literacy . . . about $8.00 plus handling.
The New Literacy: The Language of Film and Television, 1979	Harold Foster	National Council of Teachers of English, 1111 Kenyon Road, Urbana, Il 61801	Discusses ways to use film and media in English classroom settings.
Seeing Ourselves: Visualization in a Social Context, 1983	Edited by R.A. Braden and A.D. Walker	133 McBryde Hall, Virginia Polytechnic Institute and State University, Blacksburg, VA 24061	Contains 344 pages of papers presented at the 14th annual conference of the International Visual Literacy Association held in Vancouver, B.C. Canada . . . about $12.00.
Teaching Reading Through the Arts, 1983	Edited by John E. Cowen	International Reading Assoc., 800 Barksdale Road, Newark, DE 19711	Explores ways of using the arts — drama, television, music, art, and creative writing — as a means of integrating with reading instruction.

Publication Name	Author/Editor	Source	Short Synopsis
Teaching Tips from Kodak, (#AT-18), 1979	Eastman Kodak Company	Education Market Services, Eastman Kodak Co., Rochester, NY 14650	Presents 275 teacher-proven ways to use photography in the classroom. Short abstracts are presented, K-12.
Visual Literacy Enhancing Human Potential, 1984	Edited by A.D. Walker, R.A. Braden, & L.H. Dunker	133 McBryde Hall, Virginia Polytechnic Institute and State University, Blacksburg, VA 24061	Contains 417 pages of papers from the 15th Annual International Visual Literacy Association Conference held in Bloomington, IN . . . about $12.00.
Visual Literacy Languaging, and Learning: Provacative Paper Series, #1, 1978	John L. Debes & Clarence Williams	The Visual Literacy Center, Gallaudit College, Washington, D.C.	The second chaper to this five chapter monograph presents "in the classroom" ideas that can be supplemented by the creative teacher.
Visual Literacy Programs That Work. (#VR-6), 1975	Eastman Kodak Company	Education Markets Services, Eastman Kodak Co. Rochester, NY 14650	Presents case history summaries of eight visual literacy curriculum projects.
Visual Literacy through Picture Books K-12: A Curriculum Approach	M. Laughlin	ERIC Document Reproduction Services No. Ed 198 814	Shows how to use picture books found in most school libraries to teach visual literacy activities.

APPENDIX B

VISUAL LITERACY JOURNAL AND ASSOCIATION RESOURCES

Name of Journal	Address	Sponsoring Agency
Performance & Instruction Journal	1126 16th St., N.W., Suite 214, Washington, D.C. 20036	**P & I** is the official publication of the National Society for Performance and Instruction. Published 10 times per year, the journal is dedicated to the advancement of performance in science and technology.
Educational Communication and Technology Journal; (formerly **AV Communication Review**)	AECT 1126 16th St., N.W. Washington, D.C. 20036	A quarterly journal which documents research and applied theory in the fields of educational technology, administration, industrial training and other related fields.
Instructional Innovation (formerly **Audio Visual Instruction**)	AECT 1126 16th St., N.W. Washington, D.C. 20036	A journal which is published 8 times a year and covers new developments in AECT. New products and technologies are included in each issue.
Journal of Instructional Development	AECT 1126 16th St., N.W. Washington, D.C. 20036	A quarterly journal, devoted exclusively to instructional development. Articles focus on techniques, theories, reports, case studies and reviews of products and systems.
Journal of Communication	Journal of Communication P.O. Box 13358 Philadephia, PA 19101-9916	A quarterly journal which covers a wide range of the communication arts. It offers communication research and

291

Name of Journal	Address	Sponsoring Agency
	•	analysis, news of the field and coming events, and book reviews of the latest publications in the field of communications.
The International Journal of Educational Technology and Language Learning Stystems	Pergamon Press Fairview Park, Elmsford, NY 10523	This international journal is devoted to the applications of educational technology and systems thinking in a broad sense, covering problems of foreign language teaching and learning. Concentrates on the technology of teaching language, particularly the teaching of English as a second or foreign language.
Phototherapy	Institute for Psychosocial Applications of Video & Photography, University of Houston, Clear Lake City, 2700 Bay Area Boulevard, Houston, TX, 77058	A semi-annual journal containing manuscripts pertaining to the therapeutic uses of still photos, moving film, video and holography in the areas of practice, research and theory.
Visible Language	Visible Language Box 1972 CMA, Cleveland, OH 44106	A quarterly journal concerned with research and ideas that help define the unique role and properties of written language. It presents interesting and unusual typographic treatments which go beyond the barriers of normal type.
Montage	Eastman Kodak Company, Attn: Richard R. Ball Education Markets Services, Rochester, NY 14650	**Montage** is published 3 times a year. It includes articles pertaining to the way photography and photographic images are used in creative ways to develop more effective learning in the classroom.
Media & Methods	Media & Methods Institutes, Inc., Division of North America Publishing Co., 134 N. 13th Street, Philadelphia, PA 19107	**Media & Methods**, published nine times a year, is dedicated to educators who are attempting to use media methods and materials as ways of helping students plug into our modern culture.

Name of Journal	Address	Sponsoring Agency
School Media Quarterly now called **School Library Media Quarterly**	American Association of School Librarians, 50 E. Huron Street, Chicago, IL 60611	A quarterly journal for building-level media specialists, district supervisors, and others concerned with the selection and purchase of print and nonprint media. Covers development of programs and services for preschool through high school libraries.
Technology and Mediated Instruction	Academic Publications University of Louisville, 2301 South Third St., Louisville, KY 40292	**Technology and Mediated Instruction** is currently published 3 times a year. The journal deals with the effective use of media in all areas of instruction.
Journal of Visual/Verbal Languaging	Lida Cochran, JVVL Managing Editor, 35 Olive Court, Iowa City, Iowa 52240	This journal, published semi-annually, is the official journal of the International Visual Literacy Asociation. The journal is dedicated to the study of visual languaging and visual literacy and to their inter-relationship with the verbal literacies.
Visual Literacy Newsletter	International Visual Literacy Association, Inc., P.O. Box 5622, Bloomington, IN 47402	The **Visual Literacy Newsletter** deals with ways to use visual communication media in educational settings and offers reviews of work done in visual literacy.

APPENDIX C

PICTURE TESTS (NONVERBAL)

Name and Author of Test	Sources	Description and Purpose
Expressive One-Word Picture Vocabulary Test by Morrison Gardner	Jastak Associates 1526 Gilpin Ave. Wilmington, DE 19806 or Western Psychological Services 12031 Wilshire Blvd., Los Angeles, CA 90025	110 pictures are used to assess expressive verbal ability. Level 1 used for students 2 to 12 years old; Level 2 used for students 12 to 15 years old. Standardized, individually adminstered, and yields deviation IQ, percentiles, and mental age equivalent scores.
Receptive One-Word Picture Vocabulary Test by Morrison Gardner, 1985	Jastak Associates 1526 Gilpin Ave. Wilmington, DE 19806 or Western Psychological Services 12031 Wilshire Blvd., Los Angeles, CA 90025	Untimed, individually administered test designed to assess receptive vocabulary levels for children ages 2-0 through 11-11 years. Child selects picture that matches word presented orally by examiner. Results can be compared with those of **Expressive One-Word Picture Vocabulary Test** to determine differences in receptive versus expressive language levels.
Picture Story Language Test by Helmer Myklebust, 1965	Western Psychological Services 12031 Wilshire Blvd., Los Angeles, CA 90025	Group or individually administered tests of written expression for students aged 7-17. Normal and handicapped children write a story based upon a picture card stimulus. Each composition is evaluated according to productivity, syntax, and meaning.

Name and Author of Test	Sources	Description and Purpose
Peabody Picture Vocabulary Test-Revised (PPVT-R) by Lloyd and Leota Dunn, 1981	American Guidance Services Publisher's Building Circle Pines, MN 55014-1796	Individually administered measure of receptive or listening vocabulary which uses a graduated series of 175 picture plates. After examiner says stimulus word, child or adult points to picture which best illustrates word's meaning.
Pictorial Test of Intelligence by Joseph French, 1964	Riverside Pub. Co. 1919 South Highland Ave. Lombard, Il 60148	Individual test for normal and handicapped children between 3 to 8 years of age. Children respond to visual stimuli after hearing oral instructions. Six subtests measure different facets of mental functioning.
Visual-Verbal Test by M.J. Feldman and J. Drasgow, 1981	Western Psychological Services 12031 Wilshire Blvd., Los Angeles, CA 90025	Individual test designed to distinguish between groups of normals, neurotics, schizophrenics, mentally handicapped, and brain damaged. Examinee formulates two different concepts for each of 42 stimulus cards. Concepts such as color, form, size, structured similarities, naming and position are tested.
Picture Readability Formula (PPF) by Rune Pettersson, (1983)	Rune Pettersson, CLEA Stockholms Universitet Inst. for ADB S-10691 Stockholm, Swedan	A picture readability index or scale is provided which can be used in the design and production of visuals for instruction. The index provides an indication of the relative ease or difficulty with which a visual can be read. Twenty-one variables are used to rate pictures.
Picture Potency Formula, (PPF) by Anthony Mango and Alice Legenza	In **Language Arts, 52** (8) Nov/Dec 1975, pp. 1085-1089.	The PPF yeilds a score for the language stimulation value of a picture. The administrator tallies the verbal response of a subject who is viewing a picture. A rating scale is provided, yeilding four language stimulation values.

AUTHOR INDEX

SUBJECT INDEX

A

Aesthetic literacy, 1-32, 17-18
Analogic codification, 98-102
Analysis
  and verbal superiority of the left hemi-
    sphere, 74
Associative learning, 182-183
Audiovisual instruction, 168
Auditory motor and sequential processing,
  102-104
Auditory nerve, 5, 13

B

Blissymbols, 204-206
  parallels to traditional reading, 205
Brain evolution, three levels
  reticular activating system, 110-111
Brain functions, 75-79
  axonal and dendritic growth, 80
  cognitive maturation, 76
  dependence upon the environment, 81
  lateralization, 125-129
  myelination, 76-78
  role of the corpus callosum, 76-78
Brain organization, verbal and nonverbal
    learning, 137
Brain research, 61-65
  blood flow, 62
  brain wave activity, 62
  damaged or diseased brain, 62
  Mac Lean's Research, 82-84
  need for future studies, 140-141
  sensory motor system, 62
  split brain findings, 63-65
    role of the corpus collosum, 64
    Sperry and Bogen findings, 64

C

Cerebrum (Neocortex), 82
Children's thinking, 8
  active reconstruction, 57
Cognitive abilities, 149-150
  and expressive abilities, 70
  development, 6-7
  Guilford's structure of the intellect model,
    149-150
  maturation, 76
  process model, 111-114
Composing, 173-181
  relationship to synthesis, 173-174, 181
  visionary aspect, 178-179
  use of figurative language, 192-198
  visual composing, 164-166
Comprehending, 173-181
  pictures, 163-166
    principle of conservation, 163
  relationship to synthesis, 173-174, 181
  role of analogies, 198-199
  visionary aspect, 178-179
Computer literacy, 32-40
Computer technology, 34-37
Conceptualization, 10, 146-149
Connectedness, 11, 14
  inner development, 5, 13-14
Configurational processing, 74
Corpus callosum, 189-199
Creativity, 199
  applied to writing, 188-199
  role of synthesis, 199
Curriculum applications, 41-42, 46
  art, 31-32, 41
  audiovisual instruction, 168
  cameras, 207-210
  guides, 37

V

Verbal literacy, 30, 89-107, 137-138, 161-162
  foveal fixation, 91-95
  sequential processing, 89-97
  visual periphery, 94-97
Vision, 178-179
Visual composing, 16-166
  dual involvement of hemispheres, 166
  nonverbal/verbal interaction, 167-168
  relationship to other literacies, 164-166
Visual compositions, 219-232
  constructing compositions, 220-222
  composing process, 227-229
  functions, 224
  holistic process, 222, 232
  levels of literacy development, 230-232
  mental processing, 222-224
  steps in arrangement, 227-230
  strengths of approach, 232
Visual configurations, 249-252
  comic strip sequencing, 250-251
  Greek crosses, 249-250
  picture board displays, 250
  signaling idea direction, 251-252
Visual language, 204-206
  Blissymbols, 204-206
Visual literacy, 13, 18, 45, 161, 162
  acceptance problems, 45-46
  artist, 31

  building blocks, 20
  curricula, 41-42
  definitions, 55-57
  environmental stimulation, 58
  essential components, 24
  interfacing, 41-43
  lack of teacher training, 48
  vs. media literacy, 48
  nonverbal schemata, 20
  oral language, 13-14, 18-19
  perspectives, 45-49, 59
  representational communication, 28
  research problems, 49-51
  university curriculum, 49
  written, 18-19

W

Wada test, 72
Wechsler Adult Intelligence Scales, 133-134
Wechsler Intelligence Scale for Children, 133-134
Written language acquisition, 18
Written literacy, 145-149, 163-164
Writing
  figurative language as stimulus, 192-196
  interhemispheric interaction, 183
  prevision, 178-179
  revision, 178-181
  role of imagery, 185-189
  vision, 178-179

DATE DUE			
12-01-09			
REC'D JUL 1 7 2007			